ANTHROPOLOGY, FILM INDUSTRIES, MODULARITY

Duke University Press Durham and London 2021

ANTHROPOLOGY, FILM INDUSTRIES, MODULARITY

RAMYAR D. ROSSOUKH AND
STEVEN C. CATON, EDITORS

Typeset in Garamond Premier Pro and
Din by Westchester Publishing Services

Library of Congress Cataloging-in-Publication Data
Names: Rossoukh, Ramyar D. [date] editor. | Caton, Steven Charles,
[date] editor.
Title: Anthropology, film industries, modularity / Ramyar D. Rossoukh
and Steven C. Caton, editors.
Description: Durham : Duke University Press, 2021. | Includes
bibliographical references and index.
Identifiers: LCCN 2021005910 (print)
LCCN 2021005911 (ebook)
ISBN 9781478013969 (hardcover)
ISBN 9781478014904 (paperback)
ISBN 9781478022190 (ebook)
Subjects: LCSH: Motion picture industry—Cross-cultural studies. |
Motion picture industry—Social aspects. | BISAC: SOCIAL
SCIENCE / Anthropology / Cultural & Social | PERFORMING ARTS
/ Film / History & Criticism
Classification: LCC PN1995 .A584 2021 (print) | LCC PN1995 (ebook) |
DDC 791.43—dc23
LC record available at https://lccn.loc.gov/2021005910
LC ebook record available at https://lccn.loc.gov/2021005911

Contents

Acknowledgments

The direct source for the ideas in this book was the panel "Film Industries" organized by Ramyar D. Rossoukh for the 2013 Annual Meeting of the American Anthropological Association, for which Michael M. J. Fischer and Steven C. Caton were discussants. We would like to thank Michael M. J. Fischer and the eight panelists, Sherry Ortner, William Mazzarella, Kevin Dwyer, Mary Steedly, Tejaswini Ganti, Sylvia Martin, Young-a Park, and Marieke J. Wilson, for their stimulating papers and insightful comments. In 2017, Steven C. Caton gave the lecture "Ethnography of Film Industries" at Cleveland State University and at Carleton College (as the guest of its Middle East Studies Program), and he would like to thank Professor Gregory M. Sadlek (dean of the College of Liberal Arts and Sciences at CSU) and Professor Noah Salomon (director of the Middle East Studies Program at Carleton College) for the opportunity to address students and colleagues at their respective institutions. The value of their feedback was inestimable. Even earlier than the 2013 panel, courses on anthropology, cultural studies, and film, both at the University of California, Santa Cruz, and Harvard University, helped prepare the groundwork for thinking about the film industry as a subject for study in anthropology. The contributions of students in these courses to the formulation of ideas in this book was critical, and we want to thank them for their generous feedback and intellectual stimulation throughout the years. The authors would also like to express their profound gratitude to the anonymous press readers of earlier drafts of this book for their helpful suggestions, all of which were taken seriously and incorporated in multiple revisions, and that we are confident improved the final product immensely. And, of course, thanks to Ken Wissoker for having seen the potential of this book in the first place and having encouraged us to pursue its publication with Duke University Press, and always pushing us to make it better. Steven C. Caton would like to thank his husband, Donald M. Scott, for having been such a stalwart supporter of our project. And Ramyar D. Rossoukh would like to thank Asad Ahmed for the opportunity to participate in the 2015 Brown-Harvard Pakistani Film Festival, "Love, War, and Other Longings," and Naghmeh Sohrabi, Namita Dharia, and Jared McCormick for listening to his rants.

Introduction

RAMYAR D. ROSSOUKH AND STEVEN C. CATON

As world economies in the last half century have moved away from manufacturing to communication and information technologies, film industries have concomitantly become more important and more prevalent than at any time in cinema history. "Globally, more than 3,000 feature films reached movie theaters in 2006, bringing in $23.8 billion in box-office revenues. And total global annual revenues across all distribution channels such as video and DVD, cable, television, and mobile sources were forecasted to be at $450 billion by the end of 2007, according to the Motion Picture Association of America (MPAA). The largest distributors of feature films in 2006 were India with 800, the U.S. with 599, and China with 255" (Young, Gong, and Van der Stede 2008, 28). These figures reflect the prerecession (2006–2007) economy, but not even the recession could dint the upward spiral in film production that we have seen since. Nigeria has one of the most dynamic and profitable film industries in the world (known as Nollywood) and produces more films per week than Hollywood and is second only to Bollywood. According to *Fortune* magazine, "in 2014, the Nigerian government released data for the first time showing Nollywood is a $3.3 billion sector, with 1844 movies produced in 2013 alone" (Bright 2015). Other thriving film industries are to be found in Turkey, Iran, Hong Kong, South Korea, Japan, and in several Central and Latin American countries (Mexico, Brazil, Cuba, and Argentina). In China, super magnate Wang Jianlin built Qingdao Oriental Movie Metropolis, a vast entertainment center whose movie-production facilities are intended to rival Hollywood's (Shih and McGee 2015). However, not all national film industries are successful, and some that may at one time have been dominant have now greatly diminished (arguably this is the case, for example, for the Egyptian film industry). And with the shift from analog to digital media, film industries are facing a major challenge, the exact nature and impact of which has yet to be determined but which is bound to be profound. It is anybody's guess which film industries will survive, let alone prosper. Making films may be big business, but it's also risky business. We address these changes and challenges in this introduction.

Not just making money, though, is at stake in film industries; they are also about power and influence. As political agents from nation-states to social movements realize the potential of films for drawing large publics into their political projects, they too have shown increasing interest in creating, supporting, and controlling or otherwise tapping into film industries. "Motion pictures aren't only a significant source of revenue for many countries—they're also instrumental in shaping worldwide impressions of a country's intellectual, historical, and cultural environment" (Young, Gong, and Van der Stede 2008, 28). One need only think of South Korean, Iranian, or Chinese cinema to support this claim. Their respective governments are willing to financially underwrite or in other ways support national film industries because of their symbolic capital, especially when their films win international film festival awards. Social movements are also known to use films for their political purposes. Al Gore's *An Inconvenient Truth* (2006) shaped public awareness about climate change and reenergized the environmentalist movement. Feature films can also have that kind of influence. One need only consider the movie *Selma* (2014) or, in an earlier civil rights era, the 1970s television miniseries *Roots*, which was remade in 2016 for television audiences: both are concerned with injustices to African Americans that have spurred today's Black Lives Matter movement. The documentary *Who Killed Vincent Chin?* (1987) also mobilized the Asian American community into forming its own social movement. In another part of the world, less high-profile perhaps yet nonetheless very potent, is the example of Christian evangelicals in West Africa (Meyer 2015) who produce feature films that communicate Christian messages to their born-again audiences. Film industries are being used the world over for political projects of all kinds.

We distinguish analytically between the notion of cinema and film industry. We define cinema as the production of films associated with a certain political (usually national) agenda or a certain aesthetic or cultural movement. Consider in that light Italian Neorealism or the French New Wave or even American independent cinema with its attempt to examine unconventional topics and be culturally or politically edgy: they are all committed to making films in a certain way or to communicating a certain vision of the world. In practical terms, however, they are still dependent on a film industry or industries for their making. The burden of this introduction is to explain what we mean by film industries, but for the moment let it suffice that they get financing for their films and recoup investments through ticket sales (and/or government subsidies); they make their films in a standardized way, even though the content may be anything but standard or conventional, by hiring personnel skilled in those crafts; and that process involves what we call modules (script writing, on-location shooting, cinematography, etc.) that may be outsourced to sites equipped to carry them out anywhere in the world. Empirically speaking, the study of any one film will in all likelihood require both analytical frameworks. The term "cinema" has been used in film studies literature to cover both senses that we wish to distinguish analytically. In the above discussion of various independently produced films, for example, a film like *An Inconvenient Truth* may be analyzed in relation to a transnational environmental movement cinema, but that does not, in and of itself, help us understand how it was made within the parameters of film industries, which is another question altogether. One might ask, if one wants to understand the influence of Gore's film, is there any need to understand the process through which his film was made, watched, and commented upon? We claim that there is. Gore's film could not have been made, let alone seen by millions of viewers, had there not been an industry that produced, marketed, exhibited, and reviewed it, not to speak of movie theaters in which it was shown and a global cable television network that broadcast it.

With this distinction in mind, in the following pages we look at film industries in a way that privileges the notion of modularity. Without getting into details here, we argue that modularity has emerged as the key concept for understanding film industries today, after the collapse of the studio system and the outsourcing of filmmaking tasks around the world. But before we explain in more detail what we mean by "film industries," we provide a brief history of work done in anthropology on film industries that has either been ignored in film studies or is not known. It is important for anthropologists and film studies scholars to be aware of this history. We wish to create a voice for anthropology and its research on film industries in order for it to be better heard by other disciplines that also work on this subject, disciplines with which we wish to be in dialogue about our mutual interests. There are several such disciplines, and again we cannot be exhaustive in our coverage of them, so we have selected two that we sense are closest to the ethnographic work of anthropologists on film industries: production studies and world cinema.[1] At the end of the introduction, after some thoughts on the profound impact of digital media on contemporary film industries that raise the questions of what remains of our objects of study, film and film industries, we summarize the chapters in the volume and their contributions to an anthropological understanding of film industries, and in particular of the ethnography of modularity.

A Brief History of the Anthropology of Film, Television, and Media

Our volume carries the key word *Anthropology* in its title for a reason. Anthropology has studied film industries for over seventy years, and in the last twenty years the number of anthropological works devoted to research on film industries has grown exponentially, thus warranting the claim that it has become a significant subdisciplinary field within the anthropological study of mass media (Spitulnik 1993; Dickey 1997; Mahon 2000; Askew and Wilk 2002; Ginsburg, Abu-Lughod, and Larkin 2002; Mazzarella 2004; Ruby 2005). And yet, what is striking is how few scholars outside of anthropology seem to be aware of the depth and breadth of this field of film industries. Therefore, the introduction reviews the depth and scope of this field, without attempting to be exhaustive (a thorough overview would require a chapter in itself). The aim is to draw attention to the fertility of this field and to argue that it has something distinctive and important to offer the study of film with its emphasis on film industries.

Anthropologist Hortense Powdermaker was very much ahead of her time in studying film industries, not only in her book *Hollywood, the Dream Factory* (1950), for which she did fieldwork in Hollywood on the personnel of the producer and the writer in film production, but also in *Copper Town: Changing Africa* (1962), which looks at the effects of what we call cinema on a segment of African society; in this instance, certain kinds of films that the colonial administration showed to African audiences. At the same time, however, she is concerned with the material or infrastructural side of this "mobile cinema" and how it exhibited its films, an aspect we call film industries. She reflected on how she did her pioneering fieldwork in her memoir, *Stranger and Friend: The Way of an Anthropologist* (Powdermaker 1966), which to this day remains a methodological guidebook for anthropologists of film. In her time, however, the study of cinema, let alone of film industries, was considered outré, and Powdermaker remained an exception, even an outlier within anthropology. For one reason or another, film was not considered a scientific object of study, if indeed an object of study at all.

It was not until the 1980s—thirty years after Powdermaker's groundbreaking work—that anthropologists began to take up the study of film in a serious way, informed by many theoretical studies of film that had developed in the intervening years.[2] The anthropological approaches tended to reflect the prevalent focus at the time of film theory on the filmic text that offers a window on a cultural world or as a powerful form of representation that can construct that world (a wonderful example being Elizabeth Traube's [1991] *Dreaming Identities*; see also Dickey [1993] and Armbrust [1996]).

A different type of study from this era is Steven Caton's (1999) *Lawrence of Arabia: A Film's Anthropology*. While Traube looks at a whole set of films made in roughly the same period and asks how they construct identities such as class, race, and gender, Caton focuses on a single film and the process of its transnational production and exhibition; in other words, he asks how the film was exemplary of a film industry at a particular moment in its history. The process entailed what we call modules in film production. These were location scouting (in Jordan); script writing (there were two writers for this film in the end) that looked critically at the story of colonialism in the Middle East (through the adventures of its colonial agent); on-location shooting in "exotic locales" (which included Jordan, Morocco, and southern Spain), in order to draw audiences away from studio television programming; and cinematography that involved special-effects lenses to capture mirages on camera, not to speak of heavy, bulky equipment needed for large-format film stock and lighting equipment to lighten shadows, because high-contrast desert sunlight made shadows appear black, if not opaque. Sound was another important module in this production. Special sound recording equipment captured nuances of sound that were heard in wraparound theater speakers, which gave an immersive aural experience to match the visual one. Personnel were no less important to the film's commodity value. There were highly trained international crews and actors that made the film appear international and a famous director who was making the shift from national to international cinema and from a small-screen to the large-screen Super Panavision format; and finally, transnational marketing and exhibition were crucial modules in the film's ultimate financial success (i.e., investment could not be recouped on domestic ticket sales alone).

The point of an anthropological analysis is to show that what we call the film is in myriad and sometimes profound ways the product of this complex industrial process and attendant technologies, which are missed if we focus only on the filmic text and its reception by different publics. Take, for example, the filming of the desert in which T. E. Lawrence campaigned: in order for it to be seen at all on the wide screen, each frame had to be artfully filled with visual details, not only so the viewer's eye would be pulled laterally across the wide screen but so that depth of field could be created to provide visual perspective. The technology of wide-screen filming required special lenses and rather large, bulky equipment, which had to be made mobile through tracks on sand dunes so that the camera could move fluidly with the actors in the mise-en-scène. Such filmmaking translated into a more dynamic and sensuous or embodied image on the screen and turned it into a more competitive commodity with audiences used to watching television screens. What Caton could not do was carry out fieldwork on this industrial process of filming, which he had to reconstruct by working in the archives on the film and by research on the nature of the film industry in its day; yet what was provided was an anthropological framework nonetheless for studying the industrial side of film production.

While anthropologists like Faye Ginsburg (1991) did pioneering work on indigenous peoples' media practices such as video filming that were used for cultural programming or in identity politics movements, it would be difficult—and probably inappropriate—to place such practices within the industrial framework developed in this volume. The process of filmmaking was less about standardization and production values, let alone commodification, than about utilizing small, easy-to-operate, and mobile media for largely political-cultural aims. Fieldwork was based not so much on the making of such films, as in Powdermaker's earlier pioneering study, as on film reception by publics and critics, and explaining those in terms of specific cultural and historical contexts or in terms of class, gender, race, and other cultural identities constituting film-viewing publics.

At roughly the same time that Ginsburg was doing her work on indigenous media, the anthropological investigation of media expanded to television (Kottak 1990; Naficy 1993; Rofel 1994; Dornfeld 1998; Mankekar 1999; Abu-Lughod 2005) and to different national television programming and its publics, especially melodramas, and of late attention has also turned to television news as well (see chapter 3, this volume, for example). The question of industry has been kept in the background of most of these anthropological inquiries, if not occluded entirely, with emphasis instead on the politics of reception in the public sphere. Yet with television, the question of industry is inescapable, unlike the smaller-scale, artisanal mode of production that has marked indigenous media, and it behooves us to bring this framework into sharper focus. For example, writers, directors, and actors move across film and television industries, working in both media, and many movies are made for television or, if they are not made for television, are broadcast on television, broadening their reception.

In our view, one work on the television industry needs to be singled out because it has been ignored or underappreciated, and that is Barry Dornfeld's extraordinary ethnography published in 1998, several years ahead of the curve in the scholarship on television. It is a major ethnography of a production unit within public television that created the seven-hour television series *Childhood*, which aired in the United States and England in 1991–1992. He was hired as a researcher for the series and throughout the production process had access to the television program's producers, writers, and directors. Through his extensive prior experience as an independent filmmaker, he also had an insider's perspective on the television and film industries. Dornfeld situated his contribution within the then-burgeoning field of anthropology of media studies. Yet there are clear overlaps between Dornfeld's seminal study and what would later become production studies, launched by John T. Caldwell's (2008) celebrated *Production Culture: Industrial Reflexivity and Critical Practice in Film and Television*, which we talk about in detail below: for example, the focus on the production process (in dynamic interaction with reception), analysis of this process in terms of film industrial constraints—especially the bottom line—as well as their creative possibilities, and going beyond the technical issues of production to include its social aspects, especially the way the creators are constantly trying to imagine how audiences might respond to their message. Finally, Dornfeld looks at the cultural production of public television as an agent within American public culture at large, an especially urgent question given the large audiences its flagship series usually attracts, and one that is of particular interest to anthropologists. The result was a pioneering work, and yet Dornfeld's study is hardly ever cited in the production studies literature, let alone discussed.

Despite Dornfeld's pioneering work, attention to film industries was not entirely absent in the late 1990s and early 2000s, as evidenced, for example, in the work of anthropologist Brian Larkin (2008; see also Acland [2003] on mid-1980s commercial movie business). He shifted the problem of understanding film industries away from commodification to one of materiality and specifically of urban infrastructure (which becomes central in the work of Jacobson [2015]); nonetheless, his is still an ethnography of the Nigerian film industry under colonial rule for the most part, or how films were made and exhibited within that system and as impacted by certain infrastructural materialities.

By the early 2000s, the anthropological analysis of film industries took off, in terms of the numbers of such works as well as their empirical richness and theoretical sophistication. Kevin Dwyer's (2004a) *Beyond Casablanca: M. A. Tazi and the Adventure of Moroccan Cinema* is in many ways seminal in this regard. To be sure, he uses the term "Moroccan cinema" rather than Moroccan film industry to describe the object of his study, the oeuvre (rather than a single film) of Moroccan film director M. A. Tazi, whom Dwyer knew and proceeded to have a long-term conversation with (building on his theoretical and procedural notion of dialogue; see Dwyer 1982); yet we would claim that its concerns are about film industries nonetheless. Some of the main questions he poses of Tazi and his oeuvre are: What are the conditions—economic, social, political—under which he, as a filmmaker, had to work, within both Moroccan and global film industries? And given such conditions, how can a filmmaker like Tazi be creative according to his own artistic lights?

At this historical moment in the field, one might have expected a return to Hollywood, Powdermaker's earlier terrain, but it was instead non-Western hegemonic film industries that came to the forefront of ethnography, most notably Bollywood in trail-blazing works by Rachel Dwyer and Jerry Pinto (2011) and Tejaswini Ganti (2012a). Fieldwork since then has been done on other regional powerhouses such as the Tamil industry known as Kollywood (Pandian 2015), the Nigerian film industry or Nollywood (Jedlowski and Santanera 2015; Miller 2016), the Bangladeshi film industry (Hoek 2014), the Hong Kong film industry (Martin 2017), the Ghanaian video film industry (Meyer 2015), and many others. Independent cinema, under the shadow of Hollywood's hegemonic production forces, also became the object of ethnographic inquiry at this time, most notably in Sherry Ortner's (2013) investigation of U.S. independent filmmakers and how they view their themes and filmmaking practices as an alternative to Hollywood. Young-a Park's (2015) study of a collective of independent South Korean filmmakers and their efforts to change society through their filmmaking is a non-U.S.-based example of independent cinema, and another instance of how anthropology's cross-cultural and comparative approach contributes to a broader understanding of independent film outside the U.S. and Europe.

We believe this is a good moment for an edited volume such as ours on the anthropology of film industries that captures the range and depth of this ongoing fieldwork, and we hope it will attract readers from a large number of disciplines concerned with visual and media studies, economics, culture, and politics. Anthropology raises to the fore the interesting question of whether the histories of cinema and film industries around the world are simply the same history (because of an industry that got its start in Hollywood and was exported globally) or whether we have to speak of histories (because of distinct national industries that were entangled in different economies as well as distinct political and cultural projects), or both (which is more likely the case). Dwyer's chapter in this volume is an attempt to write a history of the current moment in Moroccan film industry and cinema that parallels research done on the history of film industries and of Hollywood in particular (Gubak 1969;

Schatz 1981; Balio 1985, 1993; Neale and Smith 1998; Bordwell, Staiger, and Thompson 2003; Gomery 2005; Scott 2005), but shows how the Moroccan film industry's particular history (especially due to colonialism and nationalism) and specific cultural circumstances make it distinct. In this regard, it is closer to the work of film historian Priya Jaikumar (2006), who shows how the Indian film industry changed in the period 1930–1940, due not to the stimulus of cinema, whether national or global (like Hollywood), so much as the lure of colonial film markets. This comparative perspective is also what an anthropology of film industries can provide that is often lacking in other approaches mentioned above that focus on a single industry such as Hollywood or Bollywood (for an exception, see Curtin 2007; Govil 2015a; Jin 2020).

To repeat, anthropology brings to the study of film industries a comparative perspective that allows one to see their differences or uniqueness as well as their commonalities by being part of global film industries. Anthropology also shows how film practices are grounded in other cultural practices that are not necessarily particular to film industries but shape them nonetheless; and vice versa, how film industries influence the sociocultural world they depict and at the same time operate within. All the chapters in this volume talk about one aspect or another of this grounding of film practice in local realities.

Our Dialogue with Other Film Studies Approaches

Production Studies

As the anthropology of film burgeoned in the 1990s, another somewhat related approach, which had the virtue of doing fieldwork on film industries, came to fruition under the name of production studies, though its origins are in film and media studies programs rather than anthropology departments. In the 1990s, largely as the result of John T. Caldwell and his students at UCLA, production studies came into being that looked critically but also ethnographically at film (as well as other) industries. And yet, though it crisscrossed many of the theoretical interests and methodological practices of anthropology, it is surprising how muted, awkward, and even strained the conversation between the two has been to date. Production studies has tended to see its relationship to anthropology largely in terms of method (and to some extent also theory, especially that of Clifford Geertz), but it does not seem to acknowledge that anthropology too has been constructing film industries as an object of study for its own disciplinary sake for quite some time (reference to Powdermaker being the extent of its obligatory nod to that history).

Broadly put, production studies questions the assumption made by people in film industries that their practices are purely technical and aesthetic, or supposedly value neutral, by demonstrating that they are cultural or culturally constructed. Consider Caldwell's (2008) *Production Culture: Industrial Reflexivity and Critical Practice in Film and Television*, a major book on film and television, whose fieldwork took ten years to complete (1995–2005), which is a foundational text in production studies. It draws from the ideas of Clifford Geertz (1973) on culture as a text to argue that film industries (a singular and totalizing view is explicitly disavowed) produce a plethora of often conflicting views about the making of a movie that can be traced in promotional literature, documentary films about the making of a movie, and appearances on television by the film's director and actors. The deeper point is that these commentaries are not only about a specific film but film industries at large, the roles of filmmakers in them, and the way they want others, including the general public, to view themselves and their artistic projects. He calls these "critical industrial practices" and suggests that they construct "a kind of indigenous cultural theory that operates outside of academia" (Caldwell 2008, 5).

One of the many impressive qualities of this book is the rich array of ethnographic practices Caldwell brings to bear on his study of film and television industries, including interviewing hundreds of industry personnel, attending countless industry meetings, and going to many film festivals, not to speak of extensive archival research to get a sense of the history of the practices he is studying. Another of the book's achievements is its "studying up" (Nader 1974), or the ability of the investigator to contact people at the highest industry levels, access to whom is usually jealously guarded.[3] Another milestone in production studies is Vicki Mayer's (2011) imaginative *Below the Line: Producers and Production Studies in the New Television Economy*, which concentrates on those laborers in media industries that are not the producers, writers, directors, and actors who were the subjects of research by scholars such as Rosten (1941), Powdermaker, Gitlin (1994), and Caldwell, but rather the mid-rung and even low-level workers whose contributions to film and television production frequently remain invisible and certainly unheralded. Such below-the-line workers range from offshore laborers who assemble the television sets on which programs are watched back in the U.S. to reality-show videographers in the soft-core porn industry, and several other labor sectors in between. Unlike above-the-line workers like directors, producers, script writers, and actors, these film industry workers do not have the power to deny or restrict access to the investigator, and in fact often have powerful reasons and incentives to talk to him or her about their position in the industry and how they are exploited by it. This shift to below-the-line was not only occasioned by the difficulties of studying industry higher-ups, however, but also by economic restructuring of both film and television industries from the 1990s onward. This was a time when production became more decentralized and transnational by being outsourced to offshore production facilities such as color labs, sound studios, and editing houses. What Mayer adds is an important political-economic analysis of media industrial labor that was either missing or underanalyzed in previous production studies research (for a similar critique of production studies, see Curtin and Sanson 2016, 9). In her ethnography we see how workers are often underpaid, have little job security, and usually do not have guilds or trade unions to protect them from abusive labor conditions.

Despite its affinity with anthropological field methods, production studies has not engaged very deeply with the anthropology of film and media. Caldwell (2008, 11) inexplicably states, "I do not consider this book [*Production Culture*] necessarily anthropological (in part because of the cross-sector, cross-industry scope of my project)." Why an anthropological approach might preclude an examination of such scope is not altogether clear. Instead, he offers, "I do hope that by attempting to describe new developments with more precise terminology this book may at least have some *pre*-anthropological and *pre*-social science value" (11, emphasis added). Such an attitude may betoken either excessive modesty, or an unexamined discomfort with being closely associated with anthropology and the social sciences more generally, or an attempt to carve out a distinctive and separate field, or perhaps all of the above. To anthropologists like ourselves, however, it seems apparent that Caldwell's ethnographic gaze and theoretical framing are significantly connected to our own, whether production studies acknowledges this or not.

Since Caldwell's and Mayer's contributions to production studies, two edited volumes have been published (Mayer, Banks, and Caldwell 2009; Banks, Conor, and Mayer 2016), perhaps in an attempt to consolidate diverse research under one rubric (which, of course, our volume tries to do as well). Their essays attempt to extend the field's theoretical insights, media industry coverage (besides film and television, also included are radio, comic strips, sports, and popular music), and to some extent production studies' interdisciplinary reach (however, the work is still squarely situated within film and media studies). And though the transnational dimension has been expanded, it is significant that there are only two—albeit excellent—ethnographic essays on non-U.S. and non-European film industries (Jedlowski 2016; Lo 2016). As one of those ethnographers admits, "With a few exceptions, the emerging field of production studies has dealt mainly with the analysis of Western film industries, thus leaving out [*sic*] of its radar the wide range of experiences that has developed over the past few years around the African continent" (Jedlowski 2016, 176).

What is also telling about the above citation is its restriction of film industries to Africa when, of course, anthropological studies of film have now ranged across many regions in the world, including but not limited to the African continent. The need is to examine these industries in comparative perspective, as our anthropology of film industries calls for us to do. The comparison is not only a question of how Hollywood has dominated other national cinemas, or outsourced its production to media facilities abroad, as important as these trends continue to be; it is also a matter of understanding how states and private capital abroad are building their own film industries, whether successfully or not, which tap into local audiences as big as or even bigger than Hollywood's, and they do this within local contexts of labor and commodity markets, politics, and social organization, not to speak of distinctive local traditions of visual representation that are never quite the same across these burgeoning film industries. Furthermore, while film industries are emerging around the globe and to some degree share certain technological and aesthetic practices in common, they are nonetheless grounded in their own historical and cultural specificities that end up shaping their practices and products. This comparative perspective is what anthropologists have been investigating for some time now and offers a powerful corrective to the Euro-American focus in production studies.[4]

World Cinema

Insofar as our collection of essays looks at the question of how film industries have gone global in their production and reception (for example, filming in multiple international locations, using internationally known stars, doing their image editing in a studio located in one country and their sound editing in another, aiming for crossover audiences in different parts of the world, and so forth), it intersects with the concerns of world cinema.

World cinema is concerned precisely with the question that has come late to the former fields but has been at the forefront of the anthropology of film industries since its inception; that is, whether local cinemas and film industries can arise outside of hegemonic Western forms such as Hollywood, and whether new and different kinds of theory about film might emerge as a result of analyzing them. World cinema's "poly-centric approach" focuses on national, transnational, diasporic, and realist cinema projects through in-depth examination of specific cases that represent each project or a combination of them (Nagib, Perriam, and Dudrah 2012).[5] The point of having such a focus is the claim that new theorizations of cinema might emerge that go beyond the psychoanalytic frameworks that dominated film studies beginning in the 1970s (e.g., Mulvey 1975). World cinema sees itself as strongly connected to transnational cinema (which has been around since at least the 1980s), though claiming to have a more politically radical bent, including questioning ideas about filmmaking imposed by a national cinema or a hegemonic film industry that marginalizes certain agents in the filmmaking process.

Finally, and here the intersection with our volume's approach to the study of film industries may be most profound, world cinema is interested in how filmmaking, though powerfully transnational in all the ways adumbrated above, nevertheless has to come to terms with local social realities, be they economic, political, or cultural, that affect the artistic/theoretical/activist projects they are committed to.

In that regard, the work of Ashish Rajadhyaksha (2009, 2012) might be the most illuminating. He posits the question of what a theory of cinema might look like that can accommodate "Indian cinema" (i.e., a national project). In many ways, his answer to that question entails an analysis of film industries as developed in this volume, including capital that goes into financing Indian cinema, but it also highlights that industry's relationship to the Indian state. Indeed, his argument is that the Indian state is particularly important for understanding Indian cinema as a national project, and not for the reason that one might assume, by supporting cinema in its formative stages, but rather the opposite, by keeping its distance from it. The Indian state deemed Indian cinema illegitimate, largely because of its decentralized filmmaking processes that seemed to elude quality control and other concerns. But that relationship to the state changed in the 1980s as the Indian film industry became transformed, and it now receives both state ideological support and substantial corporate investment. How has that changed relationship then also changed Indian cinema?

World cinema has several important intersections with the anthropology of film industries, but it might be fair to claim that the latter has a clearer and stronger commitment to fieldwork. The idea that new theory can emerge in the study of non-Western cinema parallels the anthropological notion of theory being grounded in place-specific fieldwork. That is to say, anthropological theory is not simply about analytic categories derived from abstract postulates and their logical or systemic interconnections that are then applied to local realities in order to make sense of them; it is also about the creation of new analytic categories when more abstract theory fails or lacks the ability to make sense of those concrete realities. Those ideas or categories emerge in the course of doing fieldwork in new places, and we speak of them as being grounded in that sense. If those analytic categories then have legs and can be applied to fieldwork in other places, they become generalizable; yet the cycle will start over again, and newly grounded theory will yet again emerge in the process of applying such categories. It is one of the strengths of all the chapters in this volume that they put forward new ideas or new perspectives that emerged from fieldwork conducted on film industries in quite different places in the world.

What Is the Anthropology of Film Industries?

If earlier we delineated a brief history of anthropological work on film, that is not the same as attempting to delineate a field that we call the anthropology of film industries. We turn to this task next.

We acknowledge our indebtedness to a large literature in film studies on the economics of film industries that has dealt with sources of financing, marketing and distribution, labor, organization of work in terms of studio systems, and so on (among others, Guback 1969; Allen and Gomery 1985; Balio 1985, 1993; Wasko 2003; Mayer 2011; Curtin and Sanson 2016). In this volume, what we talk about with regard to financing and markets is directly related to their concerns. And Kevin Dwyer's chapter on the Moroccan film industry also intersects with some of their concerns and methods (particularly statistical).

However, our approach to film industries draws on a different genealogy of political economy than the scholarship above. We are not as much concerned with describing the economics of specific film industries as with exploring theoretically the categories needed to analyze such industries. For us, those categories go back to the Frankfurt School, particularly the seminal essay by Max Horkheimer and Theodor Adorno ([1944] 1989) on the culture industry, as well as key figures of that era who were in conversation with them, namely, Walter Benjamin (1969) and Siegfried Kracauer ([1947] 2004, [1960] 1997, [1963] 1995). According to Marx, alienation is the general malaise the worker succumbs to in the capitalist system of production, and Benjamin and Kracauer in particular saw film as a "distraction" from the tedium of the workplace and its alienation, reinvigorating the worker's senses. We might add that the relief is only temporary, the worker being sent back into the workplace and suffering from alienation all over again, the result being that the capitalist system is, in effect, an "iron system" from which there is no escape.

A significant theorist in the background of the Horkheimer and Adorno essay is Max Weber, and, indeed, their formulation of the culture industry as an iron system (a system that is inescapable and in a sense imprisoning) echoes Weber's indictment of legislative rationality as an iron cage. One of their formulations of a culture industry is that it standardizes the production of artworks as commodities in order to produce them quickly and for the masses. This standardization is part of a larger calculus or rationality in which the means and ends of production are connected to each other in the most efficient, logical, and profitable way (however these values may be understood). Besides rationalization, another key Weberian idea is reenchantment, which is connected in fact to rationality. One of the effects of rationalization, according to Weber ([1922] 1958), was the loss or marginalization of the spiritual in daily life, and one might argue that film is a key way in which this reenchantment is achieved in modern life.

How, then, have these theories informed our understanding of film industries if it is not film as an object or text, nor even the relation of such an object or text to a complex historical or social context, that is the primary issue here? We lay out our theory of film industries below in terms of the following main ideas: commodification, standardization, or organization, and modularity (perhaps the most important feature of film industries).

Commodification

To answer these questions, attention has to be paid, first of all, to the fact that a film is, as Horkheimer and Adorno ([1944] 1989) reminded us more than half a century ago, a commodity and therefore part of a capitalist system. In their day, the exchange value of film commodities was primarily with other film commodities, but with the rise of television in the 1950s, film industries faced serious competition for commodity sales with television industries. The relationship of these industries is a complex one, and Amrita Ibrahim's chapter in this volume looks at this relationship with regard to Indian television news and Bollywood dramas. Whether we are talking about film or television industries, however, what Horkheimer and Adorno pointed out about commodity thinking and profit making that affect casting and plot, the casting of the actors based on the bankability of the star of the moment, and scripts on the popularity of a certain story line, still applies: it is about standardizing the commodity so that it can be mass produced in a quick and efficient manner to make a profit.[6] (We talk more about standardization in our discussion of film practices below.)

Having made the distinction of film as a commodity, we hasten to add that we do not conceptualize film industries in a base/superstructure relationship, where industries are the base and culture or politics is the superstructure;

rather, we see film industries and their attendant ideologies as thoroughly imbricated. Conversely, to understand the commodity side of movie making also means more than following the financing of films (either by governments or private investors) or their profitability or the wage-labor pools their production taps into: it means studying the way a film production is organized to deliver a certain commodity or filmic product.[7] We also speak of industry in the plural, or industries, in order to suggest that there is no monolithic business model of how films are made worldwide.

While the criticism is often voiced by independent filmmakers and others that film industries limit if not stifle individual artistic creativity by subjecting artists to the bottom line—which is why they seek other kinds of financing and pursue their work out of passion for their projects (Ortner 2013)—it is nonetheless arguable whether independent or alternative cinemas could exist without mainstream film industries; the talent is often the same in both, and independent filmmakers are dependent on industry studios for distribution of their works (many mainstream industry companies even have their own independent or alternative film units with their own budgets and production targets). There have also been cases where a film industry has been mobilized for something other than profit, as was the case for the American and German film industries during World War II, which means that an understanding of film industries cannot stop at or be reduced to its commodity aspects, and yet such moments are episodic and hardly the norm. The example of Soviet cinema also shows that films can be made without the commodity being foremost in the filmmakers' reckoning of their artistic product, and yet the ways in which such products were made nonetheless closely resembled commercial film industries in the West (Roth-Ey 2011).

In other words, films are part of business enterprises that are supposed to make money, and we propose that their workings be studied ethnographically. Being part of global capitalism, film industries require anthropological analysis like any other industry such as mineral extraction, agricultural production, or pharmaceuticals.

Organization of Film Industries

Perhaps it is easiest to see what we mean by "structure" of film industries by going back to the beginnings of Hollywood, when the making of a film was explicitly modeled on the automobile assembly line innovated by Henry Ford, a point alluded to by Powdermaker (1950) in the subtitle to her book on Hollywood, *The Dream Factory*. Business models have tended to see the organization of classic film industries such as Hollywood in terms of the vertically integrated studio, whose personnel acquire the financing, hire the talent, and market the final product; that is, as a centralized system of production under a powerful studio or production company (Schatz 1981; Balio 1985; Bordwell, Staiger, and Thompson 2003; Gomery 2005; Scott 2005; Jacobson 2015). These studios also owned theaters across the country that showcased their films. We do not need to go into the details of what happened next, but the studio system began to break up at the end of the 1940s when the courts abrogated the studios' monopoly over the exhibition part of the film industry, followed by the freeing up of actors to work outside their studios. By the 1970s, which is often called the beginning of post-Fordist capitalist production, the vertically structured firm, including the Hollywood studio system, began to decentralize and lateralize—that is, the component parts of commodity production such as photography, editing, sound, music, and so on were contracted out to specialty production houses around the world because the cost was lower without sacrificing quality—while the main creative forces behind the film (the producer and director) were responsible for assembling and refining the pieces of the film into a finished product and often under a production company name.

Whereas films for the most part today are not produced in the centralized and hierarchical, top-down fashion they were in the heyday of Hollywood, that organizational structure hasn't gone away either (the example of China's Qingdao Oriental Movie Metropolis cited earlier dramatically underscores the fact that it is by no means defunct), and powerful production studios like Disney, Amazon, and Netflix are now reinventing the model of the vertically integrated firm in the way they hire directors to make films that they finance for viewing exclusively on their subscription-based streaming platforms. How, then, do we conceptualize film industries in such a way to accommodate both a centralized and a decentralized model of film production while retaining the fundamental idea that it is organized?

Let us try to clarify what this complex organizational structure looks like in terms of three different models.

1   To maintain national film industries (whatever they might look like) and national cinemas; this is a case where a film industry on the model of Hollywood or Bollywood is maintained (even in the face of forces mitigating against it). This swimming against the stream may be in order to gain symbolic capital for countries with prestige film industries or political projects that want to keep control over their film industries rather than outsourcing their production tasks.

2 To persuade film companies to film inside their countries because of (a) the perceived beauty of their landscapes or the cutting-edge look of their cityscapes (what has sometimes been called "harvesting" or "mining" for scenery), and (b) infrastructure, where countries or cities become a global film industry hub by providing film companies with state-of-the-art production and postproduction services and facilities (in-country transportation services, traffic management, and police protection, as well as generous tax breaks and other economic incentives).

3 To build giant global media companies that produce and create their own content, which they sell on their own network platforms to individual subscribers. These conglomerates are in a sense a return to the older-style hegemonic film industry of yesteryear (Hollywood), except that they produce content in an array of media in addition to film, particularly television programs. Because of the complexity (and newness) of this model, we elaborate it at the end of the introduction.

Some countries strive to achieve just one of these endeavors; others, some combination of them. All but one of the contributors in this volume have done fieldwork on national film industries and cinemas, and arguably even the exception (Jessica Dickson) traces what appears to be an emergent virtual reality (VR) film industry in Johannesburg, South Africa. But Johannesburg also conforms to (2) above in that it has become the preferred cityscape of an imaginary apocalyptic urban space in many contemporary Hollywood sci-fi movies, which is then incorporated into action sequences through digital effects achieved in its postproduction studios. As Dickson also discovered, South African filmmakers are now trying to build on their virtual reality expertise by creating a national cinema of their own aimed at imagining an African future (1). Arab Gulf countries like Abu Dhabi, while not necessarily building their own national film industries (like Iran or Egypt) or advancing a cinema particular to the Gulf, have nevertheless built an infrastructure—in terms of both facilities and trained personnel—to allow international film companies to film inside the UAE without having to re-create or transport their production infrastructure overseas. This is in keeping with the UAE's larger global business model, which is to become a world hub for the global flow of ideas, money, and people. In addition, the UAE has certain iconic urban landmarks that are transnationally recognizable, such as the ultraluxurious Emirates Palace in Abu Dhabi or the Burj Al Khalifah in Dubai, the tallest building in the world (2), which have been filmed on location and then inserted digitally into action sequences shot in film studios in Hollywood (Vivarelli 2015).

In order to trace these differences in organization, we propose to look at film industries cross-culturally, ranging from Hollywood to Bollywood, and from Iran to Hong Kong, in order to reveal their diversities, distinctiveness, and commonalities. We will examine both dominant or hegemonic forms of such industries as well as alternative or subdominant industries.

Standardization: Personnel, Practices, and Training

Standardization may be more important than profit making. We just mentioned the great Soviet film industry that was not capitalist driven, and yet it was an industry because it exhibited many of the same standardized modules that are present in capitalist film industries such as Hollywood. On a lesser scale the same can be said for the Cuban film industry (at least with the rise of its communist regime). And there are mixed examples (Iran for one) of a prestige national cinema that is heavily state subsidized alongside commercial cinema that is paid for by capital investment and market sales: both operate according to standardized procedures.

Let us, then, try to grasp more clearly how films are made in standardized ways. First, filmmakers are personnel, or specialized workers identified by the roles they play in film production such as producer, director, actor, technical crew, writer, cinematographer, publicist, and so forth; and though a single person might take on more than one role in any given production, the roles are nevertheless thought of as distinct, entailing different yet well-defined tasks. Film professionals are those people in the industry who have attained standards in their tasks that are recognized by other fellow professionals (or certified by training bodies). These personnel may also belong to unions and guilds that help regulate film production in order to protect workers, guarantee a respectable wage, and ensure the artistic values of the final product.

Second, personnel are expected to carry out their tasks according to certain standardized practices. For example, a cinematographer is expected to know how to operate the camera and use lighting; an art director, how to acquire or make props and decorate sets; a sound recordist, how to capture the sounds of the film, like dialogue and background noise; an actor, to have rehearsed their lines and be prepared to take direction; wardrobe and make-up crew, whose tasks are probably self-explanatory; and so forth.

Third, the labor for carrying out these standardized practices has to be trained, which can take at least three distinct forms. Personnel are usually trained (often in film schools and/or apprenticeships) in order that they might perform their tasks rationally and up to certain industry standards. As Lotte Hoek (2014, 74) explains for the Bangladeshi film industry, "in lieu of filmmaking institutions, filmmaking skills were and continue to be passed along through apprenticeship." Anand Pandian (2015, 11) makes a similar point about the Tamil film industry: "Young men—more rarely, young women—come as apprentices into trades as varied as cinematography, choreography, and editing with almost no formal training." But on-the-job training is important as well and is not the same as an apprenticeship (even though apprentices usually learn their art or trade while working with a master). On-the-job training is exactly what the term implies: learning the skill while working on a job and being supervised by whatever skilled technician is at hand. The worker's relationship to the expert usually ends when the job does. Probably no industry relies only on one of these forms of labor. Even Hollywood relies on apprenticeship, especially because of the strong guild system that it works with. Countries with film industries that have neither film schools nor guilds, or weak ones if they do, will rely on apprenticeship and on-the-job training to build personnel.

But successful filmmaking can also be irrational in relation to standardized practices and safety codes mandated by certain film industries. What is interesting is the deliberate transgression of this standardized process, as Sylvia Martin explores in chapter 6, on "edgework," or when filmmakers ask their crews and actors to take risks to secure the "stolen shot," the shot that entails certain dangers that excite audiences and presumably sells at the box office. The risks often contravene industry safety codes or general public safety, and even though filmmakers are aware of these rules, they break them anyway.

Modularity

Besides commodification and trained personnel practicing their trade according to certain standards, our concept of film industries stresses the modules through which films are made, marketed, and exhibited. Several recent ethnographies of film industries have in fact stressed this idea using other terms. In *Reel World: An Anthropology of Creation* a Tamil film producer by the name of G.D. says as much to anthropologist Anand Pandian: "Very soon after we first met, G.D. began to draw a triangle onto a page on his daily planner. 'Filmmaking is a *process*,' he explained, dividing up the figure into a stack of five horizontal slabs, 'a process of step-by-step activity.' The script was the foundation. Then came the cast and technicians, then the shooting and the studio work, and finally, at the apex of the triangle, marketing and distribution. All of these layers, the producer declared authoritatively, 'add value' to the project" (2015, 41, emphasis added). Pandian does not necessarily subscribe to this bottom-up or hierarchical vision of Tamil filmmaking, suggesting that the process is, if not entirely haphazard, certainly more open-ended. For example, if control over the production process is an ever-present anxiety, it is no more so than in the camera work, especially as most shooting takes place on location rather than in the studio and is thus subject to the vagaries of outdoor lighting (109–110). Further, Pandian suggests that this is not an exceptional instance in the Tamil film industry; rather, it is one of its defining conditions, a contingency of external factors that can impinge at any moment upon the filmmaking process to cause an alteration of plans or expectations, to which filmmakers must respond (as the subtitle of his book suggests) creatively (141). Of course, even classic Hollywood movies have been made in the face of contingencies and uncertainties of one sort or another. Consider the making of *Lawrence of Arabia* (1962) by the fastidious technician David Lean, who faced the difficulties of filming in wind-swept desert terrain with large, unwieldy camera equipment, not to mention political opposition within Jordan to filming in the country in the first place, and a budget overrun so enormous that the producer had to reign in the production and complete it in Spain and Morocco. All of these contingencies required creative solutions on the part of the director, the film crew, the actors, and the producer. And so the questions are: Is it about a difference of degree or scale of film industries that make them more or less vulnerable to contingency or chance; or, more interestingly, is this contingency or chance a generative or creative principle within film industries generally? The process of filmmaking is always subject to contingency or chance, but the latter rarely destroys the process outright or makes it superfluous. Studies attuned to the process of the filmmaking, thus, allow us to recognize the indeterminacy of the work: the ways that it is shaped and the result of constraints and possibilities found in diverse contexts, some not readily apparent in the locations of their production. It allows us to appreciate how a work not only has different meanings and stakeholders at different times but how it is the accumulation of all these that result in the final text.

In her ethnography *Cut-Pieces: Celluloid Obscenity and Popular Culture in Bangladesh*, Lotte Hoek (2014) also takes up the idea of process to talk about the Bangladeshi popular film industry, which she describes as having "components" such as script writing, set building, sound mixing, fight direction, or comedy acting. She argues that these component tasks have "relative autonomy" from each other (77). For example, it is clear that a set is not designed or built from scratch to suit the setting of a particular film story; it is rather a "generic" idea of what a slum, say, looks like, in which the film's action takes place. "Every set could be organized under basic categories like 'godown,' 'hospital,' or 'bar'" (78) and could be rented from the Bangladesh Film Development Corporation, or FDC, if it was too expensive to build from scratch. The result is that many films have an "FDC look" to them (and not necessarily to the detriment of their artistic integrity or audience appeal). Something similar occurred in the classic Hollywood film industry, where studios would rent their outdoor locations or their prefabricated town sets to companies making cowboy westerns (Jacobson 2015, especially chapter 5). What Hoek is talking about is what Brian Jacobson calls "infrastructure" (see also Larkin 2008), or the materials and construction that go into the making of the set, and from our point of view what is interesting is the industrial or standardized aspect of their production. As Hoek writes, "Yugantor's team [Yugantor is an FDC staff member who instructed set builders] built standardized sets for most films in production at the FDC, irrespective of the intricacies of a particular plot" (2014, 78). Another example of what we call modularity comes out of the work of film historian Daisuke Miyao (2013) and his book *The Aesthetics of Shadow: Lighting and Japanese Cinema*. He is concerned with the emergence of a certain look that Japanese filmmakers promoted in their films, in part to make their films more distinctive and appealing to Japanese film audiences in the 1930s, that foregrounds shadow. This is not a minor or insignificant technical feat, for it requires film lighting experts who were learning from each other across world film industries (for example, Japanese cinematographers promoting certain Hollywood lighting techniques that in turn required certain kinds of film stock as well as lighting equipment) and testing these out in their films. The point for us is that aesthetic questions of the filmic text were inextricably tied to the modularity of lighting in global film industries at the time.

Does this modularity itself have a structure? Ethnographies that have been attuned to the processes of filmmaking have suggested at least two: hierarchy (usually in the form of a director and producer) and linearity or sequence of modules being performed (as in the traditional tripartite division of preproduction, production, and postproduction). Lately, however, there has been some controversy among film theorists surveying film industries in the wake of digitization (see below) as to whether linearity or sequencing in the process has given way to simultaneity combined with spatial dispersion (that is, outsourcing of production modules to studios around the world, with the production head assembling them into the final product). That this simultaneity and dispersion of production modules is taking place seems undeniable, but even theorists like Hye Jean Chung (2018) who have advanced the study of digital film industries concede that modularity of production is still key. For similar reasons, modularity is the centerpiece of our theory of film industries.

To think about standardization in film industries more precisely, the notion of modules is helpful. (Among the modules that have become standardized in film industries are production, script writing, directing, acting, on-location shooting, cinematography, editing, marketing, exhibition, censorship, critical reviewing, and, lately, postproduction digital visual effects.) A module specifically conveys the notion of a standardized part that an industry deploys to produce an automobile or a building. But there is another aspect to modularity, which is that a module moves from one domain or area of production to another, depending on need or desire. Though it may be standardized internally, it is not stable or fixed but can move flexibly to be part of another production, another movie. Finally, though each module is in a practical sense discrete, it still needs to be coordinated with other modules for the final product to emerge. Modularity may imply movement, but that movement is coordinated to fit with other modules in the production system. Modules are the reason that different aspects of a film can be uncoupled from each other and then made in different countries of the world—depending on cost or production values—with color printing being done in a Paris studio, editing in London, sound mixing in Los Angeles, and visual effects in South Africa. Modules are why film crews can be international and still ensure a standard production value, because they depend on commonly held expectations of work and excellence. And because these modules are found in other media, personnel can move from one media industry to another; for example, from film to television to the music industry and back again.

Modules are deliberate and received ways of thinking about filmmaking, the things that filmmakers talk about when they describe how a film is made. As an example, note in Pandian's ethnography of the Tamil film industry how G.D. talks about the things that make up filmmaking and their structural relationship to each other. Nevertheless, it is also the case that the practice highlighted in a particular filmmaking module may also occur in other modules, often in a discrete, though still self-conscious way. For example, editing is a module typically associated with the creation of the final cut, when an editor, often with the input of the director, splices footage, according to the guidelines of the script. But editing may also occur in exhibition, when censors insist that a film be altered, or when a film is cut by the distributor because of its length, perhaps to increase ticket sales. And before a film is released, it is sometimes previewed by audiences (the reception module) who are shown alternative versions, typically of the ending, to judge which they prefer, and the film is edited according to their tastes. The fact that filmmaking practices foregrounded in a particular module migrate to other modules foregrounding other practices does not invalidate the theoretical notion of a module per se, though it does complicate how we analyze empirically the way filmmaking practices and modules relate to each other. It might help to think about the difference anthropologically, in terms of the distinction between emic and etic categories, where emic categories are the modules of filmmaking and the etic categories are how these are realized in actual filmmaking, with all its contingencies.

It is again important to reiterate that modularity has not gone away as an analytic for understanding how films are made industrially even in digital media. The sequencing of modules is now less important because different modules can be worked upon simultaneously in the production process in different places. For Chung (2018), this is an argument for seeing spatialization of production as being more important than its temporalization, though perhaps it is more fair to assert that both temporal-spatial frames have been affected in ways that we have yet to fully understand. Rather than thinking of sequencing, perhaps we should think of reflexive reiteration (repetition, of course, also being a temporal process) as important in today's filmmaking, where the director and producer can see the filmic text produced in outsourced locations and ask for corrections or changes to be made. In any case, this spatialization is made possible by outsourcing the work of making a film to different studios around the world that specialize in that module's production, something that Dickson explores in chapter 7, on South African VR production, and a factor that Thomas Elsaesser (2013) argues has increased in the digital age with profound economic effects on digital industries. A modular approach to the study of film production helps us find commonalities within and across different industries and better grasp the links and influences among them, while also suggesting what makes industries distinctive in specific contexts.

Fieldwork and Ethnography

Several of the disciplines that work on film industries claim to be doing qualitative fieldwork, including what is arguably the hallmark of social anthropology, "participant observation." But despite these claims, this fieldwork often comes across as little more than interviews with industry personnel (whether above or below the line) as well as attending industry functions and parties, with almost no participation in the actual processes of making films themselves. Ganti (2014) has made this criticism in her comments on how film industries have been studied in media and production studies. It is argued by many industry scholars that such participation is virtually impossible given how closed and guarded the industry is, and yet anthropologists have done just that (Rossoukh in chapter 2 and Martin in chapter 6, this volume, are cases in point). How much an industry is closed to outsiders varies from one industry to the next, and given anthropology's more non-European/American reach, it may be easier for anthropologists to do this kind of participant observation in film industries such as Bollywood or Nollywood than Hollywood; but it is not necessarily precluded in Hollywood either.

We must remind ourselves that most anthropological fieldwork cannot be done in a few weeks or even a few months, not because of the scope or scale of what is studied (traditionally, this has in fact been relatively modest—a village here, a group of people there, or at several sites at one time to see how global phenomena flow through them) but rather that the object of study doesn't come into focus right away but over time. It is true that we enter the field with some preliminary sense of what it is we are after, but that sense changes as time goes on, making the object a moving target, so to speak. (Again, see Ganti [2014] for a similar point.) So much of fieldwork in production studies (and media industry studies) starts with the assumption that the object of inquiry, the production process, is what is to be studied, and the challenge is to glean what that process might mean to the personnel involved in it, including differences of point of view. But long-term fieldwork on that process is likely to reveal (a) that what people say they do and what their discourse means is quite different from what they say it means on other occasions and to people other than the researcher, let alone what they do in their work setting; and (b) that the analysis of what is being said and done in and about the process keeps changing, depending on where one is in the process and what one learns about it over time. In other words, both temporality and positionality are key to anthropological fieldwork, and neither is adequately addressed in the film industry literature.

Fieldwork (the methods by which data are obtained and collected) and ethnography (the semiotic forms in which the results of the fieldwork are presented in print or other media) are deeply contested practices within anthropology, and we do not propose to resolve the contestation by offering our own definitions or prescriptions. Rather, our plea is to be as inclusive and capacious as possible in our use of anthropological methods.

For example, filmic textual analysis may not have seemed anthropological to anthropological readers of such texts as Traube's or Caton's, because such analysis was not part of a conventional or traditional repertoire of fieldwork practices (being associated primarily with film studies); and yet there is no reason to suppose ipso facto that textual analysis couldn't be considered a field technique like textual translation, kinship diagrams, or property surveys and mapping, which have long been the staple of anthropological fieldwork. An analysis of the film's text (understood as the sound-image nexus that is present on the screen when the film is viewed) is not the same as understanding one of the film industry's key modules, the script or screenplay (and the difference between that screenplay and what ends up on the screen is investigated by Rossoukh in chapter 2 as well as Caton, in chapter 5, and Ganti, in chapter 1), and so what may seem like a throwback to an older form of film studies should not be discounted when it still proves to be useful. The notion of the filmic text has been imaginatively reworked by Constantine Nakassis and Amanda Weidman (2018), drawing on film theory, to talk about the sound-image as being not only representational but performative (see chapter 5, this volume, for a deeper discussion of their ideas). Or consider phenomenological analyses of the screen such as by Vivian Sobchack (1992) in her book *The Address of the Eye*, in which she argues for the screen's subjectivity that is on par with our own, the screen being able to address the viewer and make him or her over in in its own image (and we might add sound). Whether representational, performative, or subjective, the filmic text and its analysis are indispensable to film industry approaches.

What we include within the rubric of fieldwork is much greater than that, such as interviews with film industry personnel and film audiences, the study of film industry publicity such as professional magazines, participant observation in film industry modules such as acting, directing, photography, marketing, and cinema exhibition, and the ways in which film industries try to guide film reception through trailers, advertisements, and film reviews. The object of study has widened from the filmic text to the social context, and now from the social context to the global industry that produced the film commodity.

Having distinguished between fieldwork and ethnography, something needs to be said about the latter, which anthropology claims for its own as a distinct genre of writing. This gets us back to positionality in fieldwork, in fact, or the point—political as well as intellectual—that we come from when we study something like film industries. We have said that fieldwork is a process that unfolds over time, with the result that we understand what we are looking at differently at different points in that temporal flow, and no one point (for example, the end of the process) is necessarily definitive. Furthermore, we tend to encounter what we are looking at from a particular perspective, depending not only on our own interests but also the particular circumstances in which the work is conducted. These multiple and different ways of knowing are all valid in writing up what we claim to know about any given subject, and ethnography should reflect these epistemological aha moments and not just report the findings. The chapters in this volume engage in this kind of reflexive ethnographic writing, in which the authors share with the reader how they got to know what they claim to know about the film industry in question.

The stylistic methods for how this is achieved vary from chapter to chapter (in chapter 2, for example, it is by Rossoukh talking about his encounter over the long term with the filmmakers of a particular film and their dissatisfaction with its filmic text, and then how they tried to rectify it with a digital editing process newly introduced to the Iranian film industry at the time).

Digital Media and the Question of Film Industry

Film industries have constantly transformed themselves through the invention of new technologies or in response to the emergence of new media that compete with them. Consider the more dramatic or blatant examples of those shifts. The introduction of sound threatened the way films had been made in the earlier silent era, with their reliance on the close-up, the gesture, and dramatic bodily movement, but it ushered in the talking picture, in which dialogue opened up new possibilities of acting, not to mention storytelling. Black-and-white photography reigned supreme for decades, leading to the glories of film noir, until the introduction of color in the 1930s, not to mention 35 mm and then Super Panavision soon thereafter. Many decried the shift, while others welcomed the richer palette of colors and greater expansiveness of the viewing experience. With the introduction of television to audiences in the 1950s, the film industry responded by creating the wide-screen theater, photographing in Super Panavision, and filming in exotic locales. Rather than television eclipsing film, as was feared in some quarters, the two media have grown alongside, and in fruitful interaction with, each other. In each instance of technological change, film industries have adapted and continued to thrive.

Today the emergence of digital technology seems to pose the same challenges as did these earlier technologies for film industries (for a review of anthropological work on digital media, see Coleman [2010] and Horst and Miller [2012]; for a stimulating discussion of digital processes' impacts on filmmaking, see Casetti [2015]). Analog processes, on which earlier film and television depended, record information about image and sound as continuous, with varying degrees of intensity or amplitude in the wavelength. Digital processes record the same information differently, parsing the wave into bits of information (with their own degrees of intensity or amplitude) and then using high-speed computers to combine these bits in just about any way the producer or listener wants. Image and sound manipulation are immeasurably enhanced, and while film industries have always been interested in that, the question is whether a matter of degree is leading to a difference in kind (i.e., that what we have been calling film industries is no longer tenable). Imaging is no longer a matter of the iconic-indexical representation of the world but a matter of creating a virtual world, one that exists purely as a projection or product of the modes or media representations themselves. The difference would be between a world whose events physicists are able to represent through complex mathematical representations and worlds that exist because they are the logical outcomes of mathematical equations or theorems, regardless of whether they exist or not in the natural world. Much of our world has been transformed by digital technology, from computers and CDs to medical interventions and working robots, and the film industry is no exception.

For the most part, films are still made using analog processes, but now visual effects can be inserted or computer generated alongside them (for example, the film *Who Framed Roger Rabbit* in 1998), and high-tech studios are built in which such films can be tweaked or enhanced in the postproduction process through computer-generated digital media (see chapter 7, this volume). Whereas the use of visual effects in *Roger Rabbit* was revolutionary in its day, it has no comparison to the importance of such effects in films today. "Of the 25 top-grossing films of the 21st century so far, 20 have been visual-effects showcases like 'Avatar,' 'The Avengers' and 'Jurassic World.' (The other five were entirely animated, like 'Frozen.') The typical blockbuster now spends about a third of its production budget on visual effects" (Picket 2017, 68).

The real question is whether film industries are entering into a brave new world of film production by adopting digital technology, leading to the near replacement of traditional industry personnel by digital media and their highly skilled operators, and leading to a highly flexible and essentially nonlinear process of image execution and work (though a process nonetheless). Another way to imagine this is to say a digital film is still created using modules, but they are now performed by the computer as directed by highly specialized programmers and in just about any order that they want. Digital media have allowed different understandings of representing reality that could not be entertained before, due to the influence of video gaming, virtual reality, and augmented reality, for example.

Not only production is affected but also the viewing experience, ranging in materiality from the screen on one's smartphone or personal computer to the immersive home theater experience of a mounted wall screen with surround sound. This proliferation of the ways in which a film can be exhibited raises the question of what a film is when it is reformatted and reedited to fit the different sizes of exhibition (though arguably this question has always been raised regarding film made for theaters that is reformatted for television). Is it the film formatted for release on theater screens around the country and the world? Or is it the film reconfigured for viewing on one's smartphone? In all probability it is both, and other versions in which it can be seen or experienced, without necessarily threatening the film's ontological reality. But what happens when film viewers can download a film on their computer and then digitally alter it according to their own whim, which is now the case? Has a line been crossed? Perhaps at this point it is less film as a product or object that we are talking about than a complex process of appropriation or re-creation through which multiple agents can make filmic events and view them flexibly in different venues. Digital media literature speaks of "remediation" (Bolter and Grusin 2000) and of "convergence" (Jenkins 2006) to capture the way images presented in one medium can be manipulated by audiences in another medium for their own purposes.

But if that is the case, this only reinforces the view of film as a process, except that now it is expanded across different media and not just within them. That is, consumers can now become creators of film, not just consumers of a finished product. Or what was once the consumer of an image product now is also the creator of it and the marketer on YouTube and other platforms. In our terms, this is a new type of personnel made possible by digital media. Of course, what hasn't changed is that we are still talking about commodities, though made primarily for individual or collective consumption. But if such film processes are to have any life in the market, they will have to be produced according to certain standards set by the media-networking world and in line with that community's expectations. We are thus back to professionalization and standards, one of our defining criteria of film industries. It is noteworthy that in digital media industries (Elsaesser 2013) the question of personnel as a module does not disappear, only that some personnel within that module disappear while others newly emerge. For example, a more prominent role in classic narrative film, such as the scriptwriter, now may be more in the background of the production process, whereas the digital media artist is now on a par with the older cartoon animator. Even actors have been transformed as performing artists before the camera. Personnel is thus an analytic of lasting salience in film industries even though the roles are constantly shifting. It's not that expertise disappears but that it gets redefined.

Even if analog versions of film were to disappear except as curated or archival objects and the production of film through digital media completely replaced them (just as the computer replaced the typewriter), we would still be faced with the problem of studying them as part of an industry, albeit the exact features and organization of which may not as yet be clear. This may perhaps be the most exciting emergent form of film industries that ethnographers can work on today.

In the introduction to their book *The Promise of Cinema: German Film Theory, 1907–1933*, Anton Kaes, Nicholas Baer, and Michael Cowan write:

> The rise of digital media has provoked no shortage of debates about what cinema has been and will become. To some observers, film seems to be a thing of the past, an artifact of twentieth century visual culture, a relic of the Fordist era with its industrial rhythms and distinct division of labor and leisure. Others point to cinema's unanticipated afterlives in film festivals and retrospectives, compilation films and museum installations, online archives and virtual cinephilic communities. From the latter perspective, cinema is not so much disappearing as morphing into exciting new forms and hybrids, whose uncharted trajectories bear an uncanny resemblance to the cinema's beginnings more than a hundred years ago. (2016, 1)

Let us remind ourselves that the diversity of filmmaking forms and practices at the beginning of the twentieth century were in the interest not only of art but also of the commodity, and that this in turn was embedded within a sprawling, inchoate industry. The same no doubt can be said about digital media. While allowing artistic breakthroughs of numerous kinds, they are still driven by the same interests, and capital is bound to organize those interests in the form of an industry, whose outlines we have yet to discern. And if film studies can look to the beginning of the film industry to see what seems to be emerging now with the spread of digital media and the proliferation of platforms it has encouraged, let us suggest that anthropology can compare what is happening in the world of filmmaking today and perhaps paint a clearer, more comprehensive picture of it. Even if modes of appropriation and re-creation are now individualized or democratized (where, in a sense, anyone with the basic digital equipment and platforms can be their own filmmaker), individuals or groups making such films are still cultural agents operating within social relations and groups—hence requiring anthropological analysis.

The Contents and Organization of the Volume

Earlier work on film industries tended toward a stage model of film production, from production to postproduction and finally exhibition and reception. What our discussion of film industries here suggests is that this stage model is no longer helpful and that modularity, the key theoretical concept in our understanding of film industries, should replace it. This does not mean that modularity does not have issues of temporality built into it, but that it transcends fixed or stable notions of either space or time in the production process. In some ways, modularity is the key idea of work and production in the COVID-19 era: work need not have to be done from nine to five or in a fixed office space; now it can be done anywhere that is deemed safe and secure and coordinated temporally with the locations of colleagues also working away from their traditional work spaces. Modularity is a key facet not only of industrial production, including film, but of our everyday lives.

The modules we have proposed as a convenient way of tackling the ethnography of film industries also informs the organization of the essays (with one exception, to be discussed below), with each essay focusing on one or more of a film's modules in the process of its production. Above all, they show how an industrial perspective teaches us something about film we have not discerned clearly enough before.

We do not see any necessary order to the chapters as they appear in the volume, nor did we strive for comprehensiveness in our coverage of film industries. Rather, we hope the chapters, singly and in combination, drive home the main arguments the volume is making. To grasp these, we do suggest that the chapters lend themselves to comparison because they show what is the same across film industries in the ways we have defined here but also, and more crucially for an anthropology of film industries, what is different about them due to the grounding and embedding of industrial practices in distinct political, economic, and sociocultural contexts. We argue that this is not simply a matter of specificity or particularity but rather a deep interconnection or entanglement of industry with location and place, which is why we use the plural "industries" to talk about our subject matter. A comparison of chapters also reveals the nature of anthropological fieldwork and the thickness of ethnographic description that is required not only of film production but also of the locations and places in which the production takes place. Most anthropologists who study film industries also study the society and culture in which such industries operate, and they go more deeply into these contexts as a matter of course. It is hoped the reader will appreciate that anthropological fieldwork at its deepest goes beyond the interview or the attending of film industry events but is a matter of digging in the ground that the film industry presupposes for its work but whose students rarely undertake. To put the point differently, anthropological fieldwork often begins where such production studies fieldwork leaves off.

Chapter 1, by Tejaswini Ganti, examines what we would call a module in certain film productions, namely that of dialogue translation and also dubbing (where a professional—often an actor—speaks the lines of a film's character in a local language shared by the film's audience, and does so in a way that matches the lip movements of the on-screen character). Dubbing, of course, has long been a concern for animated or cartoon films, but these don't necessarily entail translation problems, a particular concern for films shot in one language and then distributed for foreign exhibition to audiences who speak a different language. Such is the case, for example, in the Hindi film industry's rereleasing of Hollywood blockbuster movies for local audience consumption. Because of the fact that they are significant money makers for the Hindi film industry, the number of such releases for the Hindi market is on the rise, occasioning the questions of good and effective translation and dubbing for Hindi film professionals who want to challenge past stereotypes of shoddy work in this area of the Hindi film industry.

In her analysis of what professional film translators and dubbers say and do about their practices, Ganti performs an ethnography of language or of basic notions and values of language Hindi-speaking professionals harbor that go beyond the production but in the end deeply affect it. She asks what linguistic ideology professionals of a certain social status and educational level share about language translation for Hindi film audiences, and how such ideas affect the way they render spoken English into idiomatic, colloquial, and class-inflected Hindi. Not only is this chapter an ethnographic look at a key film industry component rarely considered in production studies, it is also a contribution to the linguistic anthropology of spoken Hindi.

The module Ramyar Rossoukh focuses on in chapter 2 is editing, a process that was profoundly changed at the very time the film he analyzes, *The Willow Tree*, went into postproduction. The change was the introduction of a new technology, specifically digital editing systems (which have supplanted their earlier analog equivalents) with the power to quickly and almost seamlessly change the order of the frames, insert new frames as needed, and even alter the look of frames to suit the artistic aims of the director. As Rossoukh demonstrates in his meticulous recounting of the making of the film, the filmmakers were disappointed in the test screening of the rough cut, lamenting the fact that the Islamic allegory that was to be imparted by the story somehow got, in Freudian terms, repressed. The irony was that the high professional standards the director brought to the making of the film seemed to expunge its spiritual message. The editing challenge was a return of the repressed, or a revival of the Islamic message, through constant dialogue between the filmmakers about the revised (and re-revised) filmic texts made possible by digital editing.

One has to understand how the Iranian film industry is connected to deeper issues in Iranian society, a matter that can only be explored ethnographically. Digital editing takes on nontechnical meaning for the way it brings the spiritual meaning of the film to life, which is why Rossoukh refers to it as the "digital divine." But there is an even more profound point that would be lost were the ethnography to stop with the production itself. It is necessary to understand how film production is entangled in a larger history and context of the uses of film to reenchant society with religious fervor. Putting the editing module within this Islamic project helps us better understand the deep entanglement of film industry and society. It was not just the film as an artistic project that was saved (in a religious sense) but the film industry, or so it is hoped.

Chapter 3, by Amrita Ibrahim, is about a crime-show genre on Indian television news that uses Indian cinema to narrate its stories. As such, it conforms to the modules of script writing and editing in film and television industries. This is an example of how industries have ties to each other in terms of the flow of labor, ideas, and capital, alluded to here. It does not help us understand this interindustrial exchange by analyzing film and television as separate entities. Film and media scholars have referred to this as "transmedia storytelling," arguing that this is becoming more prominent today (Jenkins 2006; Casetti 2015). Ibrahim's chapter can thus be read as an ethnography of this phenomenon in the Indian context.

Ibrahim tells a rich and complex history of Indian television, arguing that it shifted from event programming to "flows" (Williams [1974] 2003) in which viewers experience television as subtle rhythms and moving images rather than as programming content. One reason for this shift had to do with the opening up of Indian television to private investment and international cable networks in the 1990s, when viewers gained access to a much larger number of channels and could switch between channels to establish not only their own content choice but also their own viewing rhythms, or flows.[8] The main creative agents of this fusion of news and cinema are not the journalists working on the scene to cover a crime but particular journalists working in the newsroom as writers and editors who create a story that can be narrated by drawing from their deep knowledge of, and work experience in, Bollywood cinema. Naturally, it was those personnel in the editing room with deep knowledge of film and work experience in the film industry who had a leg up in creating the kind of news that television channels were looking for. The editors retrieved filmic scenes, musical tracks, and iconic dialogues from their vast knowledge of popular film culture and through them narrated a crime story. Ibrahim argues that these personnel are creative as "cultural vectors," who, by example of their own careers as "self-made" men in the television industry (and they are almost all men), provide a neoliberal alternative to the traditional story of self-fashioning dependent on wealth, caste, metropolitanism, and religion. Unintentionally, their biographies become vectors of individual transformation for others within the Indian public sphere, calling for an ethnography that goes beyond the production.

Lotte Hoek's essay, chapter 4, is unique in its ethnography of film criticism (in the guise of film censorship), a relatively neglected topic in the study of film industries. It is also important to note that ethnography here goes beyond the film production to an ethnography of the state (the censorship board), with the result that production within the film industry is immeasurably enriched and complicated. One of the main points to be gleaned from Hoek's analysis of Bangladeshi film censorship is that it attempts to set the conditions for the production of an exhibition film rather than an effort to control it after production is over. Or, as she puts it in her chapter, "it is at this point that censorship becomes a part of the film production process (a site in the industrial process of making a film) as well as a critical reflection on that process." She refers to "cinematic discernment" as being central to film censorship, notions of what constitutes not only "proper" but also "quality" film production in all of its various modules. For example, it might be objected that the cinematography and acting are below industry standard or that the script is "not a narrative." More interesting still is that this discernment is a matter of artistic taste as much as it is of legal judgment, thus troubling the distinction between law and art that is often invoked in the realm of censorship (that is, that censorship supposedly operates in the realm of law and not in artistic or sensorial experience).

This emphasis allows her to go more deeply into the question of what censorship is and how it operates in context, a relatively neglected topic in film studies. She claims that censorship in the Bangladeshi film industry is different from what William Mazzarella (2013) found for the Hindi film industry (and most other cases of censorship examined to date), in that the former is less about something objectionable about the image or the scene's content than it is about artistic form. The notions of what is or is not artistic freedom, of how much government should regulate film production, if at all, and of the separation, if any, between art and its esthetic imperatives on the one hand and government and its sense of civic obligation on the other are not the same in this context (and the broader South Asian one) and what film industries in the U.S. and Europe face.

The relationship of the filmic script to politics is something that Steven Caton also addresses in chapter 5, discussing a Yemeni film, *A New Day in Old*

Sanaʾa (2005), except that the censorship in that case has to do with content rather than form. The other point to note is that in contrast to other essays in this volume, which examine full-blown film industries from Bollywood and Hollywood to Hong Kong and from Iran to Morocco, Caton's contribution looks at the other end of this industry spectrum, involving a country, the Republic of Yemen, with no film industry to speak of, though with ambitions to develop one. The production of the film was meant to be the incubator for this emergent industry. But even before production began, the film got into trouble, and the essay traces what Caton calls the "politics of culture" swirling around the controversies of the Old City as a cultural space in which on-location shooting was embedded. Cultural studies gave us an understanding of culture conflicts that surround artistic works, and Caton draws inspiration from this approach to delve into the politics of culture surrounding the Old City of Sanaʾa as an "Arab capital" as well as cultural conflicts around certain Western artistic performances that took place in its urban space. But the ethnography reveals that these conflicts went deep into the production, from script writing to on-location shooting, a subject not often considered by cultural studies. Political problems intensified when on-location shooting began because production was seen as an alien and threatening force in a deeply gendered and religious urban space.

The rest of the chapter is an ethnography of the Old City as that culturally coded space and the normative strictures on seeing and being seen that the production violated, occasioning bitter and at times violent local opposition. To unsettle the film industry's naive assumption that the film crew can parachute down unproblematically in a landscape or a city, to do its on-location module, and then leave as if nothing was disturbed in the process, Caton develops the idea of dis-location shooting to capture the precariousness of the actual situation. But to reiterate the broader point that connects back to an anthropology of film industries, it was only an ethnography of urban space whose insights were then brought to bear on film production that deepened the author's understanding of this dis-location.

Sylvia J. Martin, in chapter 6, examines the practice of "shot stealing," film industry jargon for filming a scene on location without getting permission from, or financially compensating, the people who are being filmed or the owner of the property. Shot stealing is done by directors to enhance the excitement or spontaneity or memorableness of a movie, and hence its commodifiability, and Martin argues that shot stealing goes back to the earliest days of film with its "cinema of attractions," when collisions, explosions, and chases of one sort or another were built into stories for the visual excitement they provided and to draw audiences into the cinema houses (nickelodeons as they were called). The kind of work shot stealing requires Martin calls "edgework." She extends this analysis of edgework from stunt workers and camera operators to actors more generally on the set. And the analogy is extended to other risks and dangers of filmmaking, such as on-location shooting in illegal or dangerous places or engaging in dubious financing.

In addition to the complicated logistics of setting up these shots, Martin was concerned with the ethical difficulties film productions face in putting crew and actors—some of them minors—at considerable physical and emotional risk on the set. Having worked in two different film industries, Hollywood and Hong Kong, since 2003, she compares edgework and its ethics in the two, showing how differently these two industries respond to ethics because of their particular economic constraints: downsizing (and competition from Hollywood, in the case of Hong Kong) that has exacerbated job insecurity on the one hand; smaller budgets and tighter film schedules that have increased pressures on directors, crews, and actors on the other to speed up filmmaking; and cutting corners to enhance the bottom line that compromises safety standards on the set. The relative precarity of workers in the two industries has also affected the tendency to protest or strike for improved labor conditions, including greater safety for edgework. Martin's essay reveals the importance of comparison across film industries to show that, despite certain universals such as commodification, standardization, and so on, these do not play out in the same way when these industries are grounded in complex local economies and political circumstances. It is an ethnography of the latter that takes us beyond the productions to the wider contexts in which such production is entangled.

The comparison of film industries Martin does in her chapter, we would like to extend across the next two chapters by comparing two different but related film industries at the most macro level. The two chapters deal critically with the question of the relationship between a film industry and a cinema. What is necessary within a film industry to make possible a certain cinema? What challenges do cinema projects face in terms of their economic viability? These questions get us back to one of the main arguments of our volume: the analytical distinction between the concepts of cinema and film industry.

Jessica Dickson did fieldwork at a Johannesburg, South Africa, film workshop, attended by VR innovators and film creators from both the Global South and North, in which the challenges of using VR were debated, and where examples of films that employed it were shown and evaluated. The larger cultural context in which this emergence of VR in Africa has to be understood, as was made clear by participants in the workshop, is an ongoing debate about postcolonial visions of Africa's future, which Dickson lays out in all their complexities. For the VR workshop participants, the more specific question was whether and to what degree VR is especially suited to imagining Africa's futures within African (as opposed to a non-African hegemonic) cinema, however configured. As with the emergence of anything else new, the debates over both VR and African futures are unsettled, leaving us with no lasting answers or clear-cut directions, and Dickson's careful, complex, and nuanced ethnography brings this out while at the same time capturing something of the excitement of this creative moment in African film cinemas.

But the workshop Dickson attended also contained a cautionary tale for creative artists hoping to tap into VR, which was offered by film industry specialists from the Global North: the industry might not yet be in place in South Africa to make this venture possible. None of this visionary project will take off unless there is an industry behind it. And they don't really know what that industry looks like. Where will the financing come from? How is production organized? Where is production done? Who will control it? How will it be coordinated? And that's only the production side. How will the films be marketed and exhibited? In other words, one can imagine a cinema that is both culturally stimulating and politically important, but without an industry to base it on, it can't take off. The tensions between cinematic aspirations on the one hand and industrial conditions of possibility (or impossibility) for those cinemas on the other are very real and poignant.

This difference between a cinema and an industry is also explored in Kevin Dwyer's chapter on Moroccan cinema, an established and critically acclaimed world cinema that is nonetheless facing enormous economic challenges. But the question is not just one of economic challenges but about how modularity is dispersed spatially across different countries, both in order to save money and to maintain or enhance quality. Dwyer scales up the analysis of film industries from particular modules to the most macro level and over a longer period of time, what we might call the pattern of the parameters of film industries. Dwyer shows how Moroccan filmmakers, for example, often contract with film production sites in France (whose government partially subsidizes the work as a form of foreign assistance) for this work. Understanding these complex national and global interdependencies and their impact on small-scale film production such as Morocco's is one of the key questions anthropologists of film industries need to grapple with. However, Dwyer's essay is really a critical examination of the Moroccan film industry as a whole over several decades and the complex and even delicate balancing that had to take place between national and transnational forces, between state and private financing, between censorship and freedom of artistic expression (a point also raised in the essays by Hoek and Caton), and a host of other macro factors.

Another key parameter is the interdependence of media industries such as film and television, which Dwyer analyzes in chapter 8 for the Moroccan case, as do also Ibrahim and Martin in chapters 3 and 6, respectively. This interdependence is critical for understanding how film professionals can survive when their industries are ailing by moving into television, and vice versa (see also Martin 2017). Technological interdependence extends to global production sites within national film industries. Thus, some pricey filmmaking modules such as music and sound effects or editing can be completed more cheaply and at a higher standard by specialized studios in other countries (what Martin [2017] calls assemblages).

What this last point underscores but is revealed in each chapter is the importance of modularity in understanding film industries, and perhaps at no other time more so than in the present. The module is universal but gets entangled in local realities. And an accounting of those realities requires an ethnography of those local realities that then loops back to the understanding of the module to show how it depends on contingencies outside itself. We have to practice ethnography on two levels, the ethnography of the wider contexts in which the production is entangled and the ethnography of the production, and then to understand the dialectical relationship between the two.

Notes

1 Of course, film studies (including the history of film), production/reception studies, and cultural studies have long been at the forefront of film analysis and criticism, and they inform our work in important ways, but they seem less concerned with the question of film industries per se than the latter.

2 Among the exciting theoretical developments were Soviet and French film criticism (such as the *Cahiers du cinema*) and before that the 1930s Frankfurt School and its attendant scholars (Benjamin and Kracauer) whom 1980s scholars were reading arguably for the first time when translations became available. Semiotic-structuralist analyses of the filmic text from the perspective of the subject's gaze (Metz 1982) and Lacanian-inspired feminist theoretical perspectives (Mulvey 1975) dominated 1970s film theory, followed by critiques of these approaches from a Foucauldian framework of the subject's discursive (as opposed to psychoanalytic) construction (Copjec 1994), or from a Frankfurt School–Habermasian framing of the public sphere (and counterpublic sphere) where the viewing subject might identify with the screen's representation and organization of experience (Hansen 1991). As innovative and influential as these theories were, it is fair to say that they concentrated their attention on the camera apparatus and on the film as a filmic text rather than on film industries. Even Marxist

film criticism (Eisenstein 1949), one of the oldest film criticisms in the literature, was more concerned with a formal analysis of the filmic text, particularly of montage editing, than it was with film as an ideological apparatus connected to film industries and the capitalist system.

3　This is something that Todd Gitlin's *Inside Prime Time* (1994; originally published in 1983), a study of American television in the 1970s and 1980s, had also accomplished. But with regard to access, it turns out that these works are very much the exception, and as Sherry Ortner (2010) slyly suggests, "studying sideways" may be a more practical alternative to studying up (that is, to talk to these highly placed industry personnel about some shared commonality with the investigator such as cultural or political interests, education, identity in terms of class, race, gender, or sexuality, or even age, and to approach indirectly more sensitive and critical issues about their privileged positions).

4　Like production studies, media industry studies has obvious connections to the anthropology of film industries. Media industry studies is a field that was launched by Jennifer Holt and Alisa Perren (2009; for an update on this field, see Holt and Perren 2019; Herbert, Lotz, and Punathambekar 2020). There have been some sharp criticisms of this field (Govil 2013; Schatz 2014), not a few of them by people who have contributed to it. But we ask, what are the theories and methods that can be said to be distinctive of this nascent field? Or is media industry studies a conglomerate of other fields doing the heavy lifting, more about facilitating the exchange of knowledge across fields than it is about bringing a distinctive set of questions, methods, and analytical framings to bear in the study of media industries?

5　There is now a vast literature on national cinemas and some important critical anthologies (Hjort and MacKenzie 2000; Williams 2002; Vitali and Willemen 2006). Some film scholars have proposed the term "transnationalism" to capture the complex interplay of global, national, and local forces involved in contemporary film production and exhibition (Berry 2010; Ďurovičová and Newman 2010; Higbee and Song 2010; Elsaesser 2019).

6　To be sure, Adorno (1975) had some second thoughts about his critique in his essay "Culture Industry Reconsidered," and it has been pointed out numerous times that he tended to give little critical agency to the viewers of film in the public sphere. But to argue, as some have, that this failing is somehow reflective of the Frankfurt School's approach as a whole is a gross oversimplification. Jürgen Habermas ([1962] 1989) is arguably the last member of that school, and he was very much concerned about the possibilities of reflexive and critical debate in the public sphere, which logically includes film. Film theorists such as Miriam Hansen (a student in fact of Adorno) combined Habermas's idea about the critical public sphere with a theory of film-viewing audiences to talk about counterpublics and identification with subjectivities constructed on the screen (Hansen 1991).

7　For a complex discussion of the forces of capital, labor, and media production, see Michael Curtin's (2007) concept of "media capital."

8　For a fascinating comparative case study of the transformation of the television industry in Japan during roughly the same period, see Lukács (2010).

1. "ENGLISH IS SO PRECISE, AND HINDI CAN BE SO HEAVY!"

*Language Ideologies and Audience Imaginaries
in a Dubbing Studio in Mumbai*

TEJASWINI GANTI

"What's a simpler word for *paristhiti*? [circumstances]," asks Deepa, a dubbing director at Mumbai's Synchron Sounds, during the dubbing of a 20th Century Studios film into Hindi. Her colleague, Parul, answers, "*Paristhiti is simple.* It is *colloquial.* If we don't use that, then Hindi itself will be finished." Deepa replies, "I'm not sure—*paristhiti* seems like a heavy [*bhaari*] word." Parul responds, "Okay, let me Google that, but for 'hypothetical' why not say, '*Yeh saare baatein kaalpanik hai*'? [This whole discussion is imaginary]." This exchange carried out in Hindi (with the exception of the words "simple" and "colloquial," which were in English), which I observed during fieldwork in July 2016, is a small example of the daily negotiations that take place around language in dubbing studios in Mumbai.[1]

Since 1994, when *Jurassic Park* was dubbed into Hindi and enjoyed unparalleled commercial success for a Hollywood film in India, the number of Hollywood films dubbed into Hindi and released in the Indian market has been steadily increasing. Nearly all of the major animated, action, superhero, horror, and monster films are now released in India in dubbed Hindi versions. According to the 2017 *Media and Entertainment Industry Report* published by the consulting firm KPMG, nearly 40 percent of English releases have been dubbed into at least one Indian language, usually Hindi. In addition to Hindi, many of Hollywood's large franchise or tentpole films get dubbed into Tamil and Telugu as well. Dubbing allows Hollywood studios to broaden their audience base in India, which leads to increased overall revenues from the Indian market. The FICCI-Ernst & Young report of 2018 pointed out that the box-office collections of Hollywood films constituted 13 percent of the total theatrical box office in India, whereas in the past it was only about 4–5 percent (Ernst & Young 2018, 79).

Based on fieldwork in a dubbing studio in Mumbai in 2016 and 2018 observing Hollywood films being dubbed into Hindi and interviews with voice artists, scriptwriters, and dubbing directors (from here on referred to as dubbing professionals), this chapter examines the prevalent conceptions and representations of Hindi and English—what linguistic anthropologists call "language ideologies"—that are articulated, performed, and manifest during the dubbing process.[2] It describes the varied ways that dubbing professionals navigate and negotiate the complex act of rendering dialogue in Hindi when the original lines are written in English, and illustrates how dubbing, a form of audiovisual translation, is not just a meta-semiotic activity (Gal 2015), but also a language ideological project whereby discussions of linguistic difference, intelligibility, and skill are deeply entangled with assertions of social difference (Woolard and Schieffelin 1994). I argue that a Hollywood film dubbed into Hindi not only represents interlingual translation—that is the expression in Hindi of what has been said, written, or done in English—and a movement across semiotic systems (Gal 2015, 227–229), but also represents a movement across different regimes of value (Appadurai 1986; Myers 2001) from being a high-status foreign import to a low-status local product. Such a movement engenders efforts by dubbing professionals to counter the stereotype of dubbed films as poor and shoddy translations of Hollywood.

While scholars have pointed out that institutions such as the law, the state, and schools rely on the "ideologization of language use" (Woolard and Schieffelin 1994, 56) whereby language is linked to issues of social inequality, group identity, morality, and knowledge production, I contend that media industries and media production are also key sites to examine the imbrication of linguistic and social difference. Language plays a critical role in the political economy of media industries. From the earmarking of subsidies for filmmaking in specific languages (Ganti 1998), to the promotion of a particular dialect as a normative standard in advertising (Davila 2001), to the daily translations undertaken by news agencies (Davier 2014), to film studios' local-language production strategies (Donoghue 2014), language is a category of sociopolitical identity, form of labor, set of commodified skills, and object of market exchange (Irvine 1988). Dubbing, by being an instance of translation and hence a site of metalinguistic discourse, is a particularly productive arena to examine beliefs about language, which emerge from particular social positions, and how such beliefs are articulated as justifications for its structure and usage (Woolard and Schieffelin 1994, 57–58).

This chapter is divided into four sections. First, I provide some context by describing the general process of dubbing a feature film from English to Hindi. Then, I detail how dubbing professionals discuss the challenges of translating English dialogue into Hindi and how these linguistic ideologies are connected to audience imaginaries. Third, I discuss the disdain that dubbing professionals display toward the idea of the literal translation, a trope they use to explain the lower cultural status and diminished reputation of dubbed films, and how they attempt to efface the signs and traces of dubbing. Finally, I outline efforts by dubbing professionals to localize content in a manner that displays their cultural and linguistic expertise, working to counter the stereotype of dubbed films as poor and shoddy translations of Hollywood, which can have the effect of recalibrating the relative positions of Hindi and English within the Indian public sphere.

The Dubbing Process

As mentioned earlier, about 40 percent of the Hollywood films released in India are dubbed into Hindi. The decision to dub a particular film for theatrical release is taken in India by the Indian executives of Hollywood studios such as 20th Century Studios, Disney, and Warner Bros. headquartered in Mumbai, who then hire a local dubbing studio to carry out the scripting, dubbing, and sound mixing of the film. When taking the dubbing industry into account, the boundaries between Hollywood and the Mumbai-based Hindi-language film industry better known as Bollywood appear blurred and porous (Ganti 2021). For example, all of the personnel doing the labor—scriptwriters, dubbing directors, voice-over artists, and recording engineers—are located in Mumbai, and many frequently work in the mainstream Hindi film industry. Furthermore, the same distributors and exhibitors who distribute mainstream Mumbai-produced/Bollywood films also distribute and exhibit the Hindi-dubbed Hollywood films. In fact, since dubbed films are part of the same distribution and exhibition apparatus as mainstream Hindi films, the release schedule of dubbed Hollywood films is now calibrated with the release schedule of Bollywood films and vice versa. High-profile Bollywood producers avoid releasing their films on the same date as a heavily anticipated Hollywood film, which would be dubbed into Hindi, and Hollywood studios avoid releasing their high-profile projects opposite a heavily anticipated Hindi film.

The first step in dubbing a film is for the core team—scriptwriter, creative supervisor, dubbing director, and sound engineer—to preview it in the dubbing studio. In order to safeguard against piracy, films that have to be dubbed are delivered electronically on a secure server to the dubbing studio, and scriptwriters who are freelancers hired by the dubbing studio are only allowed to see films there. Films are previewed inside an individual recording studio on a monitor, and the version that is available for preview, referred to as P1, is a heavily watermarked one where special effects and other postproduction work are often incomplete. Since India is now part of Hollywood's day and date release schedule—films release in India on (or sometimes even before) the same date as in the U.S.—dubbing studios keep receiving versions of a film as it gets completed, so dubbing professionals have to be ready to redo, add, or sometimes even jettison entire scenes if the final version of the film is different from earlier ones. Dubbing professionals therefore work within very tight timelines; the turnaround time for dubbing a Hollywood feature film averages four weeks for a theatrical release to a week—or even less—for nontheatrical (satellite TV, DVD, streaming) outlets.

After the writer views the film in the studio, he or she is given the original English script as the source text from which to write the dubbing script. The English script is heavily annotated with explanations about slang, idioms, humor, pop culture, and historical and cultural references to help the writer in the translation process. Examples of such annotation range from a simple clarification of a contraction, "That's = 'That is'"; to an explanation of idiomatic usage, "give up on = colloquial phrase, meaning to stop having faith or believing in"; to a detailed exposition of American pop culture, "Muppet = a part of an ensemble cast of puppet characters known for their self-aware, burlesque, and meta-referential style of variety-sketch comedy." While scriptwriters acknowledge that such annotations are useful, they emphasize that an important dimension of writing a script for dubbing is to be attentive to issues of synchronization—matching lip movements, facial expressions, and the length of utterances—which becomes difficult without continuous access to the film. Since decisions about word choice and dialogue length are in relation to the written text (English script) rather than the performed text, the writer comes into the dubbing studio after having written the first draft to do a read-through with the creative supervisor and dubbing director, where they watch the film again while the writer simultaneously reads aloud the script in Hindi. During this time, the dubbing director and creative supervisor provide feedback to the writer on the translation and offer suggestions for revising the script. While it is uncommon for the translated script in its entirety to be vetted or approved by the Hollywood studio, writers are sometimes required to submit an English translation of a portion of their Hindi dialogues—referred to as a "back translation"—as specified by the studio, which becomes a way to monitor that the translation is capturing the essence of the original's tone.

In parallel with the scripting process is the voice casting process where the creative supervisor and dubbing director choose the voice artists for the various characters in a film. The amount of autonomy dubbing professionals have over casting is connected to the scale and release strategy of the film project, as well as which Hollywood studio is the client. For high-profile theatrical releases, dubbing studios have to send the auditions, referred to as "voice tests," of the principal characters to the international dubbing divisions of the Hollywood majors based in the U.S. While the U.S. office exercises the final approval over the voice casting, all of the dubbing professionals and Indian executives of the Hollywood majors I spoke with in Mumbai emphasized that studios usually went along with their judgment and approved their recommendations.[3] Although Hollywood studios send casting guidelines for each film project that includes character descriptions, which consist of the age and voice description, they are neither country nor language specific since they are prepared generally for the international market. Instructions such as "Please use established voices when possible/available. If no established voices available, please match the voices and performance as close to the original version character as possible," and voice descriptions like "a medium-range voice that is textured and has some resonance" or "a medium-range voice that is raspy throughout but warm," give dubbing directors a great deal of room for interpretation. Experienced dubbing directors have a vast knowledge of voice actors and their vocal styles and hence can often cast a project without auditioning several actors. When assessing whether a voice artist is a good fit for a particular character, dubbing directors pay attention not only to character synchrony (Bosseaux 2015, 59)—audience expectations of what a particular type of character based on age, class, occupation, and narrative function should sound like—but also to how quickly and skillfully the voice actor can complete the assignment.

Once the script and voice artists are in place, the dubbing commences, and, depending on the length of the film, number of speaking parts, and amount of dialogue, it can take anywhere from three days to two weeks to complete. The dubbing coordinator first schedules the voice artists who will dub for the principal characters, and they are individually booked for large periods of time—from two to five hours per session, and, depending upon the number of lines of dialogue, a voice artist may require multiple sessions to complete the part. Given the concern with piracy and spoilers, voice artists are not given the script in advance, nor can they take it with them to practice their lines. The dubbing director briefly summarizes the plot of the film and describes the particular character and their role to voice artists when they first arrive for their dubbing session.

The dubbing studio assigns a recording studio to a particular project so that over the course of the dub, the equipment and space remain consistent. The recording studio consists of two rooms: the larger, outer control room with a full audiovisual console, monitor, and seating where the dubbing director and sound engineer work, and the smaller inner room with heavier soundproofing and a window that makes it possible for people in the outer room to see the voice artist inside. This inner room is equipped with a microphone, headphones, speaker, screen, chair, and a stand or a desk with a small light where a hard copy of the script can be placed. Prior to the start of a session, the sound engineer adjusts the height of the microphone in the interior room and instructs the voice artist as to how far they must be from it for optimal recording quality.

The dubbing director gives instructions through a microphone to the voice artist inside, who watches the film on the screen and listens to the pilot track (the original English dialogue) while saying the Hindi dialogue. Sanket Mhatre, who has voiced for Matt Damon, Ryan Reynolds, and Brad Pitt, described the multitasking of physical and sensory skills involved in dubbing as akin to swimming: "You're standing with a script in front of you; you have a headphone on; the left ear is listening to the original pilot that is being played; the right ear plays back what you're saying; you're reading off a script, and you're trying to pause and talk along with the lips of the character that you're watching on-screen" (interview with author, August 6, 2016). Dubbing a film involves a great many rehearsals, takes, and retakes and is a very repetitive and painstaking process. The dubbing director and sound engineer have to pay attention not only to issues of synchronization and language but also to sonic quality. Their aim is to have the vocal track free of any extraneous sounds, and I observed many instances when a line had to be redone because of misplaced breaths and a variety of minute sounds—referred to as "clicks," "nose noises," and "snorts"—made naturally during speech.

What becomes apparent from observing actual dubbing sessions is that the task of translating and adapting a film is not solely the scriptwriter's but also critically involves the dubbing director and voice artist. Not being able to consult the film while writing makes it difficult for writers to draft a script that resolves the problems of synchronization—phonetic, kinesic, and isochrony.[4] Dubbing directors and voice artists frequently have to change and improvise dialogue to fit the lip sync and length of utterances on-screen so that the script serves more as a skeletal outline than a definitive and authoritative text. However, each film comes with a list of "key notes and phrases," mandated by the Hollywood studio, that either have to be retained as is, in the case of proper names and brands, or translated literally or explained rather than localized in the case of certain historical events or concepts central to the narrative.

Before a dubbed film is released, it undergoes a series of revisions as a result of the Q-C or quality check process. Once the dubbing is completed, the creative supervisor and/or head of the dubbing studio carry out the Q-C, which entails viewing the entire film with the dubbing director and sound engineer present. The dubbed film is assessed for the quality of synchronization, voice artists' performances, clarity of pronunciation, grammatical accuracy, narrative intelligibility, idiomatic language, and how conversational the dialogue sounds. The supervisor points out mistakes and areas that need revising, and the sound engineer flags those points on the audio track's timeline—referred to as placing markers—and enters a brief description of the required correction into a dialogue box that opens up via the audio editing software on the monitor connected to the recording console.[5] After this initial Q-C, the voice artists who need to redo portions of their work are notified to come to the dubbing studio to make the corrections. Once all of the corrections have been made, the film is screened for the representatives of the Hollywood studio, who may demand further changes and revisions. Once the dub track has been finally approved, depending upon the client, the film's final sound mix can either be done in-house if the dubbing studio has the technology and capacity or sent to the U.S. for mixing. During my fieldwork, I had the opportunity to observe all of the various stages described above. At every stage, discussions about translation and language hinged on questions of audience comprehension, identification, and pleasure, which is the topic of the next section.

Linguistic and Audience Imaginaries

In August 2016, while previewing the Hindi versions of the trailer for an American shark-survival film, Meena Ganguly, the head of Synchron Sounds, said, "*Chuttiyon manaane ke liye?* What does 'Be ready to enjoy your holidays' have to do with the film? How is it connected to what is being shown on-screen? What's the original in English?"[6]

Parul, the dubbing director who was supervising the project, played the English version, which stated in an ominous tone, "This year, plan your getaway. *The Shallows*—not just another day at the beach."

Parul pointed out, "We need a word in Hindi that means both vacation and escape."

Meena agreed and said, "Yes, but we also need some options for 'another day at the beach.'" She then muttered to herself, "Why hasn't Mohan given us some options?" She told Parul, "As soon as Mohan comes in, you need to have him write some taglines for the trailer, including for the title since 'shallows' means nothing in Hindi."

After Meena left the room, Parul lamented, "What to do about this 'getaway'? Is there a word in Hindi that has this sort of double meaning?" She spent the rest of the afternoon vexed by how to find an appropriate Hindi equivalent for "getaway" that would represent both senses of the word. She kept asking different people in the studio for their thoughts and input about whether they could think of a Hindi equivalent for getaway until Mohan the scriptwriter showed up and declared, "There's no word like 'getaway' in Hindi."

When dubbing professionals spoke about the challenges of translating scripts from English to Hindi, they often contrasted the two languages in terms of communicative efficacy and accessible vocabulary. Mona Ghosh Shetty, the owner and head of Sound & Vision India, a leading dubbing studio in Mumbai, echoing Parul's dilemma about the word "getaway," stated, "English is a very precise language. There are so many words for specific things, and at the same time some words can have double meaning so easily. We can't always tread that line in a local language" (interview with author, August 8, 2014). Divya Acharya, a dubbing director who worked at Sound & Vision India, elaborated upon this point: "Many a times, an English word, a single word encompasses a meaning [that], if translated, is a long sentence. To find an equivalent in Hindi—it's not that there isn't such a word in Hindi, but to find a colloquial word in Hindi becomes a tough job" (interview with author, July 29, 2016).

"Colloquial" is a term used with some frequency by dubbing professionals to signal accessible and conversational—hence desirable—vocabulary choice. However, the film genres that are most frequently dubbed, such as superhero or science fiction, pose particular challenges, as the Hindi translations for terminology commonly used in such genres are regarded as occupying the exact opposite register and are usually described as *bhaari* or "heavy." Talking about science fiction and space-oriented films, Ghosh Shetty related:

Nowadays, there is always everything about outer space; there is galaxy, there's so many words just for space, y'know? And then the words in Hindi—that's the other thing—you know in English everything that sounds colloquial, the moment you translate it, sounds really heavy in Hindi—very formal, and very hard language! So, like, if I had to say, "Would you like to go into space?" and I say, "*Kya aap antariksh mein jaana chaoge?*" You would have never heard the word *antariksh* or a spaceship—*antariksh-yaan*—and you can't just say *jahaaz* [ship] because it's not a *jahaaz* technically, so some of these things don't translate very well! Some of the concepts in a lot of these science fiction [films]—like atom-molecule—I mean, the moment I even start saying some of these words in Hindi, it sounds like a science class more than a feature film, y'know? The word "science"—*vigyan*—is just, so less used! (interview with author, August 8, 2014)

While her comments may seem reminiscent of colonial-era ideas about Hindi being inadequate to express scientific concepts (Dodson 2005; Prakash 1999), Ghosh Shetty was not complaining about the absence of Hindi terms, but rather their register. Discussing the experience of dubbing *The Hunger Games*, which was retitled *Maut ka Khel* (Game of death), Ghosh Shetty stated:

There was a host of terms that we had to deal with—what are we going to say for "donor"? What are we going to say for "candidate"? What are we going to say for so many things? It's not that you don't have a Hindi word; you have; there is. There exists a Hindi word for everything. I'm sure of it, but the point is, can we use it? Is it familiar? Because see, again the point is, who are you dubbing it for? You are dubbing it for people who speak a lot of Hindi, but are they very literate? To really know everything, to understand everything?

In Ghosh Shetty's statements, we see how the discussion of register quickly shifts into a discussion of audiences. The question of translatability here is not about the deficiency of Hindi as a language, but about the deficiency of Hindi speakers' comprehension.

Asserting that while Hollywood films in English are made for a wide English-speaking audience that encompasses a broad range of socioeconomic strata, Ghosh Shetty explained that in India she had a different target audience. She said, "We find that the kind of people we're dubbing for is not the same people that the film was made for, because there are literacy issues, as they may be of a poor economic background." Abul Ansari, a dubbing director who had been working at Sound & Vision India for nearly a decade, described that they were dubbing Hollywood films not for educated people (*padhe-likhe log*) who would in any case watch the films in the original English, but for people who were very unfamiliar with English, so unfamiliar that they barely knew of its existence (*aise logon ke liye hoti hai jo English se kam aashna hai, jinko pata hi nahi hai ki English kya hoti hai*; interview with author, July 30, 2016).

Dubbing professionals' representations of audiences for dubbed films as primarily working class with very little understanding of English is highly reminiscent of mainstream Hindi filmmakers' descriptions of the "masses" as the main audiences for Hindi cinema up until the mid-2000s (Ganti 2012a). Such descriptions are a key element of the Hindi film industry's audience imaginaries, which are the discursive constructions of the vast filmgoing public as opposed to actual socially and historically located viewers. When executives of the Indian divisions of the Hollywood majors such as Disney, Fox, Universal, and Warner Bros., spoke of their criteria for deciding which films to dub for theatrical release, they expressed audience imaginaries that created a clear hierarchy of film taste and viewing preference based on geographic location and linguistic ability, similar to audience classifications expressed by members of the Hindi film industry (Ganti 2012a). According to the three executives at Disney India whom I interviewed, anything that was "a little intelligent, thinking, or [had a lot of] dialogue" would never get dubbed for theatrical release, as such films would be "limited to three or four main cities," and only people who knew English would want to see them. These three individuals explained that films with too much dialogue would be hard for Hindi-speaking audiences to relate to and hence would not be commercially successful.

All of the dubbing professionals I spoke with kept emphasizing how their job was to simplify concepts and language so that the "Hindi audience" could comprehend these films. The underlying assumption is that those who only know Hindi are unable to grasp complex concepts and vocabulary. Referring to science fiction and films set in space, dubbing director Divya Acharya explained:

> It's not just you and me that's watching, and it's not just people of metros watching, in the interiors also—people watch, and if they don't understand, I will not have a repeat value when another of my Hindi-dubbed movies is released. That person would not want to go, because of too much of English *kuch samajh mein nahin aaya* [didn't understand anything], so we have to cater to them also. So we take those liberties and, as far as possible, want to keep it simple. We don't want to use sci-fi language—it's too much. Maybe term it and explain it, or not use it at all, and twist it in a way that it becomes simpler. (interview with author, July 29, 2016)

Making the content easier or simpler, however, was not a straightforward task but a difficult one, according to dubbing professionals. Ansari pointed out that it was important to avoid "bookish" language and make sure to use conversational Hindi (*bol-chaal ki bhaasha*) so that audiences would easily understand what is happening on-screen. In addition to not knowing English, audiences for dubbed Hindi content are presumed not to have a very extensive Hindi vocabulary either. Anju Jamwal, a voice artist, dubbing director, and the codirector of Mayukhi In-sync, which focuses primarily on dubbing American television content, described the Hindi used in dubbing as "audience-friendly Hindi." Explaining that the market for dubbed programs was in the "interiors" rather than the cities, Jamwal stated, "*Ab interiors ko hum itni* heavy Hindi, *shuddh Hindi denge joh unki samajh mein nahi aayegi, toh woh nahi dekhenge* program. [If we use a really formal and pure Hindi, the kind they can't understand in the interiors, then they won't watch the program.] The idea is to catch their attention. *Aur unko woh program ka* addiction *ho.* [So they get addicted to the program.] We don't focus on *shuddh* Hindi [pure Hindi]. It is like *joh samajh mein aaye—waisi* Hindi [the kind of Hindi that can be understood]" (interview with author, August 6, 2014).

An allied concern, which further shapes dubbing professionals' translation choices, is their sense that audiences are hypersensitive and can be easily offended, especially when it comes to religion. Dubbing professionals relayed many anecdotes to illustrate this point. One voice artist, during a lunch break, offered the example of an animated children's show on the Cartoon Network where the Hindu god Krishna took on the guise of a student and attended a school where his evil uncle Kamsa was the principal. He recounted, "People who were upset by this took out a *morcha* [protest] in front of Cartoon Network's offices, so they changed all the references. They kept the boy blue and the principal evil, but removed all references to Krishna's life." A dubbing director who was also listening to this anecdote nodded and said, "Yeah, it becomes really difficult. We have to be really careful with what names we use and what references we put in the films." Dubbing directors mentioned how they would rarely translate "God" as "*Bhagwan*" (one of the Hindi words for God) as that appears too Hindu, but would tend to use a term like *upar-waala* (the one above) as that is perceived to be neutral. In other cases, dubbing studios make such changes at the behest of the client. For example, a dubbing director who supervised the Hindi dubbing of one of the *X-Men* films related how the client, in this instance the Indian representative from 20th Century Studios, objected strongly to dialogue that was translated as "*Mandir-masjid gira denge!*" (We will tear down the temple and mosque!), as they felt that was too incendiary. The dubbing director then replaced the words *mandir* and *masjid* with *prarthana-sthhal*, which means a place for prayer (literally, "prayer-place"), but neither is it a commonly used term, nor would it be considered colloquial. These examples illustrate not only how audience-seeking/oriented media producers preemptively exercise self-censorship but also how audience imaginaries are central to the translation and dubbing process.

Rather than being idiosyncratic or individualized, dubbing professionals' translation choices are shaped by their role as media producers and guided by their broader assumptions about audiences for Hindi-language content in India. Their discussions about the differences between English and Hindi are also discussions about the perceived differences between English and Hindi speakers. While dubbing professionals explain their choices in terms of attraction and accessibility for the Hindi audience, another important aim is to make sure the films do not "sound dubbed," as that is a source of diminished status for these films, a topic I address in the following section.

The Problem of Literal Translation and Sounding Dubbed

While observing dubbing, I noticed that dubbing directors would frequently criticize portions of the dub script for being too literal, which usually meant that with its fidelity to the English, the Hindi dialogue ended up either conveying the wrong point or was rendered in an odd syntax. Anecdotes, frequently humorous, of the bogey of literal translation abound within the dubbing industry, often serving to socialize new entrants into the field or as a form of origin narrative for writers. Divya Acharya, the dubbing director at Sound & Vision India, narrated a humorous story she heard when she first started working as a dubbing director about a writer who was notorious for his literal translations. She said, "So for a gangster movie where a goon is asking for his money—the line was 'rest after the job,' which the writer translated as, '*Kaam ke baad aaraam karo!* [You should relax after you do the job]." Ashiesh Roy, a voice artist and scriptwriter who had written the scripts of *Dark Knight, Finding Nemo*, and *Happy Feet*, among many others, narrated the literal translation story that made him turn to writing dub scripts in addition to being a voice artist. Mentioning that he had a master's degree in English literature and was familiar with idiomatic English, Roy said:

> I suddenly started noticing that we needed to correct a whole lot of stuff that was written and given to us to dub because the meaning, the idiom, the context was all rotten! The writer who had written [it] had obviously no clue. . . . The first scene they were dubbing for—a man was sitting in a bar and there's a woman who comes in and obviously she's late and she says, "Sorry I'm late. I got caught up—I had this, I had that, I had a terrible

day." And he just says, "Come, join the club." And to my horror, I saw that it was being dubbed as "*Aao, club join karlo*," which is not the idiom! It is that something similar has happened to me also and so come join the club. You have to know. If you're writing, you have to know your slangs, your idioms, your modalities. If you don't, you have to learn. (interview with author, August 9, 2014)

While in the previous section I discussed how dubbing professionals represented their audiences as lacking English competency, both Acharya's and Roy's anecdotes point to scriptwriters' poor English skills, which in a sense reduces the distinction between dubbing professionals and their target audiences. Expressing disdain or derision at literal translations helps to distance dubbing professionals from the poor knowledge of English associated with their target audiences.

The other problem with literal translations is that they call attention to the disjuncture between the visual and the verbal on-screen; they highlight the fact of translation, that the film sounds dubbed. The primary objective of dubbing professionals, however, is to ensure that the film does not sound dubbed. In other words, the language should sound conversational, and there should not be a disconnect between the on-screen actor and the off-screen voice.[7] Acharya elaborated:

First of all, it has to sound natural, just the way you and I would speak to each other, so it need not be literary language, but it has to be grammatically correct at the same time. Sentences can't be long and twisted. They have to be straight, short, and simple. So we take ample pauses, because there are certain sentences in English which are long, and their construction is the reverse of what happens in Hindi. "I've met you before, Mr. Buffet." "Mr. Buffet, *main aap se pehle bhi mil chuki hoon.*" So the construction has been reversed. We can't twist the construction because then it will sound twisted, and it will sound forced. And it will sound dubbed, which we don't want. (interview with author, July 29, 2016)

Stating that while earlier films "looked and sounded dubbed," Acharya explained that currently the aim is to make dubbed content appear as natural and conversational as possible. She detailed how much effort dubbing professionals undertake to erase the traces of dubbing:

It's like two people talking, naturally. Like, make it as believable as possible that this was the original work, which is why we also pay close attention to the closed lips: p-ph-b-bh. Wherever there is a close-up shot and somebody has said a word in closed lip, we try to match it with an equivalent in our language where there is a closed lip. Like if somebody is in danger and he says, "Please!" We can say "*Bachao!*" [Help!] there because it's a closed lip. If it's a close-up shot, we try as much as possible to match those closed lips so that it looks more natural, as if the person has said that, the very thing that has been dubbed.

While Acharya spoke of effacing the traces of dubbing in terms of lip synchronization, Shakti Singh, a veteran voice artist who has been the Hindi voice for Jeff Goldblum, George Clooney, Morgan Freeman, Anthony Hopkins, Daniel Craig, Kevin Spacey, and many more, spoke of the importance of erasing the traces of English. He discussed how it was absolutely critical that one did not speak Hindi as if it were English. In other words, the goal was to make the dialogue so effortless and seamless that audiences would forget that the film was ever in English. He said (in Hindi), "It should not occur to you that the film was also in English. It should appear to you that this person is actually speaking in Hindi, and, after watching for a little while, you'll even forget that this person is white. It will appear to be totally plausible to you that, 'Yes, this person is able to speak Hindi.' So it is absolutely necessary to keep this in mind, that people are convinced" (interview with author, August 6, 2016). Singh discussed further how he always attempted to bring whichever film he was working on closer to a Hindi sensibility to reduce that sense of rupture and disjuncture caused by dubbed films. In the next section, I detail how dubbing professionals attempt to reduce this disjuncture further through the ways they adapt and localize Hollywood films.

Cultural Expertise and Creativity in Adaptation

The Disney executives who decided to have *The Jungle Book* dubbed spoke at length about their decisions and strategies for the film as well as their general brief for films they choose to dub. They mentioned that when they brief a writer about adapting a Hollywood film, they tell him that it should "be more like a Hindi film" with "localized humor," as the "local connect is very important." Figuring out the "local connect" was frequently referred to by dubbing professionals as a "transcreation" rather than a "translation," as script writers felt that a literal translation could never be successful either linguistically or culturally. Mayank Jain, who has written the dub scripts for numerous Hollywood films like *Independence Day*, *The Martian*, *Deadpool*, *The BFG*, all three *Kung Fu Panda* films, all of the *Ice Age* films, *X-Men*, and many others, had strong views about what would and wouldn't work within a Hindi-speaking milieu. He stated bluntly during our interview, "I always believe, and I still believe, two languages cannot be translated literally. They never can be, and if somebody says, you have to literally translate, I say, it cannot be. At a point you have to adapt, you have to go regional" (interview with author, August 5, 2016). Jain then proceeded to describe how in his adaptation of Spielberg's *The BFG*, he created a language for the giant that was a hybrid of Hindi and Bhojpuri since in English, the giant speaks in a peculiar dialect. He also listed the ways that he adapted the giant's unique terminology for animals and vegetables into Hindi:

> The giant, who is the main lead in that movie, speaks a very different language, like he calls hippopotamus "hippo dumplings"; he calls giraffe "girage" or something like that; and crocodile "croco-dial-a," something weird like that. For us, if we had written the same words in Hindi, it would have sounded very stupid. So the giraffe became *jeera-saunf* [cumin-fennel]—very Hindi context. The hippo-dumplings became *hippo-motalo*—*Hippo mota hota hai* [hippos are fat], and the crocodile became *agar-magar-much*—*Agar-magar hum boltein ha na?* [Don't we say if-but?] *Jaise unki sabzi thi* [Like his vegetable]—snooze-cumber— again it was a made-up vegetable. I made a combination of *kakdi* [cucumber] and *kharbooja* [cantaloupe]—I made it *kakad-bhooja*, because I also had to be creative.

Jain's neologisms were part of his effort to generate humor by playing with the language. He maintained throughout our interview that translating the English dialogue literally would never produce an enjoyable viewing experience.

Mayur Puri, a screenplay and dialogue writer for the mainstream Hindi film industry who has been writing dub scripts since 2015 for Disney films such as *The Jungle Book*, *Captain America: Civil War*, *Finding Dory*, *Angry Birds*, and *Avengers: Infinity War*, spoke at length about how it was more important to "translate emotions," by which he meant the intentions of the original screenwriter, than to translate words.[8] He gave two examples from *The Jungle Book*. The first was a scene between Mowgli, the little boy who was raised in the jungle by wolves, and Baloo the bear, where Baloo asks Mowgli to climb up a steep cliff to fetch honey for him. Mowgli's response in the English version is "Are you kidding me?" For Puri, this line communicated that the writer wanted to portray Mowgli as a savvy, wisecracking kid rather than an innocent babe in the woods. He then explained how he decided to write that line in Hindi:

I realized that they're trying to make Mowgli cool, like a guy that kids today would identify with. When I'm translating that in Hindi, the easiest way to do that is to say, "Do you think I'm a kid?" and the translation would be "*Baccha samjha hai kya?*" which people use in colloquial language, but then I wanted to go a step beyond that. I wanted to make him even smarter. I wanted to have that sense of repartee, so what I've written actually is "*Subah se koi mila nahi kya?*" "Haven't you found anyone else since the morning?" Now this is a colloquial term that we use, that we say when somebody is trying to pull a fast one on you: "Do you think I'm an idiot?" "Haven't you found anybody else to fool today?" Now, this is a very slang thing; this is a very cool thing to say in the Indian perspective, [but] if I back translate this, they will not understand it in Burbank. (interview with author, August 1, 2016)

Puri's second example had to do with the term "red flower," which was the way the animals referred to fire. In the film, the animals speak of the threat that humans pose to the jungle because of their possession of the red flower. Commenting that the term evoked a sense of mystery, beauty, and fear from the animals' perspective, Puri pointed out that if he literally translated the term as *lal phool* in Hindi, the effect would be the opposite, since *lal phool* was too generic and ordinary. He said, "*Lal phool* is used for many flowers—rose and this one and that one, and it's very romantic, and it's very sweet—there is no threat!" Therefore in his treatment note for Disney outlining his ideas for the translation, he suggested the term *rakht phool*, as *rakht* means blood. Puri asserted, "Now that creates a feeling of mystique. . . . When you say '*rakht phool*,' an Indian will have the same sense of mystery, same sense of beauty, and at the same time a sense of threat and awe. All these things will come to your mind when you say '*rakht phool*' or 'blood flower,' but not 'red flower'—'red flower' will be comic for us. It won't work."

Much news was generated in the trade in 2016 when *The Jungle Book* became the highest-grossing Hollywood film ever in India, earning an estimated 2.5 billion rupees—more than many Bollywood films, including superstar Shah Rukh Khan's *Fan*—and about 58 percent of these revenues were generated from the dubbed versions in Hindi, Telugu, and Tamil (KPMG 2017). In fact, even though initially more English versions were released theatrically than Hindi, by the third week, the ratio of Hindi to English had flipped, with more Hindi versions playing in theaters. Puri suggested that the reason for *The Jungle Book*'s success in its dubbed Hindi version was the fact that Disney India had given him the freedom to adapt the film in his own manner. He said in our interview,

"The reason why the Hindi version of *Jungle Book* became more popular than the English version was that the word-of-mouth was so good. Everybody was saying, 'This movie, you gotta watch it in Hindi, because the Hindi dialogues are damn funny. They are very good!'" Implicit in Puri's statements is the idea that audiences who normally would have watched the film in English chose to see the dubbed Hindi version.

Another film that was being celebrated within the dubbing community as an example of very successful localization was *Deadpool*, a satirical take on the superhero genre of films based on a Marvel character of the same name. Both Mayank Jain, the writer of the Hindi version, and the dubbing director, Kalpesh Parekh, were very proud of the way the Hindi version turned out, especially given that the source material posed a lot of challenges in terms of profanity and sexually explicit dialogue, which they knew would never pass the CBFC (Central Board of Film Certification) if they tried to replicate it in Hindi. Parekh, who relayed during our interview how *Deadpool* was among his favorite dubbing projects, mentioned a number of places where they took, in his words, many "creative calls" to adapt the material that avoided all of the problematic elements but still stayed true to the film's irreverent humor and entertaining nature. He stated (in Hindi), "If you watch and compare *Deadpool* in English and Hindi, then you will realize how different they are from each other" (interview with author, August 1, 2016).[9] Sanket Mhatre, who voiced the character of *Deadpool* in Hindi, reinforced Parekh's point in his interview. Referring to a specific scene where after a major shoot-out Deadpool inhales the smoke emanating from his gun and quips, "Tonight I'm definitely touching myself," Mhatre said, "Now that's not gonna happen in Hindi, so in Hindi, we had to work around, we went back and forth, and finally what we decided was "*Aaj main apni bandook ki nalli saaf karoonga*" [Today, I'll clean the barrel of my gun], which is like an innuendo, but it's not a direct thing" (interview with author, August 6, 2016). About the process of dubbing, Parekh explained (in Hindi), "Once you dub a Hollywood film into Hindi, it's not the same. You're almost creating a new film. It's as if you're directing a new film because you have to think about everything from scratch." Jain, *Deadpool*'s Hindi scriptwriter, took a great deal of pride in his work, stating, "My entire idea is to make the Hindi better than the English, because I've been paid for that. So then I look at it as a Hindi product. I'm very confident while saying that sometimes our English Hindi movies are better than the English" (interview with author, August 5, 2016).

Both Puri's and Jain's comments about the Hindi dubs being better than the English originals can be seen as a response to dominant perceptions and stereotypes expressed by members of the Bollywood industry as well as general media coverage in India. Dubbed Hindi films are generally characterized as shoddy translations, which ruin the viewing experience of a Hollywood film, and are only watched by viewers who cannot understand English.[10] Voice artist Mhatre acknowledged, "It's still not cool to watch dubbed films, or dubbed TV shows, because that kind of puts you in the category of an uneducated person" (interview with author, August 6, 2016). In Mhatre's statement, watching dubbed media is equated with not knowing English, which is equated with being uneducated.[11]

The association of dubbed Hollywood films with uneducated audiences positions these films as occupying a lower cultural and social status than their English originals. Both Puri and Jain alluded to this status by emphasizing how the particular films they wrote—*The Jungle Book* and *Deadpool*—had changed the paradigm and perception of dubbed films among social elites. Jain asserted, "Earlier, our dubbed movies were mainly watched by auto-rickshaw wallahs, taxi-wallahs, the masses; but now, after *Deadpool*, those sophisticated, upper-class people who saw [it] in English, when they saw the Hindi version, they said the Hindi is better than the English! And *Deadpool* was a major hit! And I got so many compliments" (interview with author, August 5, 2016). The main assumption behind such perspectives was that viewers who were bilingual in English and Hindi would never see the dubbed version of a Hollywood film and that watching a dubbed film was out of necessity, not choice or preference for Hindi. Jain's statements illustrate the imbrication of linguistic and audience imaginaries. Garnering an English-speaking audience is an index of the Hindi writer's skill and mastery and a validation of his translation. Jain's comments about the masses and narrative of cinematic improvement linked to socially elite viewers are remarkably similar to those made by mainstream Bollywood filmmakers about their own audiences and filmmaking practices (Ganti 2012a).

Conclusion

In this chapter, I have examined how discussions about language and translation are also discussions about audiences and social difference, illustrating Raymond Williams's point that "a definition of language is always implicitly or explicitly a definition of human beings in the world" (1977, 21). I have also detailed how dubbing a film importantly initiates a movement across different regimes of value. In their original English-language versions, Hollywood films—as the products of a globally powerful, successful, and technologically sophisticated culture industry—released in India occupy a register of prestige and distinction (Bourdieu 1984). They are regarded by media industry professionals as a foreign, niche commodity catering to an English-speaking urban elite, evident by their circulation in upscale multiplexes in the major urban centers of India. However, once they are dubbed into Hindi in order to reach broader audiences, these very same films lose value as they become associated with vernacular and provincial non-English-speaking audiences outside of major metropolitan centers.[12] Dubbing professionals in Mumbai, therefore, go to great effort to counter this loss of value through their deployment of linguistic, technical, and cultural skill in the hope that audiences who would be expected to watch these films in English would choose to watch the dubbed Hindi versions instead. English-educated, multilingual audiences thus represent the desired audience demographic for professionals in this segment of the dubbing industry. In their efforts to make the dubbed film more artful and prestigious, dubbing professionals simultaneously embark on an effort to recalibrate and reconfigure the symbolic capital of Hindi vis-à-vis English.

This chapter also illustrates how a focus on language and translation helps to complicate nation-bounded understandings of film industries, specifically those of Bollywood and Hollywood. While dubbed Hollywood films are increasingly characterized by the Indian and international press as threats to Bollywood, examining the production process of dubbing, however, reveals a much more complex picture. Not only do Hollywood majors rely on local companies in India to carry out the translation and dubbing of their films, but increasingly for their Hindi versions, they are eager to utilize Bollywood stars for the dubbing and employ established screenwriters from the Hindi film industry such as Mayur Puri to write the dub scripts.[13] In fact, the phenomenon of dubbed films calls into question national categories of both industry and cinema (Ganti 2021). With the dubbed Hindi version doing more business than the English original, the question arises, is the Hindi version of *The Jungle Book* a Hollywood film or a Bollywood film? Rather than taking such categories for granted, an anthropological approach to the study of film industries would examine the people, practices, discourses, and methods involved in constituting these categories and investing them with meaning (Ganti 2014; Govil 2015a).

Notes

I would like to thank Mona Ghosh Shetty, Divya Acharya, Sanket Mhatre, Shakti Singh, Abul Ansari, Mayank Jain, Mayur Puri, Kalpesh Parekh, Anju Jamwal, and Ashiesh Roy for all of their valuable input and insights that allowed me to write this chapter. This chapter began as a presentation for a panel, "Assembling Audiences, Legitimizing Languages: Ethnographies of Media Practice in Multilingual Societies," at the 116th Annual Meeting of the American Anthropological Association in

Washington, DC, in 2017. I thank Smita Lahiri for organizing that panel. Bambi Schieffelin has been an invaluable interlocutor and mentor. I thank her for being an incredible sounding board for my ideas and a tremendous resource for all things language-related. Research for fieldwork in Mumbai in 2018 was supported by an American Institute of Indian Studies Senior Short-Term Fellowship.

1 All names in this anecdote are pseudonyms.

2 Dubbing in India has a very long history, especially in the southern Indian cinemas, that predates the dubbing of Hollywood films. There are no systematic statistics, but from my conversations with dubbing professionals, television probably represents the largest segment of this industry.

3 Usually when a film is being dubbed for a straight-to-DVD or satellite release, dubbing professionals do not have to send voice tests or wait for the U.S. office's approval.

4 Phonetic synchrony refers to lip-synching; kinesic synchrony refers to making sure the translation matches the actors' gestures and facial expressions; and isochrony refers to making sure the length of the translated dialogue matches the length of the on-screen utterances (Bosseaux 2015, 58).

5 The dubbing studio where I conducted research was using the audio editing software Pro Tools 7 at the time.

6 The film is about an American woman who journeys to a secluded beach in Mexico to surf and then is stranded on a rock only thirty yards from the shore because of a great white shark. The rest of the film is about her attempts to battle the shark and escape to safety.

7 Akin to the long-standing practice within the Hindi film industry of dubbing actors for a variety of reasons—unfamiliarity with Hindi, not having the desired vocal quality, not having the time to dub for oneself (if not shooting in sync-sound), or even just being a newcomer in the industry.

8 Puri has written dialogue for Hindi films like *Om Shanti Om*, *Happy New Year*, and *ABCD—Anybody Can Dance*.

9 Changes to a media text are the norm in dubbing globally. See Ascheid (1997), Bernabo (2017), Ferrari (2011), Lindsay (2005), and Srinivas (2008) for discussions about dubbing-initiated localization in Germany, Latin America, Italy, Indonesia, and southern India, respectively.

10 This derisive attitude is not unique to India but is prevalent in the U.S. as well. An article in the *Hollywood Reporter* discussing Netflix's expansion of its dubbing practices begins, "'Localized' content has traditionally been sneered at" and then states, "Dubbing . . . is more often derided or ignored than celebrated. In the U.S. 'localization' is still mainly associated with cheap and schlocky overdubs of martial arts movies and spaghetti Westerns" (Roxborough 2019).

11 The conflation of knowing English with being educated is not relegated to just the media sector, but is quite prevalent across India (see Annamalai 2004; Jayadeva 2018; LaDousa 2014; Sadana 2012).

12 For a related but distinct example from a very different sociocultural context, see Perry Sherouse's (2015) discussion of dubbing in the Georgian film industry, where Georgian occupies an inferior register to Russian, so that many viewers were critical

of a law passed in Georgia that mandated that all foreign-language films—which were previously dubbed into Russian—be either subtitled or dubbed into Georgian.

13 For example, in *The Jungle Book*, Priyanka Chopra was the voice for Kaa, the serpent; Irrfan Khan was Baloo, the bear; Om Puri was Bagheera, the black panther; and Nana Patekar was the voice of Sher Khan, the villainous tiger. Other examples of Bollywood stars voicing for Hollywood films include superstar Amitabh Bachchan voicing for the titular character in Spielberg's *The BFG*, along with Parineeti Chopra and Gulshan Grover also voicing key parts; Arjun Kapoor voicing for Buck, the weasel, in *Ice Age 5*; Varun Dhawan as Captain America in *Captain America: Civil War*; Tiger Shroff as Spiderman/Peter Parker in *Spiderman: Homecoming*; and Ranveer Singh as Deadpool in *Deadpool 2*.

2. THE DIGITAL DIVINE

Postproduction of Majid Majidi's The Willow Tree

RAMYAR D. ROSSOUKH

Traffic on Vali 'Asr, the main north-south artery of Tehran, had come to a standstill. It was almost midnight on a Thursday. As drivers edged their cars into any available space, the grand tree-lined boulevard lost any semblance of order. Blaring horns and techno-pop filled the air. The film director Majid Majidi was driving me home after a day of reshoots for his latest film, *The Willow Tree* (2005). He now directed me to look out at the cars surrounding us. Had I noticed, he asked, the way the girls were dressed up and the boys were trying to get their attention? At their age, he was taking part in the revolution. "I spent my university years not in classes but in the streets." He didn't understand today's youth or know how to talk to them. When he tried to speak to his own teenage son, it felt like they were separated by "four generations." The media was exposing them to things he never had to deal with. Take pornography. "It used to be that a nude photograph was a rarity, something people kept hidden. Now all you have to do is turn on the satellite." Such extremes have taken a terrible toll on his generation. They all married young, but now so many of his friends are divorced and with younger women. Drug addiction, especially to opium, is rampant. Even the most committed revolutionary filmmakers have become opponents of the regime. Iran has changed so quickly, he considered. "In the West, it was a dissolve; in Iran, it's like a jump cut."

For Majidi, the promise of cinema is its potential to restore our shared humanity and connection to God in the face of such changes, even if we are unprepared to see it. "If the Prophet were alive today," he later told me, "he would be a filmmaker." Through humanistic and spiritual-themed films about children and young adults like *Children of Heaven* (1997), *The Color of Paradise*

(1999), and *Baran* (2001), Majidi had become one of Iran's most successful directors and a prominent figure in the state's project to "Islamicize" the postrevolutionary film industry. The avowed Islamic vision of his films, thus, offers a unique perspective for understanding the cultural work of the Iranian film industry in all its many dimensions.[1]

From 2004 to 2007, I did ethnographic fieldwork on the Iranian film industry, initially by working on Majidi's film projects—starting out as a production assistant, then moving to the cinematography unit, until I finally became an assistant to the director himself. During the postproduction of *The Willow Tree*, I participated in editing sessions and helped coordinate film reshoots, dubbing sessions, and communications with outside labs and studios, among other tasks. In this chapter, I focus on a three-month period in the film's postproduction, between an initial viewing of the rough cut of *The Willow Tree* and the film's premiere at Tehran's Fajr International Film Festival.

After briefly describing the different stages of the postproduction process and the way it was undertaken for *The Willow Tree*, I discuss the rough cut screening and the viewers' strongly critical reactions. Then, I examine three key efforts to reshape and reinterpret the film: first, the decision to cut down the film's length and abandon its linear structure; second, the introduction of new cinematic and editing techniques to recapture the spirit of the film's original script, such as flashbacks and voice-overs; and third, the way in which these changes led to efforts to remove the realistic elements of the film in favor of the otherworldly, which transformed the process of editing into a search not just for the film's meaning but for the divine in the mundane. In effect, not only did the world the film represented through its story become reenchanted, but so did the very filmmaking process that created it.

Postproduction: Editing

Postproduction encompasses a wide range of tasks normally undertaken after the end of principal shooting such as editing, sound design, musical composition, audio and visual effects, and the final sound mixing and processing of the finished print or copy. Though the sequence of postproduction work is fairly standard to all filmmaking projects, the length, costs, and number of personnel involved can vary immensely between industries and films within those industries.

Arguably, the most important individual in this module is the film editor, responsible for assembling the raw footage into a film based on the script and the director's artistic vision. The first step in this process is the creation of a rough cut, so called because it lacks important transition and sound effects, not to mention a musical score, among other elements. The film editor assembles the rough cut based on the script and detailed notes taken during the viewing of rushes and discussions with the director and other crew members. But some directors, like Majidi on *The Willow Tree*, can also play an active role in the postproduction process. For example, Majidi worked extensively with Hassan Hassandoost, the editor of all his feature films, Mohammad Reza Delpak, his longstanding sound designer, and Fouad Nahas, who had coproduced Majidi's previous film *Baran* and was a cowriter on *The Willow Tree*, and also solicited feedback from other members of the production team.

It is important to periodize technological innovations in any film industry, since these build on earlier technologies and infrastructures but come into being to solve other creative and logistical problems and sometimes are connected to different film projects. For example, handheld video cameras, like the Steadicam, with an active cameraman seem like a throwback to an earlier "cinema of attractions" (Gunning 2006) for filmmakers who wanted a closer connection to characters on-screen and more kinetic film experience. This was a response to an earlier style that was seen as too static and removed from the action and thus solved a stylistic problem. Similarly, the large cinema screen developed in the 1950s, which changed the way movie exhibition took place, was in reaction to television but required new technologies—film projectors and cameras and a whole new film stock—and created a different film experience. Steven Caton (1999) discussed this in terms of *Lawrence of Arabia*.

The same can be said for the Iranian film industry, which was undergoing an important technological transformation at this time (circa 2004–2005), one that would profoundly affect the postproduction of *The Willow Tree*. Before this date, almost all 35 mm feature films in Iran were edited manually, on standard flatbed editing tables on which picture and sound reels are synced, and run through a series of plates and projected through a prism on small, often hooded viewing screens. Each shot had to be individually cut and spliced together with the next shot. It was a laborious process that did not lend itself to group viewing by the filmmakers. While digital editing systems—in which the raw footage is transferred to a digital copy and then assembled through a software program—began to be more widely adopted in the United States in the 1990s, they had only recently been introduced in the Iranian film industry.[2] Digital filming and editing had already been used in Iran for small-scale video and television production but not for feature-length films. *The Willow Tree* in fact was one of the first—if not the first, according to many sources I spoke to—35 mm feature film to be entirely edited digitally. Examining this editing process for a particular film gives us a unique glimpse into a technological mediation of a film's content that was more profound than one might at first expect.

Since the late 1990s, digital film production and editing has become an industry standard, and, of course, film studies has also been analyzing its effects on all modules of film industries, including production and postproduction. There is now a substantial literature in film studies on film and sound editing.[3] As one of those scholars, Valerie Orpen, notes, scholarship on editing has tended to focus on the visual and the silent era because "sound has been perceived as limiting the editor's freedom" (2003, 6). My analysis of *The Willow Tree*'s postproduction editing will show the importance of sound and, in particular, dialogue to the editing process, an underexamined topic in film studies. While the final sound editing and mixing module of the film is beyond the scope of this chapter, a discussion of voice-overs and sound flashbacks created in the digital editing process will demonstrate this point.

However, it is important once again to periodize the use of such technology within film production, and to note that for *The Willow Tree* this was the first time that this technology was used, which subsequently became standard procedure in the film industry. This chapter asks: What happened in the moment when this technology was introduced? How did the filmmakers respond to it? And can we theorize this response in ways that address questions of temporality within the development of the technology and its continuous but changing use within the film industry? At the time or moment of its introduction and use, what transpired between the filmmakers and their new mode of assembling the bits and pieces of realistic images into a filmic text is likely to have been different from the moment it became more widespread and from the moment or period in which it became standard practice. In the most banal way, it is the eureka or aha moment that captivates and then deeply inspires filmmakers. To anticipate how I develop my argument, I argue that the use of newly available digital editing technologies mediated the transformation of *The Willow Tree* from the mundane into the divine throughout this postproduction process. It allowed for the uncanny reappearance of an Islamic spirituality in a film industrial process where it was feared to be lost. Indeed, the film itself seemed to reveal its own meaning in ways that often challenged or troubled the filmmakers' understanding, gradually emerging as a far darker story than originally envisioned. I claim that this moment of production is a magical one, in a quite literal sense of magic (something that seems almost supernatural in its powers). Suddenly, the production process became uncanny in its effects on the filmic text. I argue that this is a theoretical departure from the discussion of the uncanny in film studies, which has almost always directed the question to the filmic technology and not the production.[4]

Postproduction of *The Willow Tree*

In spite of, or perhaps because of, the difficulties involved in shooting *The Willow Tree*, editing began with great optimism and expectations. Throughout the production, the viewing of rushes or dailies became a space usually given over to celebrating the beauty of the film and acting of the cast. The silence of these rush viewings (as the soundtrack had yet to be added) was often broken by the repeated cheers of the crew, until a perceptible buzz lingered in the air. The memory of these viewings made postproduction seem like an unfortunate delay to the film's destined success. Majidi demanded that postproduction meet or surpass international production standards to ensure that nothing would get in the way of the film's international exhibition and distribution. He had experienced problems in the past due to the limitations of Iran's postproduction facilities and was determined to not repeat them. These global ambitions were mapped onto the far-flung facilities and experts he hoped to involve in the film's postproduction.

Before filming had even been completed, a plan to address the postproduction process had been put in place that seemed to spare no effort or expense. An Iranian digital effects expert, who had worked in Hollywood on films like the *Matrix* (1999) and *The Terminator* (1984) sequels and had recently moved back to Iran, was tasked with creating computer-generated effects for two crucial scenes added late in the production. He vowed to take the work to Germany if it could not be completed in Iran. Ahmad Pejman, the film's musical composer, who lived for most of the year in Los Angeles and had composed the score for *Baran*, was given approval, despite the costs involved, to record the film's music in the United States. And after the editing was completed, the film would be sent to Eclair Labs in Paris for sound mixing, final grading and matching, and printing. Finally, subtitles for the film would be created in Belgium or Dubai. Indeed, at the start of the postproduction process, the only substantial task that would be fully completed inside Iran was editing, due in no small part to the availability, for the first time in that country, of digital editing.[5]

Outsourcing postproduction processes to labs and studios in other countries, rather than carrying them out in-house within the same production company, has been a feature of contemporary film industries (as noted in this volume's introduction). Majidi's ambitions reflect a larger global context of the specialization of modules within specific film industries (sound in this industry, color in that, and so forth). But there was another, more immediate, reason for outsourcing such a task. Postproduction was widely understood within the industry to be Iran's weakest link in the film process. The handful of postproduction studios and film labs established before the revolution had not substantially upgraded their equipment. Fewer than three film processing labs existed in the whole country, and the Ministry of Culture and Islamic Guidance had closed down many of the postproduction facilities it had provided to support filmmakers. During this period, however, the availability of digital film equipment and services had begun to improve. A number of small studios—many in private hands—began to offer postproduction digital services for feature film production. And many film and sound professionals came to embrace these technologies.

In the fall of 2004, *The Willow Tree* project moved to Roashana Studios, a postproduction facility specializing in digital editing and animation, recently founded by brothers Kamran and Amir Saharkhiz. *The Willow Tree* was their first major feature film project. Located on the third floor of a newly built commercial apartment building in a quiet residential side street, the cramped studio was in a perpetual state of renovation and equipment upgrade during the many months spent working on the film. One of the main editing suites was remodeled to create space for an in-house sound studio to dub dialogue and record sound effects. A mixing studio was being built in another corner of the office.

Compared to the noise and chaos of a film set, an editing studio is quiet and the work of editing done in relative silence. In old editing rooms, with the flatbeds, one would hear the jerking sound of tape being run and stopped through spools with an occasional pause and snip. At Roashana the only sound from the equipment was the low hum of the flat-screen monitors and the periodic whirr of a fan kicking in to cool the hard drives. Even common areas were used sparingly, as work on different projects went on behind the closed doors of the editing suites.

A major challenge, according to Amir Saharkhiz, was obtaining good equipment and quality software under long-standing U.S. sanctions imposed as part of the trade and investment ban on Iran, which also inflicted penalties on foreign firms doing business with Iran. Pirated editing and sound-mixing software could be purchased for a few dollars from any computer center but not the professional versions needed for feature film work and the accompanying technical equipment and support. *The Willow Tree*, for example, was being edited using software from a Canadian company made for professional video, not film, production because only they would provide support for an

Iranian-based company. This created problems when the editing finished and the editing metadata was sent to the lab. The slight difference in standard frame rates between video and film meant the film was cut incorrectly. As a result, the Roashana team had to manually calculate the discrepancy for each shot of the film and resend the information to the lab before a print could be produced.[6]

Hassandoost, Majidi's longtime film editor, had become the in-house film editor at Roashana, and occupied one of the more spacious rooms. A long narrow desk stood at one end, with two flat-screen monitors on a raised hutch, a keyboard and computer tucked underneath. Along the opposite wall was a row of chairs and a glass coffee table for the use of visitors. To the right of the desk stood a cabinet that contained the film's production logs and reports, software manuals, and assorted film magazines. The only other piece of furniture was a large whiteboard filled with notes on scene breakdowns and time codes and in the top right corner the total run time of the film, which changed at the end of each day.

Hassandoost had spent the better part of four months assembling a rough cut of the film from the more than twenty-four hours of raw footage, considerably more than the average Iranian film.[7] Majidi stopped by most days to review the editing and offer his opinion. He was often joined by Fouad Nahas, whose opinion Majidi particularly valued for his role as a producer of his well-received and commercially successful film *Baran* (2001). A retired technology executive, Fouad lived in Canada but stayed in Iran for the duration of the film's postproduction. Majidi saw Fouad as someone who both understood his work and could provide a Western perspective on it. As the first rough cut of *The Willow Tree* neared completion, I also joined the editing sessions on a regular basis and, like Fouad, was often asked by Majidi how international audiences might respond to the film. During editing, however, I was mainly an observer, my main role being to coordinate and supervise some of the related postproduction work that emerged in the editing process, like additional film shoots, dubbing sessions, and correspondence with foreign labs and studios. Later on, I would also be asked to handle some of the correspondence and negotiations with film festivals and international distributors over the film.

At Majidi's request, Fouad increasingly took on a more central role in postproduction. He and Hassandoost occasionally clashed on editing choices, often ending with Majidi intervening and making a final decision. Most days, other members of the postproduction team would also stop by to offer their opinions on whatever was being edited. Majidi encouraged these visits and usually asked Hassandoost to play for them additional sections of the film as well. This kept editing sessions lively and unpredictable but also contributed to lengthy reviews of previously completed sections of the film and suggestions for how they should be altered. Like Penelope in Homer's *Odyssey*, Hassandoost spent his evenings undoing the work he had done during the day. "Can you imagine if they edited *Lord of the Rings* in this way?" Ahmad Pejman, the musical composer, said to me one day. "It would have taken ten years for them to finish the film." One afternoon, Hassandoost uncharacteristically dropped his accommodating demeanor and vented: if not for Majidi, he would not put up with working in this way. "Whatever we decide today, tomorrow some new idea will be suggested and it will be changed." If he could work independently, without the others present, he would have a chance to think about the film and come up with some creative ideas, but, he said, "Now I feel like my opinions get lost." Instead, Fouad went home at night and arrived in the morning with suggestions. "I am just the operator," Hassandoost continued. "Without digital editing, I would be sick of the film."

The use of digital software—a new experience for all involved—changed the dynamics of the editing process. The editing table and its stacks of canisters with reams of film and tape no longer dominated the room. As noted before, digital software allowed what would have taken hours to be accomplished in minutes. Shots could be swapped, scenes reordered, and different sections of the film viewed with a few keyboard strokes and movements of a mouse. Flat-screen monitors replaced the small screen, allowing for collective viewing. In other words, these technological changes to the editing process allowed it to be a more collective, unfettered, and experimental experience. And, to Hassandoost's frustration, the value of his expertise was diminished while at the same time his role as the operator of this equipment increased his workload. In the remainder of the chapter, I demonstrate how this process facilitated the use of new storytelling and editing techniques originally not in the script and created the space for the sacred to be reinserted into the film.

First Test Screening

About five months after principal photography had finished, a few invited guests assembled in Roashana's studio for the first viewing of a rough cut of *The Willow Tree*. The viewing was primarily for senior crewmembers from the film's production and, thus, people who knew the story and what had been filmed. The film had recently been trimmed from an unwieldy two and a half hours to two hours, which was still considered quite long by the standards of Iranian films, which range between ninety and one hundred minutes. The film was viewed on a large television monitor moved for this purpose into the studio's common area. We viewed the rough cut in the dark in silence.

This is what we saw. *The Willow Tree* tells the story of a university professor. Blind since age eight, Yusuf is happily married to a devoted wife and is the father to a precocious six-year-old daughter. After a sudden collapse, he is diagnosed with a life-threatening brain tumor and sent to France to undergo surgery. As a pious man, he asks God to grant him a miracle. The surgery unexpectedly leads to the restoration of his sight, which upends his life and leads to an existential crisis. Yusuf soon dislikes his humble home, wishes to leave his job as a university professor for something more lucrative, and ends up becoming infatuated with a younger woman. At the end of the film, Yusuf loses his sight again as he begs God for another chance to live again.

The screening ended. After we arranged our chairs in a circle, each person took turns offering their opinions. What struck me was the candor and sharp criticism leveled at the film. After months on the project, I had rarely heard anyone openly talk in such an unrestrained and critical manner about the film, much less in the presence of its director. Nearly all agreed that little of interest happened in the first thirty minutes of the film, which dealt with the initial discovery of Yusuf's illness in Iran and his treatment in France. Many thought the film began with the restoration of his vision and return to Iran. For the first time, he would be able to see his wife and family, the home he considered his "little piece of paradise," and the city he lived in. We all in some way spoke to the question of how the film might be better if it began with his arrival in Iran. This was not seen as a major issue since the film needed to be cut down in any case. Many also found Yusuf to be a character that they could not empathize with or get close to. His passivity and flat and monotonous portrayal, particularly in the first half of the film, made Yusuf an enigmatic figure. Nava Rohani, the script supervisor, in an exasperated tone asked Hassandoost what happened to all the footage shot of Yusuf as a loving husband and father who was content with his life. Without this background, why would anyone care about Yusuf or understand the radical transformation in his behavior once he regains his sight? Yadollah Najafi, the sound recordist, shared his disappointment with the rough cut by remarking that the version of the story he was telling his friends—based on what he knew they shot—was much better than the film he had just seen.

What proved particularly hard for the group to reconcile, however—and there was near-unanimous agreement on this point—was that from the moment Yusuf returns from Iran, the story became dominated by Yusuf's infatuation with Pari, a young woman he initially mistook for his wife. Many felt that it was this transgression that ultimately was to blame for his going blind again at the end of the film. What happened to the other elements mentioned in the script and further developed during the production that revealed Yusuf's wayward behavior? Even for those who did not mind this, it was noted that Yusuf never actually acts on these desires. One person asked, "Why is it objectionable to be attracted to a beautiful woman?" The focus on Pari was deemed problematic, and many urged Majidi to clarify her role in the film. If Pari was meant to represent something more than a carnal desire for Yusuf, this symbolism did not come through. In short, the screening revealed that rather than the allegorical, spiritual film they had come to expect from Majidi, *The Willow Tree* resembled a relatively conventional, if poorly told, melodrama of a middle-aged man consumed by lust for a younger woman. The sacred space of a Majidi film had been rendered profane.

In what follows, I discuss the subsequent steps taken in digital editing to address the problems in the film raised in the discussion of the test screening. (Some of these had already been identified as far back as the scriptwriting stage and had a profound effect on the structure and content of the film.) I focus on the decision to change the structure of the film and abandon its linear narrative through the use of flashbacks and voice-overs, which were primarily intended to make Yusuf a more sympathetic protagonist. (Once again, this highlights how important digital editing is not only to the image but also to the sound of the film.) But on another level, one could argue that this new experimental format was an extension of the way the film was shot. That is, the experimentation with a nonlinear narrative reproduced the experience of shooting the film out of its narrative's chronological order, a first for Majidi on both counts. Similarly, the willingness to abandon the script to find a better way to communicate the film's message and the addition of new dialogue in the form of voice-overs and additional scenes further demonstrate Majidi's inclination toward improvisation and spontaneity in the moment of creation.

Needless to say, in abandoning the original structure of the script, the editing stage opened a space to reimagine and evaluate the film anew. It created new possibilities for finding the film's message embedded within the hours and hours of discarded raw footage and discovering the qualities that define a Majidi film. In other words, one component of film production, the rough cut, could be changed through another, film editing, in order to loop back to the message in the script, produced in yet another module. This illustrates the ways in which modules that occur later in the sequence can actually undo or change (and regrettably also damage) what was produced in earlier modules, presumably in order to enhance the final product. Usually we think of modules as setting up what will be done in the next module of production, but they can also be recursive, in the sense that they can fundamentally affect what was already produced and change the outcome of the film. In the case of *The Willow Tree*, the effect was seen to be even more profound, namely, that something so precious as the film's spirituality, which the script had secured, had somehow been lost in the actual shooting or initial editing of the scenes, but that spirituality could now be retrieved or reanimated in the film in the postproduction process. Voice-overs and flashbacks became crucial ways to bring back the spiritual message of the film: the act of finding God and oneself (or, more precisely, the loss of self) through the physical and ethical journey that Yusuf undertakes within the world of the film.

But the profundity of this change goes deeper than a technological fix that magically resuscitates a seemingly moribund film. I argue that the film's story came to uncannily double the experiences of those working in the editing process (Freud [1919] 1955). In chapter 5, this volume, Caton, building on but also critically reacting to film studies and its theorization of indexicality, talks about the filmic text as an "iconic indexical" of the film production (and he makes the bolder claim that all filmic texts in a sense are references to their own production). If we take the idea of the double as congruent with the idea of an icon, then what he and I are saying parallel or double each other, but for my purposes I prefer "double" because of its psychoanalytical resonances that I explore within the context of the film's production. The story of *The Willow Tree* is a parable of blindness to the truth in front our eyes, the seduction of the profane, and the possibility of redemption by remembering the presence of the divine in the mundane. It describes a condition that exists everywhere, even in an editing room and within the film itself. And the fact that the film's narrative became a double for the actions taken in the editing room shows how the industrial process of filming became reinscribed as an Islamic experience, and contributed to the larger project of Islamicizing the film industry to which Majidi had committed himself in his film work. And speaking now to an anthropology of film industries, this volume's central theme, it shows how a process that on one level is seen to be purely or merely technological (the cultural apperception of the process from the standpoint of an impersonal, standardized, and universal mode of production) becomes infused with and even interpenetrates with a very different cultural interpretation, that of religious redemption.[8]

In other words, the postproduction process of *The Willow Tree*, particularly editing, was now dominated by the search for the film's meaning filtered through a religiosity that sought to rescue the film's sacred elements from those that were deemed profane. This process occurred on multiple levels, both within the narrative of the film and in the editing room, and, like the film itself, was closely bound to issues of both sight and sound. The act of editing opened a space for the participants to release and discover this meaning, already encoded in the materiality of the film. The use of new digital editing techniques helped to mediate this process by allowing for the rapid review and assemblage of previously discarded footage that often revealed the unanticipated signification captured during the film shoot.

Reediting the Film: Return of the Repressed

A more standard Freudian interpretation of the repressed in regard to a film production would be that psychic material repressed in the filmmakers is released or expressed by the filmic text. Indeed, such an interpretation is possible in the case under examination here. When the reedited film finally emerged after a long, laborious, and contentious process that involved not only the editors but the film crew and the director, several prescreening viewers remarked on how spiritual it was and congratulated Majidi for having produced another masterpiece. In a self-congratulatory manner, the director would later explain to me that such artistry can only be accomplished by an artist "pure of soul," and that he was merely an instrument of divine intervention. What this comment leaves out, however, is that the same viewers also privately commented to me and to each other that the Majidi who made this film was a different person from the director of his earlier films that centered on children and celebrated their innocence. These viewers also remarked that the filmic text of *The Willow Tree* was now much "darker" than anyone, including the director, had ever anticipated and that the film had become unnerving but perhaps more interesting in its moral ambiguities as seen in the character and the plot. The main character, for example, came across as "darker" and "harsher" than any character in his earlier films and, in a certain sense, can be seen as a double of the repressed side of Majidi's psyche that his self-serving comment above does not reveal.

However, I want to explore a different avenue of thought about film and the unconscious, one that builds on what Walter Benjamin meant by the "optical unconscious." The term is used in his essay "A Small History of Photography" (Benjamin 1979). He is concerned with the way new technologies allow the world to be seen in ways that it hadn't been before and, in that seeing, how an optical unconscious emerges (including the feeling of the uncanny or the double that Freud spoke about as being the return of repressed). For example, as still photography was replaced by the moving image, things could be seen in motion in ways not captured before by photography. Those new visuals, as it were, elicited unconscious feelings and thoughts that were key to the medium's reception. I want to build on this insight in my analysis of the postproduction process in *The Willow Tree*. This film was made according to the highest film industry standards of the day, including an internationally acclaimed film director and a world-class film crew. And yet the test screening, as I will show, revealed an unexpected outcome, a film that was judged flat and uninspiring by all the filmmakers. Somehow the ways in which the world was seen by the camera apparatus and the story told in the script fell far short of the divine message it was supposed to capture. Another way to put this is that the film became disenchanted in the standard industrial film process. The challenge was how to reenchant it, how to bring back the divine that seemed to have become repressed. Digital technology was a means by which the world could be seen anew (through sound and image effects), and in the process an optical unconscious could emerge that seemed divine, or, if you will, uncanny.

Returning now to the ethnography of the editing process, I discuss the importance of the particular individuals involved in this process and their collaboration to explore the ways in which these individuals and technologies interacted in the postproduction process to shape the meaning of the film. If the initial screening revealed the profanity of the film, the purpose of the editing undertaken afterward was to bring back its sacredness. This is where the question of the film's meaning took center stage and became a source of tension and struggle among the different participants in the postproduction process. However, I argue that more than just the actions of the crew, the film itself seemed to resist certain interpretations and efforts to mold its meaning and reveal itself in unexpected ways. It was within this contested atmosphere that the sacred reemerged in the film.

What follows is based on my field notes during the film's editing.

Phone call, 1 a.m. A voice in the dark that I recognize as Majidi's. It was like a voice-over. He tells me that he did not sleep after the screening. He spent the night and early morning thinking about the film. He then spent the day with Hassandoost, Fouad, and Delpak discussing changes to the film. He wished I had been there. The voice spends nearly an hour describing to me what they decided. He said that they agreed to some changes that he thinks will give new life to the film. The opening section, before Yusuf returns to Iran, will be cut to about ten to fifteen minutes. This version better emphasizes the letter at the beginning of the film which people seemed to forget about in the test screening. The voice said, "In this way the film is like a circle: it begins at night and ends at night. It starts with a letter and ends with a letter." He also tells me that at the screening he felt like he was watching the film, like we were, for the first time. "Until then I had a feeling of security but as I watched it with everyone for the first time, I saw things I hadn't seen before. In the close-up where the doctor checks his eyes, I wanted to jump in front of the monitor and not let anyone see it. I couldn't believe that I'd left that in." The voice explained that "it was like telepathy" when he heard the comments from the others after the screening.

This was the start of how Majidi framed the process of reediting his film. Freud speaks of telepathy as a kind of doubling, where thoughts jump from one mind to another. The thoughts of the film crew had jumped to the director in a doubling that was uncanny to him. Through these initial interactions between himself and his crew, with the technical intervention of the editing machine, they would be able to bring back to the surface what had been repressed or hidden.

The two key images in Majidi's comments are the circle and the letter, the idea of repetition and the contents of what is repeated, the perfect image of the Freudian idea of repetition compulsion and the return of the repressed. What I want to ask is, what is in those letters? Not just literally, but symbolically. How do they contain the secret that had to be revealed in order for the film production to be completed? Note also that the idea of the voice-over, which was to become a key device in the digitally edited film, was uncannily embodied in Majidi's phone call to me in the early morning hours. The concepts of the voice and the voice-over have received considerable attention in film studies (Chion 1999; Doane 1980, among others), and some of this material, as in the case of Mary Ann Doane, is analyzed in psychoanalytical terms that I have found inspiring, even though I go in other directions with it. In what follows, I examine the way that sound and editing techniques became a means to release the unconscious meaning repressed not just in the film's audience or even its makers but in the film itself.

The circle begins. The first twenty minutes of the film had depicted Yusuf at home before his operation, continued with the diagnosis of his illness, and then his flight to France for his operation: all of that would be excised. Now, the film would begin in complete darkness with a voice-over. For one minute, the screen is completely black. Then a slow fade-in reveals a figure on a balcony. It is Yusuf summarizing what has happened to him. But we don't know whom he is talking to. We hear the sound of a Braille machine. The voice-over continues.

The first letter. It is Yusuf narrating a letter to God. He asks why God has forsaken him and continues to cause him so much hardship. He has come to realize that his life is threatened. He desperately pleads for God not to forget him and to let him survive his operation so that he may have the chance for a new life. Then the film cuts to Yusuf's operation in France. Listening to Majidi describe the new opening, I could not help but think that he was describing how he had emerged from a long period of darkness, of aesthetic or spiritual blindness, and pleading with God for him to be able to see his film anew.

In Majidi's imagination, the voice-over would become the means by which large segments of the story would be narrated in place of the original story line. For example, the sequence of Yusuf going to France was originally told in a number of sequential scenes, but now the same sequence would be told through a combination of voice-over and images in a swift, economical manner. Most importantly, the audience would not know what his family looked like. We hear the sound of a plane. A cut to a telephoto shot of a plane in the air, a cut to Yusuf seated inside a plane, and then we see his arrival at the airport. To this point, we still have not seen his family. Large chunks of the hospital scenes would be cut as well. The testing scenes will be removed. A voice-over may be used as the doctors discuss his case. Yusuf will say, "They're making decisions for me. What is going to happen?" In this way, two critical scenes will dominate the first part of the film: Yusuf lifting his bandages to see the ants and then taking them off and playing in the hallway. "Before they were like flowers lost in the grass," Majidi told me.

Not only Majidi's spirits but everyone else's were raised in the postproduction process after it was clearer, or so it seemed, how the film would begin and be narrated, thanks to digital editing. It was seen as utterly transforming the film. The mood proved contagious as different members of the crew, some present at the test screening, dropped in over the next few days and were shown the film's new opening. Ahmad Pejman, the film's composer, called it a "masterpiece" that took the film "from a ten to a one hundred" and raised the film to an "international" level. Almost everyone commented on how the letter and voice-over had turned Yusuf into a character they instantly liked and found sympathetic. Moreover, some interpreted the black screen at the start as setting up an expectation within the audience that linked Yusuf's vision (or lack thereof) to their own. The audience no longer could be certain if what they were seeing was real or simply in Yusuf's imagination. "Everything [in the film] has turned otherworldly," Majidi said. This idea of using the editing process to blur the distinctions between reality and fantasy became more important as time went on. Over the next weeks, different ways of structuring the film were tested and discarded as the postproduction team sought, in Majidi's words, to give "new life to the film."

After this promising beginning, however, the team struggled to find a way to improve the rest of the film. Countless hours were spent reviewing footage to find new material. A consensus took shape over the next few weeks that while the film had great individual scenes, compelling and beautifully shot, for some reason they lost this quality when they were inserted into the film. The story connecting these scenes was weak, and the team began to experiment with different narrative and editing devices to find a way to construct a more compelling story.

Fouad felt the main problem was that the editing was "too flat" for the film. "The film doesn't work with a classical editing style." It made the film too "realist," which killed its intended "romance and feeling." Drawing inspiration from the new start of the film, he explained that they needed to make the film more "surreal" so the audience wouldn't know whether what they were seeing was real or imaginary. As an example, he brought up Yusuf's arrival scene at the airport. They had recently removed an establishing shot of Yusuf coming down an escalator toward the crowd waiting to greet him. It was replaced with a shot from Yusuf's point of view set at an oblique angle that slowly tracks forward as bouquets and flowers rain down on a spotless marble-tiled floor. Fouad felt this change would raise in the audience's mind the question, "Is this actually happening or just in his head?" He told me that they had discovered additional shots in previously discarded footage and ways of combining them that produced a similar "unexpected magic" and "haunting atmosphere," a quality that neither he nor Majidi expected to find. At times, though, Fouad felt frustrated that some postproduction participants were still trying to relate to the film as if it was a real story when really "it's something between reality and a dream."

Hassandoost did not agree with Fouad's criticism of the film's editing style. For him, and Fouad would probably agree, the main problem confronting them in editing was the weakness of the script. "The difference with this film is that Majidi's other scripts were much clearer. We edited according to the script. This film is not like that. I mean, the issues that have come up are because the script wasn't thought through." According to Hassandoost, this created tension in the editing room because Fouad and Majidi liked to work by "feeling," but he had to find a way to bring that meaning out. "Now, it's become a personal thing. One says this way, another says no. It's up to the director to pick which feeling is better. In some places I may not like it, but since the others wanted it, I put it in." He concluded by telling me that the lack of a good script "is why most Iranian films are made in the editing stage. It's the editing that holds the picture together, more than the story."

During this stage, there was a variety of moments when the clash of story versus feeling described by Hassandoost materialized in the editing process. One day, the team was working on a scene in which Yusuf watches but does not intervene when a young pickpocket takes the wallet from a man dozing in a crowded subway car. The scene begins with a series of shots of Yusuf seated on a bench inside the subway car, staring at the passengers around him. The pickpocket thinks he has been caught when he notices Yusuf watching him but continues with his work when he realizes Yusuf is not going to do anything about it. Mohammad Reza Delpak, the sound designer, whose office was next door and was waiting for editing to finish so he could begin his work, frequently dropped in to offer his advice. Like Hassandoost, Delpak had worked on all of Majidi's films and had been involved with the project from the start. Delpak suggested removing the initial shots and starting the scene with a close-up of the pickpocket's hand removing the wallet. Hassandoost replied that they had already tried it and it didn't work. Fouad and Majidi, however, wanted to try out Delpak's suggestion, and so Hassandoost grudgingly removed the shots and cued up the scene. Remember, the new digital editing process first used on this film made this kind of reshuffling and reviewing possible. The sense of being in a subway car was lost, and the encounter between the pickpocket and Yusuf took on an abstract quality. Delpak argued that the new version brought the scene together. Fouad agreed and felt it made the scene more "surreal." He added that it reminded him of Robert Bresson's *Pickpocket* (1959), instantly raising the scene's credibility and prestige. Hassandoost, however, was not convinced and made a last attempt to explain to the group that the key issue was to understand how it worked in relation to the scenes that preceded and followed it. Without the establishing shots, the audience initially wouldn't know where the action was taking place, and by the time they figured it out, the scene would be over. He said they had to decide whether the "story or feeling" of the shot was more important. We all turned and looked at Majidi. He thought for a moment and responded that what was important in this scene was not the story but its broader meaning, in which case the new version was more appropriate.

Another instance later in the editing process concerned Yusuf's night journey, a crucial scene in the middle of the film in which Yusuf spends an evening walking around the city contemplating whether to act on his desire to be with Pari. When he returns the following day, Yusuf lashes out at his wife, Roya, for asking where he was all night. The team kept coming back to this scene over and over again, primarily at the insistence of Fouad, who felt that Yusuf's outburst needed to be explained. He argued that they needed to focus on specific things Yusuf sees during the walk to explain how he came to his decision to pursue Pari. Hassandoost felt that in the context of the story, what was important was not what he looked at but the fact that he was out the entire evening, alone, and wrestling with this dilemma. Fouad found this repetitive and boring; the entire film consisted of scenes of Yusuf walking around without doing or saying anything. A scene had been written and shot that was meant to be inserted within the walk that could have solved the problem, but Majidi did not want to use it because it now seemed too melodramatic and clichéd. The scene consisted of Yusuf coming upon a group of people surrounding a dead body on the sidewalk. While passersby throw money on the corpse, Yusuf cannot stop staring at the figure, who has an uncanny resemblance to him. One evening when the postproduction team was once again debating the same scene, Majidi exploded: "Everyone keeps telling us to go faster, faster, faster. It's destroyed the feeling of the film! Where is Roya? Where is the street? Where is Yusuf walking? We've taken so many things out. . . . We've cut so much . . . the feeling is lost! We've ruined it! The feeling of Yusuf in the streets is no longer in the film. Instead, it's faster, faster, faster!" Needless to say, he was now contradicting what he had said earlier, which was that the larger meaning rather than the story or the feeling was what was important to him.

The session, rare for its acrimony, more or less put a halt to the removal of shots deemed superfluous to the main narrative. They had to start the circle over again. The new imperative was to strike a balance between keeping the story brisk and allowing scenes intended primarily to elicit an emotion to develop at their own pace. The crew began to review the film yet again and once again put back some of the materials that had been discarded.

The Second Letter

The perceived success of the addition of the letter and voice-over at the start of the film led to the decision to add a second letter and an interior monologue just before Yusuf undergoes his operation. Its purpose, like the first, would be to give the audience some insight into Yusuf and make him a more sympathetic character as well as more explicitly draw out the spiritual dimensions of the film. The content of this second letter to God, however, still needed to be worked out.

About a month after the screening of the rough cut, Majidi asked a friend to help him compose the letter. The friend, an Islamic scholar, had written the first letter and so was already familiar with its role in the film. He stopped by the editing office one day so Majidi could screen the film for him up to the point where the second letter would be inserted. Yusuf has just been told not only that his tumor is not cancerous but that with its removal he could potentially regain his sight. Still in shock, Yusuf sits on a bench in front of a large pool, where he writes this second letter. Majidi explained that now that Yusuf has a chance to see again, he has a further request and wants "God to complete this act of mercy."

Along with Hassandoost, they went to work on further developing the purpose and message of the second letter. The scholar quickly dismissed a suggestion that Yusuf write the letter to himself as a record of what he was feeling at that moment, saying, "The receiver and writer should be the same" in both letters. Majidi suggested another letter of supplication to God, but the scholar wanted it to address the content of the first letter. Since the first letter was a desperate plea couched in the form of an accusation that God had abandoned him, the second needed to ask God for forgiveness. "If we go back again to the idea of a plea, it won't work. We have to close it." He suggested that the letter be in the form of "a conversation with God." He went on, "It starts with him rebuking himself: 'I made a mistake in thinking you had forgotten me. Now I know my name is still on your list.'"

With the form of the letter settled, they turned to the content. The scholar felt that in the letter Yusuf should make not a promise but a vow ('ahd) and not to his wife or child but to God: "If we make it beautiful, the audience will be more inclined to sympathize with Yusuf even when he starts to do bad things." Majidi was skeptical: "If he makes a vow, the audience will know what to expect. It has to be subtle. You can't use the word 'vow.'" The scholar elaborated that a vow in such a context made sense. It is common for people in times of distress to make vows only to forget them when the moment passes.

In a dubbing studio a few days later, Parviz Parastui, the actor playing Yusuf, patiently rehearsed the lines of the new letter and worked to achieve the tone and cadence that Majidi wanted in the voice-over. It was the second time within a month that he had been brought in to dub the narration of a letter. After about twenty or so takes, Majidi felt that they had enough variety to find a recording suitable for the voice-over. On the way out, Parastui jokingly said, "They told me this was going to be a film with almost no dialogue. If that's the case, then why do I keep getting brought in to record new lines?" A few days later he stopped by the editing offices and, perhaps as a preemptive move in case there would be more letters, dropped off a CD containing several monologues he had written for Yusuf to be considered for the film. Majidi and Hassandoost gave it a quick listen and discarded it after he left.

Sound Flashbacks

Another narrative element added to the film at this stage of production was flashbacks. Their use primarily had to do with including important early scenes in the film that had been cut to improve the film's tempo and pace. It was believed that they would be especially useful in filling out Yusuf's backstory, particularly his relationship with his wife, Roya. In other cases, the use of flashbacks had less to do with providing the audience with relevant information than with finding ways to include beautiful scenes that seemed to resist being incorporated into the new framework of the film. Four or five moments were identified as potential spots to insert flashbacks.

However, one of the obstacles to using flashbacks in the film was that most of the story was told from the perspective of the blind Yusuf. Majidi initially believed it couldn't be done. "How can a blind person have a flashback?" he asked. He wasn't convinced by the argument that cinematic license gave them leeway to incorporate flashbacks from Yusuf's perspective. Soon after, the idea of inserting "sound flashbacks" became of major interest as a way out of the dilemma of a blind person having visual flashbacks. The idea was that after Yusuf regained his sight, a sound of some kind would trigger a memory from his past when he was still blind. The audience, like Yusuf, would not be able to see the scene but would only hear the dialogue or other sound elements, as Yusuf recalled them from memory.

A list was drawn up of different places to insert sound flashbacks. The fact that no one could recall a film that used sound flashbacks in such a prominent way generated even more excitement. Fouad claimed that he had originally suggested the idea but that no one seemed interested until Delpak, the sound designer, brought it up and managed to convince Majidi to give it a try. Hassandoost thought that if the sound flashbacks were inserted from the beginning of the film, audiences would get used to them and catch on. He also thought it would add yet another dreamlike element to the film, in keeping with their efforts, over the many weeks, to purge the film of its realism.

Sound flashbacks also generated enthusiasm because the crew saw them as an original technical innovation on par with something one might find in a Hollywood film. Soon after, the crew wanted to experiment with all kinds of other types of flashbacks. It was decided that Roya would have her own series of visual flashbacks to complement Yusuf's sound ones. Fouad argued in favor of making the entire story of the film a flashback, one that began with the final shot of the film. Majidi and Hassandoost briefly entertained the idea of trying to use "flashbacks within flashbacks." Finally, the crew discussed ways that they might also want to utilize "flash forwards" to keep the audience guessing. Flashbacks became for a few weeks the panacea for the perceived weaknesses in the film's narrative. It led to a tremendous amount of additional editing work, but in the end only a couple of instances were kept in the film, and these were rather conventional in nature.

The Digital Divine

Without digital editing software, it would have been impossible for the crew to improvise so extensively in the editing room and to use trial and error to discover what worked. What took minutes on a computer—moving a scene to a different part of the film, syncing the sound, replacing shots with alternate takes, and returning everything to the way it was when it didn't work out— would have taken hours or days if the team was still working with film. Rather than hastening the editing process, the use of digital editing technologies very likely prolonged it, as long as the crew felt the right combination of shots was only a few keystrokes away.

As with watching rushes, the speed and relative freedom of digital editing often led to focusing on the immediate, the fragment, and the shot. Hassandoost warned us that in the haste to make so many changes all at once, there was not enough time to process them, much less think about their relation to the overall film. But it also allowed the team to search quickly through vast quantities of footage and experiment with their juxtaposition, which often produced a sensation not of creation but of discovery. For Majidi, of course, this was an article of faith that over the months, editing the film also seeped into all our imaginations about how the film seemed to reveal itself. In an odd kind of way, Majidi, Hassandoost, Fouad, and the other members of the editing team harnessed the capacity of the digital to produce the uncanny as a means to locate the spiritual in the profane.

I argue in the remainder of this chapter that the digital and the divine became linked in this process. As we have seen already, the editing process was mediated through the spiritual. Yusuf's letters drew attention to his piety and framed his subsequent actions in terms of the "forgetting" of his vows to God. The flashbacks, while addressing narrative gaps in the script and problems of rhythm and pacing, also attempted to stylistically blur the lines between reality and fantasy. Meanwhile, those involved in the process of postproduction, like the film's intended audience, were also disciplined to understand the film as a kind of call to re-remember the binding covenant between man and God and the need to learn how to see anew and recognize His signs. The act of editing the film became a process of discovering the role of the divine in the shooting of the film. Indeed, it was through the search for the better film, the anticipated but unrealized Majidi film, embedded within the materiality of the project and mediated through the digital that one began to access the divine.

Returning from a short break in the middle of editing, I was struck by a new mantra in the editing room: the film had taken on a dreamlike quality between reality and fantasy. It always struck me as strange because prior to the screening of the rough cut, no one had referred to the film in this manner. And like any good mantra, it took on a life of its own that permeated every facet of editing over the following months, including a reevaluation of the film's production history. At one point, Majidi started complaining about the work by the film's first cinematographer. Most of the footage he shot was now deemed unusable because it was too "realist." Fouad pointedly reminded Majidi that at the time of the film's shooting, not even Majidi knew that he was after a particular aesthetic.

The mantra resonated so strongly because it was broad enough to satisfy the different interests of the film's participants. For Majidi, these dreamlike and otherworldly elements spoke to the spiritual, the view of truth as residing beyond the real, and dreams as a form of revelation. Everyday life, the mundane, is itself shot through with the unexplainable and unearthly if one only knows where and, perhaps more importantly, how to look. As such, the search for the film's meaning during editing was also a process of discovering God's role in the production process itself, the sacred in the mundane. And in the production of feature films there could be many sacred spaces, among them the temple of the film festival.

Other participants also had a stake in the mantra. For Fouad, the space between fantasy and reality was the natural home of tragedy. Increasingly, he came to insist that the only way to understand the film and Yusuf's actions is to realize the film is a tragedy, not a melodrama. "All are victims . . . unable to control their fate." He told me that he thought that Majidi and the others were finally coming around to this truth about the film. Fouad's background and history with Majidi gave him license to play an important role in editing. And "tragedy" (which also came to be picked up by Majidi and others) had the right ring for a project that aspired to success at international film festivals.

If Fouad was the film's conduit to an international audience, Hassandoost was its technical conduit to the realm of international film standards. His skill at harnessing new digital technologies and identifying the possibilities of different editing strategies, such as using voice-overs and flashbacks, gave the film its distinctive look and allowed it to be read as "sacred" but at the same time with the highest production values. Perhaps more than for any other participant, the space between fantasy and reality can also describe his own struggles on the project. I remember walking into his office early one morning to find him furiously working on a scene we had edited the previous day. He said that before anyone arrived, he wanted to restore the scene to the way he had originally edited it. He was confident that no one would know the difference. Perhaps in jest, he once told me he had prepared himself for a year's worth of work on the film. Ironically, because of digital editing, that statement proved to be prophetic.

This is not to say that those participating in this process necessarily understood it as a spiritual and divine production, but rather that the entire project was cast in such a way, regardless of one's beliefs or actual views. Mahmoud Kalari, the film's principal cinematographer, for example, returned in the final stage of postproduction to oversee the color grading and printing of the 35 mm print for its premiere at Fajr International Film Festival in Tehran. For several days, Majidi and Fouad recounted his reaction to the rest of the production team. He told them that when he joined the project, he had not read the script but worried about the film. It dealt with a topic that could easily become sanctimonious in the film. But he congratulated Majidi for overcoming those dangers and making a film that rose above any ideology and set a new benchmark for Iranian cinema. He continued that one didn't even have to be religious to understand or be moved by the film. The film got under one's skin and had a strange quality that hovered between reality and fantasy. This quality made it difficult for him to even attempt to describe it. The only way he felt he could describe the film was to say that it is a cross between a film by Krzysztof Kieslowski (*The Double Life of Véronique*, 1991; *Three Colors* trilogy, 1993–1994) and David Lynch (*Blue Velvet*, 1986). In almost the same language as Kalari, another cinematographer who worked on the film told Majidi that while watching this new version of the film he felt an "otherworldly presence" envelop him. But at the same time, one did not need to be religious to be affected by the film. This was because the film never resorts to sloganeering or preaching. It is a film that affects you because you are "human." He felt that some of the scenes he saw would haunt him for the rest of his life. He then went on to call Yusuf the second most important role in the film. The true star of the film is God, and he suggested that Majidi consider adding "God" to the title credits.

Majidi had a provisional explanation for the effects that the film seemed to have on its viewers, which was that humans couldn't help but relate to the story in the same way, even if, like Europeans, they say they are not religious. This is because we all have the same divine essence within us, even if we choose to forget it. For him, what was important was that the film would force people to reflect on how they lived their lives.

Conclusion

This chapter has examined the postproduction stage of *The Willow Tree* by focusing on a brief period between a rough-cut test screening of the film and a reedited version of the film screened at the Fajr International Film Festival in Iran. This coincided with the use of digital editing technologies that were relatively new in the Iranian film industry. Key sections of the film were cut and scenes were shuffled around in order to try to create a better story from the available footage. It was felt that these changes would require a nonlinear storytelling style, and so cinematic and editing elements not part of the original script, like flashbacks and voice-overs, took on an outsized role. While this opened up new ways for the team to edit and interpret the film, I also argue that in this process the film itself seemed to reveal its own latent or sacred meaning. What emerged was not the film that they had anticipated making, and so much of the discussion around the film at this time was couched in terms of the discovery of the film's meaning.

What was uncanny about this process was that a religious meaning that seemed to have been repressed in the film reemerged through the digital editing process (and probably would not have emerged in an analog process). Just as the film's character Yusuf saw the world in a different light once he had his operation and regained his sight, so the director and his crew saw the film in a totally different light once they could "operate" on it through digital editing technology. The filmic text was an uncanny double (or iconic) of the editing process through which it was made.

The concept of the optical unconscious helps us understand this. A technology allows the world to be seen in a new way, which in turn allows an unconscious meaning and feeling to emerge, what I have been calling the digital divine. The way the optical unconscious was conceived by Benjamin was for its revolutionary potential. I, on the other hand, have developed it for its power of reenchantment, a rather different issue. What had diminished or been lost since the Iranian Revolution, or so Majidi thought, was the infusion of religiosity throughout society, including the film industry. The optical unconscious in the film allowed this religiosity to reemerge, or the world to be reenchanted again by religious spirituality.

Production ethnography of the sort this chapter has engaged in is not enough to fully grasp the cultural importance of the digital divine. Nor can the question of the Islamic film or the Islamic film industry be adequately answered by focusing only on the filmic text or the film industrial practices that create it, market it, and exhibit it. Anthropological perspective can reveal how technology (as well as standardized film practices) is not merely a means to producing an Islamic film, but that the means also produce an end of an Islamic practice of filmmaking. That is, the vision of such projects is not only visible on the screen but also felt in the very industrial practices and technologies that the film must go through to be made. This is what anthropology through ethnographic fieldwork offers to the study of film.

Notes

1 For a comprehensive history of the postrevolutionary Iranian film industry, see Naficy (2012a, 2012b). For more on the politics and aesthetics of postrevolutionary Iranian cinema, see Atwood (2016), Decherney and Atwood (2015), Zeydabadi-Nejad (2010), Mottahedeh (2008), Sadr (2006), Tapper (2002), and Dabashi (2001). To date, Majid Majidi has received little scholarly attention; however, see Pak-Shiraz (2011) and Langford (2008). For ethnographic work on Iranian cinema, see Bajoghli (2019), Doostdar (2019), Varzi (2009), and Fischer (2004).

2 For more on the history and impact of digital technologies on film editing, see Furstenau (2018), Keil and Whissel (2016), Oldham (2012), Salt (2009), Dancyger (2007), Bordwell (2006), Crittenden (2006), McKernan (2005), Lefebvre and Furstenau (2002), and Murch (2001).

3 See, for example, Keil and Whissel (2016), Bordwell and Thompson (2008), Orpen (2003), Fairservice (2001), and Fischer (1999).

4 See Chung (2011) for an exception.

5 In the end, the music was recorded in Armenia and the subtitling and printing process completed in Iran due to budget and time constraints.

6 In spite of these constraints, shortly after work began on *The Willow Tree*, Roashana converted their editing suites to support Final Cut Pro.

7 At the time, producers of feature films could purchase up to 120 rolls of 400 feet of negative stock at government-subsidized prices, roughly equal to eight hours of raw footage. Beyond that, negative stock had to be purchased at market rates.

8 In a similar vein, the film is also concerned with the way that technological and scientific progress (medical advancements) has a cost, in this case to the loss of the spiritual side of the protagonist. With his sight restored, Yusuf transforms from a pious man and loving husband and father to one in search of wealth, who loses his way.

3. JOURNALISTS AS CULTURAL VECTORS
Film as the Building Blocks of News Narrative in India

AMRITA IBRAHIM

On a hot July afternoon in Delhi in 2009, I sat down to interview Mr. V, a journalist and former managing editor for a leading Hindi news channel. I had been introduced to Mr. V, as I call him here, by a mutual friend in the news business who told me that he would be interested in my ethnographic interest in the news as a genre of storytelling. Mr. V began by asking me what my dissertation research was about. I started to explain my broadest research goal as I had laid it out in my dissertation proposal: to map the changed terrain of news television in India since liberalization, accounting for how the news itself had changed as a narrative and aesthetic form since the days of state-run television.[1]

Emphatically agreeing with me as I began mentioning genres and storytelling, Mr. V started to tell me about a recent opinion piece he had written for a newspaper in which he "lampooned" the content of daily news (especially Hindi). He said, "The way they flit, effortlessly, between history and mythology, science and astrology and leave the viewer—the average viewer—almost convinced that this is science, or this is history, not astrology or myth . . . that is the danger." I grew confident in sharing more of my research ideas with him now that he seemed to endorse, rather than dismiss, my interest in the storytelling character of the news. He was the first person that I had been able to talk to openly about terms like "myth," "storytelling," and "aesthetics"; previous interactions with journalists and editors were met with incredulity that I was looking for these aspects in the news that they produced. This dismissal itself became a stance among journalists that intrigued me. When I told Mr. V this, he said, "They are in denial." I said that one channel in particular was marked out by those I had been in conversation with as the one that packaged the abovementioned content as news. This channel was India TV, a Hindi channel that drew high ratings, competing with other leading Hindi channels at the time, like Aaj Tak and Star News. Mr. V then gave me some background on why India TV had taken this route to rating success:

Rajat Sharma [managing editor of India TV] is on record saying that [he] came [into the market] with all the normal news properties: [he] had a show on environment; . . . a show on RTI [the movement behind the Right to Information Act, passed in 2005]; nothing worked and [he] was still battling [for audience share]. [Mr. V.] heard him at a public forum say that for one story [Sharma] wanted his journalist to get a [sound] bite . . . from . . . he didn't name [whom], maybe an Aaj Tak [top Hindi news channel since 2000] editor. So, when this journalist went to the Aaj Tak editor, that editor said, "What's the point of giving you a bite? Who watches India TV?" Then [Sharma] said, "It struck me that my media itself did not take me seriously, then I'll show them what I can do."

What Sharma did to "show them" was to introduce a range of news programming that took myth, religion, astrology, superstition, and local rumor as his channel's major content. The switch bore immediate results, and India TV was the leading channel from 2005 to 2010, including my time doing fieldwork. It was this kind of content, Mr. V emphasized, more than entertainment television, that would change Indian society as a whole. Contrary to the emphasis that anthropological studies of media had thus far given to entertainment (soap operas or film), Mr. V emphasized the enduring effects of infotainment on the industry, the public, and the state. There was, he rued, no scope for state regulation that would not also raise complaints of censorship; not much initiative for self-regulation by the news industry itself; and too fragmented a public, and so, he said, "What's happening is, they're getting away with it [the news channels]. And what happens unfortunately is that they keep blaming the public: 'They want this.' My answer to that is, for three years you've given them opium. Now you're accusing them of addiction. Obviously they will be addicted—you've supplied them with the opium . . . [slight laugh]."

The critique that television journalists were enabling the decline of public and critical thinking in India was a common refrain during the time I conducted fieldwork on television journalism in Delhi. Among intellectuals, the shift to commercial news programming had been a concern for some time, but even journalists had begun to be critical of the effects of fast-paced news that focused on scandal, crime, and sensation on the collective psyche of viewers. While this has been a focus of scholarship in media and cultural studies for some time, the specific historical and social contexts underlying changes in the

Indian television news market during the 1990s and early 2000s had not been investigated. It became clear during my meetings and observations in newsrooms that to understand how claims to truth-telling had changed in the light of a growing commercial television industry, it was necessary to understand how content production, industry bottom lines, and the revenue-generating news public were intertwined. One set of interwoven strands, which I try to explore in this chapter, bring together film and television. It is not possible to think of the Indian news industry without acknowledging its inherent semiotic and material links to film industries, and vice versa. The encounter and exchange between film and television industries has changed from the 1980s and early 1990s, when the state broadcaster had a monopoly over the airwaves, to the 2000s, when private television channels grew at a rapid pace. Where television was considered a minor medium in the past (literally being termed "the small screen"), by 2010 it was the dominant medium. Not only does television dictate tastes and trends for the film industry; it also offers film stars a means to remain in the public eye through reality shows and guest appearances when they have no promotional film events. Further, the flows of content back and forth across reality shows, news-as-entertainment and entertainment-as-news, and film have reshaped the visual regimes that structure audience anticipation and perception of what counts as credible and real (Chowdhry 2011; Tanvir 2015). In this heavily mediated terrain where diverse screens, including mobile screens, compete for viewers' attention, what is film and what is television, what is fictitious and what is real life are not clearly demarcated. In my previous work, I have explored these tensions through the way television news reports on reality shows and crime news that specifically focuses on the family. Here, I aim to discuss the flows between television and film and the industry concerns that underpin these movements.

I begin by outlining some of the major changes in television from the 1990s into the first decade of the twenty-first century, followed by a discussion of how news stories incorporate film, among other media, as the building blocks of narration and affect production. In this discussion, I focus on the flows between television and film in the larger ecology of media industries in India. "Flow" is a term that has been used with some ease when referring to the movement of media as well as experiences of viewing. Public culture studies and the affective turn in particular have made it more of a focus of anthropological investigation than ever before; however, there is a complex interplay between form and flow that makes any ethnography of media and mediation thick and substantive. In the literature, "flow" becomes a way to denote the somewhat ambiguous movement, experience, and captivating quality of mediated culture in the world. But the question how—does culture flow or is it moved along—requires that we pay attention to how elements move across differently configured mediums and spaces of encounter. In 2001, Elizabeth Povinelli wrote that meaning and translation are linked to this effort of tracking the interplay of form and flow across spaces and mediums, recognizing that there are conditions of circulation that "do not seem to be in the *text* in the way textual interiority and integrity have typically been understood.... These translation practices seem extra-textual: one life imposing its immanent structures on another" (2001, x). Dilip Gaonkar and Povinelli (2003) offer us the term "transfiguration," moving away from questions of meaning and identity as they come to us from the semiotic tradition inherited via Ferdinand de Saussure and critiqued by Jacques Derrida; moving toward a notion of circulation and mediation that comes from the Peircean work on language and performativity in anthropology. The approach to translation as the possibility of transparency in meaning across languages, genres, or semiotic systems, they write, "orient[s] us to a theory of the sign, mark, or trace and away from a theory of the social embeddedness of the sign, of the very social practices that these histories wish to describe" (Gaonkar and Povinelli 2003, 393). Transfiguration, on the other hand, offers the possibility of mapping the interplay of indexicality and iconicity, stitching together how signs of culture or symbols move through the world with the dense social contexts they come into contact with. I will discuss how film fragments move through the world, taken on by journalists as their language of storytelling. Scholars have suggested that film might even have the status of a pan–South Asian language (Punathambekar, Chopra, and Ahmed 2012). However, it is my argument that it is not only films, or their songs, where this language performs the work of identity, but also Hindi television news during the early 2000s.

Finally, I end by suggesting that journalists' efforts at storytelling are oriented less toward meaning making for others; rather, I mean to show, through the materials of news making (film fragments among others), that there is a layering of film and television, which have until recently been studied as discrete industries, where production has analytically been separated from reception. Here, I suggest that we see film and television as part of the same universe, where production and reception, consumption and circulation need to be studied as part of one universe of meaning, rather than as separated from each other, as in class cultural and media studies approaches.[2] Instead of analyzing content to arrive at a deeper level of symbolic meaning or accounting for how signs play in the creation of simulacra (what the redeployment of these symbols upon symbols means in the news), I ask what might we be able to see if we take content as the material—building blocks—that is available at hand for journalists, like brico-leurs? As Claude Lévi-Strauss writes, the bricoleur is not only reconstituting from existing materials at hand, but also, through these choices, says some-thing about himself in the reconstitution as well: "He 'speaks' not only *with* things . . . but also through the medium of things: giving an account of his per-sonality and life by the choices he makes between the limited possibilities. The 'bricoleur' may not ever complete his purpose but he always puts something of himself into it" (Lévi-Strauss 1966, 21).

The connections between film and television are established not only as personnel and technologies circulate between the two, or because corporate monopolies own interests across film and television, but also through jour-nalists themselves, who stitch together images and structures of anticipation across intermediating worlds of film and television. We could see journalists then not as participating in an exercise of meaning making and translation, but at a metapragmatic level, as forces that move culture along (Urban 2001). When journalists draw on older and recognizable narrative and aesthetic forms to anchor their address through the news, as well as their narratives of self-presentation, we begin to understand the relationship between media and publics not only as the effects of global media industries on vernacular nar-rative and aesthetic forms, but also on how elements within existing genres of storytelling are improvised upon to tell new stories and forge new genres, in this case the news. This interplay forces us to reconsider how local and global are situated in the professional field of journalism in India, which has been marked by considerable geographic and social mobility in recent years.[3] "Global" and "local" do not map only onto geocentric notions of flow, but between national, regional, and individual sites of public cultural production and circulation.

Thus, journalists are not only subjects of the cultures of circulation (Lee and LiPuma 2002) through which film and television converse (though they are also that), but they are also the agents who stitch together the semiotic to the specific social contexts from which they emerge as journalists. If we take Greg Urban's (2001, 55) exhortation to look at "sites of replication" to track how culture moves through the world, then I suggest that journalists are one such site. Being products of particular media industries, including film, they carry those media languages with them as they move through the world. This is how film moves through the world, too, through the workings of other media industries.

Television and Film in India: Events to Flows

Between 1990 and 2000, Indian viewers in the major cities saw a qualitative and quantitative increase in their choice of channels and content on television. The growth of the commercial cable and satellite industry in India has been the focus of a number of studies that have highlighted the sea change in the mediascape in India during the 1990s (Page and Crawley 2001; Singhal and Rogers 2001). The loosening of state controls over mass media is seen as heralding a new public culture of liberalized subjectivities, where identity, culture, and "Indianness" come to be mediated through the market and commodities (Butcher 2003; Fernandes 2006; Batabyal 2012). When I was designing my research plan, entertainment dominated studies of television in India; journalism was somewhat marginal. The few studies either approached news from the perspective of American influence on Indian news formats (the Foxification of news; Thussu 2009) or saw the news industry as poised on the cusp of a revolutionary period of interactive citizenship and democratic change (Mehta 2008). Since then, news in India has been the study of more focused ethnographic and media studies attention (Rao 2010; Punathambekar with Kumar 2012; Chakravartty and Roy 2015; Rodrigues and Ranganathan 2015; Udupa 2015). My own interest in the genres of storytelling in television news sought to expand the concept of publics and publicity by tracking how new forms of journalism were shaping ideas of credibility and public action. Taking sensation seriously as being materially and socially embedded, I wanted to take television news—its political economy, aesthetics, and effects—as a site to explore changing perceptions of reality, truth claims, and publicity in Indian journalism.

The expansion of television news in India began in 2000–2001, when the first news channels were launched as stand-alone channels and no longer aired as thirty-minute scheduled programming on entertainment channels. It was around this time that news channels such as Aaj Tak and NDTV, which continue to be influential in the field of television news, were launched. By 2008, there were at least twenty-five nationally broadcast news channels, catering to different linguistic and regional groups and interests in India, but also hundreds of regional and locally produced channels that competed for viewers (Kohli-Khandekar 2010). The diversification of channels, with the separation of news from entertainment programming, created a qualitative shift in the flow of television watching. From its inception to the 1980s, when television was the monopoly of the state, television could not ideally be defined in terms of flow, that is, a series of otherwise unrelated genres brought together only by the physical entity of the medium.[4] Instead, watching television was to be interpellated by the state as a national subject, experienced as a relatively discrete set of programming moments that were available through regional centers or *kendras*. With the inauguration of national programming in 1982, the national nature of the interpellation was further underscored, when every evening around 7 p.m., each regional kendra would link up to the central kendra at Delhi, with an elaborate presentation of the uplinking process itself, with text on-screen announcing the shift from the local to national time. Further, frequent communication breakdowns between the satellite and regional or national kendras would occur, bringing viewers face to face with the less than seamless workings of television as a medium, which served as a reminder of its ideological and political agendas (Ghose 2005). While it is true that the national program brought otherwise disparate televisual events under a single temporal flow, the spectacle that the audience was watching was nonetheless the crafting of a national psyche and subjectivity. The state-owned Doordarshan channel, during the 1980s and 1990s, aired didactic teleserials such as *Hum Log* (We the people) and mythological series like the *Ramayana*, along with films (popular and art), film songs, and the news as well as feature programming for rural audiences. Certainly, "flow" interpellated viewers into a flow of national time, as the switch from local to national programming evoked a sense of collective viewership to which scholars attribute the imagined community through television (Monteiro and Jayasankar 1994; Mankekar 1999; Rajagopal 2001). It could be argued that the audience was not, to paraphrase Raymond Williams, watching programs; it was watching the nation—and themselves as subjects of it—coming into being.[5]

In the 1990s, the increase in private television channels meant that Indians began to experience flow much more as Williams described it; that is, they were "watching television," not explicitly being interpellated as national subjects. Not only did the didactic horizon of the national recede or dissipate, the nature of twenty-four-hour television flow inaugurated an apparently more seamless relationship of the viewer as consumer through the television screen (Rajadhyaksha 1999). Viewers watched a variety of shows on cable and satellite channels, jumping from soap opera to news to sports and so on, in the course of the day. Different companies provided the channel with their particular content—for instance, news bulletins were regularly broadcast as half-hour shows on channels whose main focus was entertainment—Rupert Murdoch's (mostly English) STAR TV and Subhash Chandra's (Hindi) Zee TV. The content provider and the channel that acted as the medium of delivery were not the same, and complex financial agreements regulated what could be broadcast and during what times (Mehta 2008). So, even though television continued to be a domestic medium oriented to all members of the family, particularly during prime-time viewing slots (7–11 p.m.), the twenty-four-hour nature of broadcasting changed the experience of television within the home. The day's schedule was broken up by specific demographics, which in the competitive television industry are referred to as genres. Whereas under national programming, television was crafting modern, national subjects through a collective interpellation, the diversification of entertainment and news targets women, men, urban populations, youths (ages eighteen to thirty-five), and children through specifically crafted forms of address. Some of this is to be expected in any media industry, where news and entertainment would break down by language (English, Hindi, and regional) and type of entertainment (soap operas, reality shows, music, sports, movies, religious, and children's programming).

Since the separation of news from entertainment, each entertainment channel caters to distinct, sometimes overlapping, demographics and genres, except television news, which is perhaps the only space on television in India where a range of genres continues to flow in Williams's sense. While entertainment channels are able to fill most of their twenty-four-hour cycle with distinct shows and can repeat them to catch viewers at prime and nonprime times, the editors in the news genre routinely told me in interviews that continuous, insightful coverage of political and public events does not draw viewers.[6] This is also a challenge because of the limits of the medium itself—television news is not as far-reaching as newspapers are, the latter seeing substantial increase in Indian markets around the same time, in stark contrast to declining newspaper sales and subscriptions in the Anglo-American world (Jeffrey 2000; Ninan 2007). Television—particularly cable and satellite—as a whole continued to grow in the first decade of the twenty-first century but was not able to penetrate the vast rural and semirural market, where newspapers continue to have a stronger toehold in terms of how people get their news. Even in urban India, where television is much more firmly entrenched, television news comes along with or second to newspapers (English and vernacular press), which in general circulate in everyday life and mediate social relations as both more concrete and reliable sources of the news (Peterson 2010). Television news certainly provides fodder for debate, conversation, and disagreement, but there is much to suggest that the medium and its formats do not perform the work of disseminating information to the exclusion of print news and, increasingly, social and mobile media technologies and the internet. Mobile technologies have, in recent times, displaced television news as a form of information sharing, despite lacking factual corroboration. This crisis of "fake news" has prompted mobile apps like the extremely popular WhatsApp to explore ways to contain the spread of misinformation after Hindu nationalist groups used the service to organize lynchings of Muslim men (Dwoskin and Gowen 2018).

News channels, even before the rise of social and mobile media in India, have faced a challenge of mobilizing and holding on to viewers, which has led them to diversify the content they air. Apart from conventional political news, the early 2000s saw crime news stories, cricket and other sporting news, and entertainment industry news get the lion's share of twenty-four-hour airtime. This was described as the three Cs rule by editors and journalists—crime, cricket, and cinema (or celebrity). Supplementing this daily fare were horoscopes (in the morning time slots) and religious programming (afternoon time slots) on Hindi news channels, and travel and lifestyle shows on English news channels.

However, the diversity of kinds of programming on news channels was not merely a problem of how to retain viewership, or capturing eyeballs, as news editors put it; the content of television, and television news in particular, was also a function of the ownership patterns of entertainment and news channels and film companies as well as the partnerships between them during the early 2000s. I got an example of this during an interview with an executive of a leading Hindi news channel when he explained to me how one genre of shows that is very popular among the afternoon female demographic—news shows about television entertainment or teleserials—also becomes a medium of revenue generation for the channel. These shows are entertainment news segments done on the sets of popular teleserials. While Aaj Tak has a show called *Saas Bahu Aur Betiyan* (*SBB*, Mother-in-law, daughter-in-law, and daughters), Star News has one that spawned the genre, one might say, titled *Saas Bahu Aur Saazish* (*SBS*, Mother-in-law, daughter-in-law, and conspiracies).[7] The titles take their cue from the story lines of the many Hindi teleserials that have been the bedrock of Hindi television entertainment since 2000, when *Kyunki Saas bhi Kabhi Bahu thi* (Because a mother-in-law was also once a daughter-in-law) blew away television ratings points with unprecedented numbers (Bamzai 2009). Both entertainment news shows recap the nightly family dramas and the teleserials that air on Hindi GECs (general entertainment channels). While *Saas Bahu Aur Saazish* on Star News tends to focus on the shows aired on Star Plus (a leading Hindi GEC headquartered in Bombay/Mumbai), Aaj Tak's show features different shows from across channels. Both these shows are shot, edited, and packaged in the Mumbai offices of these respective channels and then digitally uploaded onto the servers from where they are picked up to be placed in the order of shows being aired by the Delhi office. Major entertainment channels regularly send clips and promos from their serials to the news channels for promotion, as part of a new way to incorporate advertising into news.

This advertising is both for the entertainment shows and for external products or services.

In my interview with that same executive, the rationale behind such specials was explained, given that the crux of the news business is advertising. No clearer justification for news networks as advertising space was ever given to me as directly by anyone during my fieldwork:

> I have to get value for my content, and also provide ad space. If Malaysian tourism wants an ad, we'll do a [title] show on location in Malaysia. . . . If an English [news] channel was doing this [and they do produce lifestyle and travel shows, which Hindi news channels do not], it would be called E-news (entertainment news) like E! [in the U.S., entertainment channels like E! and TMZ]. You have to give a twist to the language. The moment you become a Hindi channel, you become like a *Zanjeer-Deewaar* Hindi movie. You have to become mass. If not, you are competing with English, and you will be out of the market.[8]

The television industry at the time of this fieldwork (2009–2010) made up the largest share of the Indian media and entertainment industry—at 36 percent of all revenue in 2008, it stood at Rs. 295 billion (U.S. $5.4 billion). Despite the image that the film industry has of being the most prolific in South Asia, it was television that increasingly took hold of audience imaginations (Kohli-Khandekar 2010). Evidence of this hold comes by way of columns devoted to television reviews and commentary in major newspapers, a series of films featuring journalists as main protagonists or parodying the industry, and scores of young men and women who sought reality show auditions for their chance at fifteen minutes of fame. An instrument of nationalist and modernist pedagogy in the 1980s, television did not have the glamour of film and in fact was criticized by policy makers and bureaucrats for featuring too much cinematic content in its attempts to draw in audiences (Roy 2007). By 2010, not only was television creating its own content, drawing viewers away from the multiscreen movie theaters or cineplexes, but film stars found themselves drawn to television—in reality shows, talent hunts, and promotions—in order to keep their fan base and visibility high. Entertainment journalists revel in the fact that the relationship between television and film has been reversed, that it is now film that cannot do without television and not the other way around. Television became the primary vehicle that "controls, decides, and shapes the course of several other sub-segments—music, films, sports, software production, and an array of distribution businesses such as cable or DTH—that rely on television content to sell their services" (Kohli-Khandekar 2010, 55). Since the days of state-controlled television, when television hosted film content, television has today become a key medium through which film identifies its audience and deciphers their needs. Aswin Punathambekar (2013) argues that we cannot think of film industries without also accounting for how other screens and technologies, including television, make possible the publicity, distribution, and circulation of film as a commodity. While he focuses on how television tie-ins and interactive dot-com ventures expand the boundaries of the film industry, I argue that we must also include television news, where what counts as news in a twenty-four-hour cycle runs the gamut from cinema itself to crime. One entertainment journalist told me that while the film industry in Bombay had always looked down on television, now they could not afford to do without the publicity television provides—not only in terms of promotion and as supplemental to the cinema business, but for television shows as well. At the same time, the television industry has grown into an independent entertainment industry, which has established itself as distinct from theater and other forms of public entertainment that constituted it in the 1980s and early 1990s. There is, now, a whole community of television stars and workers within this industry that parallel the film industry. In Bombay, this is clearly geographically visible too, as Lokhandwala emerged as the home of the television production and acting world—literally where the stars, aspirants, and related artists live and work. Lokhandwala became to television what Bandra and Juhu as locations of the stars were and perhaps still are to the Bombay film industry. The relationship between the film, television, and news industries is therefore intertwined along multiple physical, material, technological, aesthetic, and communicative times and spaces.

Bricolaging the News

Entertainment news is not the only category of television news shows that repurposes preexisting media material. Soundtracks from popular and recognizable movies, YouTube videos, and lines from films or television soap operas are often used in Hindi crime news stories. A number of journalists in the newsrooms emphasized to me that crime as a genre of news is the most easily "reconstructed" from other materials. It is necessary to do this, one editor told me, in order to fully sketch out the contours of the story, which because of the nature of the event, the journalist can only arrive at after the fact. Indeed, reconstructions of crime scenes or whole stories leading up to the crime are often made up of film and other media fragments, relying on the audience's quick recall of similar plot lines or alliterative puns to enhance the viewing experience. Crime is that kind of soft story in which you can deploy the emotional intensities of fear, loathing, disgust, and suspense to great effect, underscoring the flows between real life and reel life at times. Scores of interns or production assistants—during my fieldwork these were almost always young women—across news channels daily scour the internet and partner entertainment network footage to categorize material that might be of use in another story—either directly reporting on the clip in question or to be repurposed as an enactment in a special story. Senior editors explained to me that this repurposing of existing media material is a common technique in an industry where most of the money comes from advertising revenue, which is not reinvested into the quality of investigation for shows but goes to pay salaries and broadcasting costs. Journalists must fight their editors for space to do critical or hard-hitting stories. One journalist told me, for instance, that she was forced to make a bargain with her managing editor that she could do what he called "bleeding heart" (*jhola chhaap*) stories as long as she also delivered stories that covered concerns of young, urban, hip Delhi.[9] Whether it was lack of financial or political will that kept corporate media houses from pursuing in-depth investigative stories during my fieldwork, it has long been a truism within the industry that when it comes to special shows, like the nightly crime shows, the main work of putting together the stories occurs in the newsroom, with script writers and editors, rather than out on the beat. The use of the cinematic as a material to build or craft crime news stories involves more than merely copying or referencing scenes, dialogue, or music from popular films that enter into language in everyday life in India. In separate interviews with the members of one crime news production team, they emphasized the cinematic form of storytelling as a methodological approach in their work. In an interview with me, Srivardhan Trivedi said:

> The stories [in the news] . . . are more or less the same. At the end of the day, you're not telling your audience anything that others [channels] are not telling them. Then what becomes important is the way in which you tell your story. I make a story on a love triangle; so do you; and so does Yash Chopra [a famous and popular Bollywood director of romantic films]. What is the reason that mine flops, yours runs just a few days, and his is a hit? We have more or less the same actors, writers, and budgets, so what makes the difference? It's how you tell the story, how you place it before the viewers.[10]

One such story in which real and reel life appeared almost as mirror images happened during my fieldwork when, in 2011, a leading Hindi channel ran a story about a young man and woman who nullified their marriage on camera by accepting each other as brother and sister. The story reported that the young woman had married under pressure from her parents but was in love with another man. She had preemptively married this man before the official marriage arranged by her parents. On camera she asserted her right to be returned to her first husband and stated that her life was being threatened by her own family. The channel ran the story in their prime-time slot, in which they showed the parallels between this story and a Bollywood hit from 1999, *Hum Dil De Chuke Sanam* (Straight from the heart). Not only did they craft catchy headlines on the screen banner to grab audience attention, they reconstructed a scene with actors playing the parts of the couple in the news story and excerpted dialogue from the film to highlight the mental anguish that the young man was going through.

It is this kind of citational practice (Dwyer and Pinney 2001) in their style and approach to the news for which Hindi journalists get a lot of criticism, often by English-language public intellectuals and critics like Mr. V. However, what this criticism of Hindi news misses is that it is the manifestation of shifting practices of production and consumption within a larger media ecology since the 1980s. As film is increasingly defining itself and assessing its audience through television, it is also losing a demographic for which film was precisely that which television was not—racy, masculine, potentially spectacle oriented (Derné 2000). Big-budget films out of Bollywood have increasingly gentrified to appeal to an urbane audience that is as comfortable in Bombay as in London or New York, which leaves the mass audience in India without a medium devoted to reflecting its desires and anxieties (Ganti 2012a). The melodramas of the angry young man of the 1970s or the street-smart hero of the 1980s have given way to gentrified, arguably realist, depictions of urban upper-class conundrums of city and transnational life. As cinema halls in big cities became more upmarket, they also edged out the single male voyeuristic viewer in favor of family-friendly or urban youth demographics. Television journalism became, in the early 2000s, the visual medium through which aspiring young men who were not from Delhi, but lived in its ambit and its shadow, could strive for visibility and recognition. Rajat Sharma's India TV, for instance, broke into the public eye with a hidden-camera sting operation on the casting couch in Bollywood (Bamzai 2005). The young men (and they are mostly men in front of the camera), who are products of films from the 1970s and 1980s and wear that subjectivity on their sleeves, flocked to staff the newsrooms as more channels opened through 2010. Several prominent Hindi journalists have criticized the *filmi* (film-like), *hero-bandi* (heroics), or *tapori* (street-rogue) character of these new entrants. Here I quote Ravish Kumar, a highly respected Hindi journalist: "There were a lot of these things in the early days . . . a strange kind of machoism, a parochialism. As though in a tiny neighborhood the hero comes running in and saves someone; grabs someone and beats them up; or gets something done for someone else. This tendency was present in Hindi journalists."[11]

The tapori is a popular figure from 1990s Hindi film, played by a leading male star in the form of a cunning and street-smart rogue (Mazumdar 2007). In their orientation to language, media forms, and genres of expression, the Hindi journalist appears as this rogue figure, breaking with earlier tropes in both film and television where the male public figure is an urbane and cosmopolitan Hindustani, apparently unmarked by religion, caste, or regionalisms. The tapori is a rebellious figure that performs an explicit relation to the regional media languages with which he grew up and was inculcated into through a series of media forms like popular magazines and journals, films, and, more recently, television itself. Kumar continues in his interview with me:

> It is true that the influence of Hindi cinema is present in the storytelling of Hindi news—they tried to capture it deliberately. They wanted it to be a cinema. Cinema was itself going through a phase of redefining itself, with new films such as *Dil Chahta Hai* [What the heart wants, 2001], *Black* [2005]—these were films that were doing new things. But the techniques that cinema had begun to find monotonous [*uub chukka tha*], those techniques came into Hindi news. For these people, there was no aesthetic, so what else could they look to? Perhaps the imagination is that of an ignorant viewer, for whom a murder story is essential viewing, borrowing from the true crime segment.

While older journalists like Ravish Kumar feel that this influence has cheapened the language of news, replicating the critique of English-educated and metropolitan-born men like Mr. V, younger (male) journalists see this mediascape as their chance to script their stories of the future. Far from a lack of aesthetic, they brazenly claim the tapori nature of their journalism as a badge of pride. Not being beholden to the forms of civility or etiquette of preliberalization, Nehruvian India, or even actively reporting and identifying against it, Hindi journalists during the early 2000s used television as a means of asserting themselves and cementing their emergence as heroes on the scale of national visibility.

I turn now to the question of what we are to make of this flow between film and television news industries. I suggest that it allows us to see, personified and in practice, how the effects of film industrial production, commodification, and circulation manifest in the figure of the journalist.

Journalists as Vectors of Culture

I have discussed how the diversification of channels, with the separation of news from entertainment programming, created a qualitative shift in the flow of television watching. In addition, the diversification of what content belonged in the genre of news from the perspective of the industry indexed an increasing diversification of languages and voices in the public domain. Hindi television news through 2010 opened up, and brought into national view, the politics of caste, class, and region in powerful ways that state television never wanted and, given its unifying national project and print, though expanding rapidly since the 1970s and particularly in the 1990s, couldn't, given its local bases of growth and expansion. In drawing on the idioms of film and television itself, among other genres of mass and performative media, Hindi television news popularized and gave national visibility to language that is not the Hindi of official state bureaucracy or Hindu cultural nationalism. The circulation of this common or *aam* language in national news culture brings the *mofussil* and the *qasba* (provincial towns and cities) into the national space in a very material and tangible sense. Journalists coming from a vast network of nonmetropolitan cities have brought Hindi from the heartland (Ninan 2007) into the center of national news making. Local cultures of consumption of media like film, television, video and audio cassettes, local and national newspapers, weeklies and magazines, and more recently mobile phones and the internet are all linked in a dense ecology of media production in news studios now located in metropolitan centers like Delhi. These circulations might well be motivated and enabled by the logics of global capital and media flows but produce specific exchanges within local and regional worlds that previous ethnographic attention to media has tended to pass over.

Journalists present themselves as public figures through their work, demonstrating that a variety of journalistic subjectivities can be traced through the forms and modes in which they tell their stories. The flows between film and television industries that I have discussed above are personified in the figures of journalists, if we see them as sites of reception of existing media texts and languages (such as film and television shows) as well as producing new texts from these languages, that is, the news. When I first met with the team that produced a leading crime news show, I met Debu, originally from Kolkata. I introduced myself in much the same way I had done to Mr. V, explaining my interest in the production of news as a genre of storytelling but keeping to myself (initially) the talk of myth, storytelling, and sensation. Many of the journalists I approached during my fieldwork were distinctly unreceptive to my preliminary efforts to engage with them, but my opening interaction with Debu was to go particularly badly. As background about himself, he mentioned that he had been more involved in film production but now had moved from Bombay to Delhi to be part of the news industry. When I asked what prompted the shift, he angrily retorted, "There are some things which cannot be shared."[12] He immediately got up and moved away from me, and I wondered what might have transpired in his move to make him so touchy. Later, by coincidence, he was assigned by the production manager for the team to introduce me to the host of the show. With the host, my encounter went more smoothly, and I was able to reveal my interest in the aesthetics of the show and how the team sought to manipulate images and narrative to secure their audience. On the return from the green room, Debu's attitude to me had changed. He said to me, "I didn't know you wanted to discuss features of aesthetics and sensation in the news! This is one of the skills I think I bring from film into the news. I can tell you a lot about that." From then on, he became much more willing to talk about his work, and even let me observe in editing suites how the stories were put together. For a time, I was not able to understand what inspired his change of heart. It was my conversation with Imtiaz, a young journalist and author from Banaras who had made it big in Delhi, that helped shed light on Debu's initial reticence.

In his late twenties, Imtiaz was already a published author in Hindi. A Shia Muslim raised in Banaras, recognized internationally as a Hindu holy city, Imtiaz urged me to write the story of young journalists like himself, for whom the changes from the mid-1990s through 2010 had meant an entry into a more urban, metropolitan, and securely middle-class existence. The hallmark of this lifestyle was its stability: "Today a journalist can do only three things: buy a nice house, a nice car, and send his kids to a good school," he said. Then he added, "Perhaps he can go on a nice holiday abroad and be happy, but that's it."[13] In becoming urbanized, as English news always was, Hindi was leaving the rural areas behind, because these are not the stories that the journalists want to tell of themselves. How he told his own story of coming to Delhi, over a cup of coffee in Oxford Bookstore in the heart of Delhi's Connaught Place, not only highlights his aspirations but also points to how closely this storytelling shares a boundary with creative pursuits like cinema or television storytelling, entry into which is far harder than the news business.

Imtiaz's education (bachelor's and master of arts degrees) was completed in Allahabad and then Bhopal, large cities in Uttar Pradesh and Madhya Pradesh, the heartland of Hindi-speaking India. He started work in journalism in print with the newspaper *Amar Ujala*, but he wanted to write more creatively. By 2007 he had decided he wanted to be in television and told me that he had been following the career of Q. W. Naqvi, who was then the head of Aaj Tak, a fellow Shia from Banaras. He wrote to Naqvi, introduced himself, gave a résumé and asked for "just one chance" (*ek mauka dijiye*) to show him what he could do. There was, unsurprisingly, no response. In the meantime, he managed to find the number of yet another managing editor, Ajit Anjum of News 24, which had just recently launched as a new channel. Anjum is also from a small town, but from Bihar.

Somehow or other, Imtiaz got hold of Anjum's cell phone number and called him directly. At first, Anjum yelled at him for having the temerity to just call the managing editor of a channel like that, without proper introductions, but Imtiaz said that he just wanted a chance to show him that he was a good writer. He got Anjum's email address from him and sent him a résumé. The next day he was called to give a test. He did well, but then when he went to the interview, he was the last to be called. His appointment was for noon, but he didn't go into the room until after all the others who had recommendations (*sifarish*—introductions through mutual contacts). The scene Imtiaz set seemed very cinematic in itself, very like a scene in *Deewaar* (The wall, 1975) where one of the leading men in the film plays an honest, poor, young man who is denied job after job because he doesn't have sifarish, that is, recommendations, introductions, and the right contacts, signifying a network and connections. When Imtiaz finally went in for the interview, it was already 7 p.m. The interview went wonderfully, and three hours later, they were still talking. After being offered a handsome salary, he started work with News 24, but he only worked there nine months, because he got a call from Aaj Tak. He finally found himself face to face with K. W. Naqvi. By this time, he had some experience and Anjum's recommendation, so he negotiated a higher salary and started work at Aaj Tak in early 2008.

What stands out in Imtiaz's account is a narrative of a self-made man who saw opportunities and took them, or, as when he contacted Anjum directly, he made opportunities happen for himself. At the same time, it was clear that he wanted more than what he was achieving in the studio, where he was an assistant producer who did much of the script writing for news stories behind the scenes. He told me that he felt a great deal of frustration in the newsroom when others pulled ahead because they were literally more visible—they had roles in front of the camera. But it was his writing that gave them the glory, for which he got no credit. Imtiaz is an author who, at the time we met, had published one novel set in Banaras and was starting another about a Hindu-Muslim love story set in a fictitious newsroom. He told me he was thinking of leaving journalism, and, indeed, two years later when I had returned from the field, I saw on Facebook that he had gone to Bombay and was working as a creative writer for teleserials. Since then, he has written two more novels set in Banaras and has directed films based on all three of them. These films have achieved not only domestic but also international acclaim. For Imtiaz, what propelled him upward and out of the confines of a small town was the feeling that there was a space now for Hindi in the big cities that had earlier been impossible, or certainly very limited.

For those like K. W. Naqvi, Ajit Anjum, Ravish Kumar, and others who became the faces and ideas behind Hindi channels during the early 2000s, the story is not too different. Many of these men continue to have connections to the small towns they came from but have integrated these connections and networks into the urban landscapes they work in, cultivating them further through the networks they create in television news and other forms of expression, including blogs and, of course, social media. This migration from the small town to the city, which has long been a feature of changing social relations in the north since independence, in the early 2000s began to bring its language, gestures, and personality with it, rather than assimilating into the metropolis. These self-made journalists are, in their narratives, the heroes of their own stories, substantially transforming the nature of news reporting and its publics in India.

Conclusion

This chapter has examined changes in Indian television since the 1980s, including the introduction of many international cable channels, that affected the flows through which viewers experienced television programming, which, in turn, affected the market for audience viewership. Given so many different options, how could programs on these channels hold viewers' attention and sell advertising? As this transformation was taking place, the Indian film industry was also undergoing changes, among them being a more porous boundary between itself and other media industries like television. What in this volume is called personnel moved from film to television (and back again), with popular film stars making guest appearances on television talk shows and appearing on television programs. In order to draw viewership to its programs, television news developed the crime news genre, drawing on Bollywood's cinematic traditions to narrate the crime event. This creative solution, however, entailed a shift in personnel that would now be at the core of the news program. No longer was it the reporter narrating what had happened at the crime scene, in accordance with the realistic conventions of objective journalism, but rather the studio editor. This editor would have a vast knowledge of Indian cinema (and oftentimes had worked as a writer or editor in the Bombay film industry) and would draw on this knowledge to select scenes, dialogue, or other vignettes through which to frame the crime story, an example of what I have called media bricolage. Much of the ethnography of this chapter consists not only of interviews with personnel such as program producers and creators but also of trips to the editing room to see how this bricolage worked. An anthropological analysis of the film industry, however, would go beyond the specific production module of editing and the personnel laboring in it to consider the wider impact these might have on Indian society. Thus, these editors/writers have become storied figures who have managed to climb to the top of the television industry ladder. Through a presentation of their successes as the product of a combination of talent, street smarts, and pluck, they de-emphasize how traditional networks of caste, class, religion, or region structure their ability to navigate the television industry, which remains beholden to these criteria. Journalists in India during the early 2000s thus become allegories of neoliberalism and, as such, I argue, also vectors of change in Indian society.

Notes

Material for this chapter is drawn from fieldwork conducted for my doctoral research in Delhi, India, between February 2009 and July 2010. The fieldwork was made possible by a generous grant from the Wenner-Gren Foundation. The project in its earliest iteration explored the links between new genres of news making and emergent publics, forms of subjectivity, and ideas of citizenship after liberalization in India. Methodologically, it emphasized a move away from existing political-economy critiques of infotainment toward an anthropological understanding of the social life of storytelling in the news and the political and social subjectivities it engenders.

1 Interview with Mr. V, Delhi, July 15, 2009.
2 See also Gabriella Lukács (2010), whose ethnography on Japanese "trendy dramas" shows the interdependence of sites of production and reception, particularly when television is no longer limited to the screen in the domestic home but also traverses other mobile and digital media such as blogs, fan websites, and social media. In her book, Lukács also shows how television production capitalizes on the shift away from signification and meaning making in entertainment in favor of the emphasis on affect as a site for identity production. Here, I am not arguing for a shift away from

signification but rather drawing attention to the materiality and social nature of the sign and the gendered universe of meaning within which it circulates.

3   Despite mobility, however, the caste makeup of all Hindi news channels remains predominantly upper caste and Hindu.

4   See Williams ([1974] 2003, ch. 4, "Programming: Distribution and Flow. Television"). Williams postulated that since the 1960s British and American television had seen a shift in programming from a concept of sequence (that is, of discrete programs following each other, depending on the time of day or even the day of the week) to a concept of flow, though he conceded that the latter was difficult to discern because the older idea of sequence often overlapped with it. Not only that, but from Williams's account, flow was often an implicit concept in television programming, one not necessarily discussed by programmers or overtly apparent to viewers, and therefore difficult to discern though nonetheless real. According to him, the shift entailed "the replacement of a programme series of timed sequential units by a flow series in which the timing, though real, is undeclared, and in which the real internal organization is something other than the declared organization" (93).

5   Williams ([1974] 2003, 94) writes, "We do not watch programs, we watch television," that is, we watch the endless streaming of shows that come on one after the other.

6   I sat with one managing editor and lead anchor of an English news channel while he was showing me the ratings gathered by TAM (the Indian agency for audience measurement, in partnership with Nielsen) for the previous week. Ruefully he showed me the previous Wednesday's prime-time slot, when the channel had aired an important analysis of documents relating to a recent political scandal, which got single figures in ratings. Comparing this time slot and choice of story to that of other channels, it became clear that a controversial reality show was instead drawing all the viewers, leaving the editor to rhetorically reflect that there is no point in doing good journalism if no one sees it.

7   Due to a change in ownership, Star News was renamed ABP News in 2012 and is no longer part of the Star TV network. I continue to refer to it here as Star News, since that was the name during my fieldwork.

8   *Zanjeer* and *Deewaar* are successful Hindi films from the 1970s starring Amitabh Bachchan, from which snatches of dialogue often circulate in parody, as citations, and in referential fragments as public words (Spitulnik 1993).

9   "Jhola chhaap" is a term that has no direct translation in English but would be equivalent to the notion of the bleeding-heart human interest story in an English-language context. The jhola is a simple cloth bag used to carry one's daily belongings, the stamp (chhaap) of which is seen derisively as a marker of somewhat outdated socialist principles in the context of India's turn to neoliberal policies and politics. Journalists who are particularly focused on violence against women, student activism, rural and agrarian debt and marginalization, and indigenous rights issues are frequently dismissed as jhola chhaap.

10 Interview with Srivardhan Trivedi, Delhi, October 9, 2009.

11 Interview with Ravish Kumar, Delhi, January 25, 2010.

12 Interview with Debu, Delhi, September 24, 2009.

13 Interview with Imtiaz, Delhi, October 14, 2009.

4. "THIS IS NOT A FILM"

Industrial Expectations and Film Criticism as Censorship at the Bangladesh Film Censor Board

LOTTE HOEK

In February 2014, I was sitting in the office of the then vice chairman of the Bangladesh Film Censor Board. As with all such offices of the highly placed, there was a constant stream of visitors, well-wishers, and supplicants. Some arrived with boxes of sweets, others with sheaves of paper. Interspersed with these, more lowly placed bureaucrats of the board came and went with forms, folders, and cups of tea for the many supplicants.

That day, one of the visitors to the vice chairman was a fellow high-ranking official and poetry enthusiast. A senior civil servant, an additional secretary at the Ministry of Public Administration, he came in for a chat with his friend the vice chairman. Upon being introduced to me, the additional secretary not only gave me a copy of his recently published poems but also said that for the purposes of my research into Bangladeshi cinema, I should really take a look at the film made by Jean-Nesar Osman. He explained that he was the son of Shawkot Osman, a famous novelist who published his important works in the 1960s and '70s, and that Jean-Nesar had studied at the Film and Television Institute of India (FTII) in Pune and had made some very interesting films. At this point the vice chairman intervened and told his friend that I would not be able see this film because "we" (the Censor Board) didn't clear it.

"An upside-down film [*ultapalta chobi*]," the chairman added. "The guy is mad."[1]

"Well, he made a good film about child labor," mumbled the additional secretary.

"What was wrong with the film?" I asked, intrigued.

"The plot wasn't right [*ghotona thik nei*]," said the vice chairman. "It was also very commercial."

"What does that mean, *ghotona thik nei*?" I asked, more intrigued still.

"He wasn't able [*o pare nei*]," the vice chairman said. "He couldn't make a film."

And with that, he changed the subject.

What sort of judgment is it by which officials tasked with executing film certification in Bangladesh reject a film on the basis of the incompetence or madness of a filmmaker? In this chapter, I take up two cases where the Bangladesh Film Censor Board has refused to certify films and has cited incompetence and inadequacy as reasons for their refusal. In both cases, the films submitted were made by film industry outsiders, that is, filmmakers who were operating within the art or alternative circuit of filmmaking and in television in Bangladesh rather than in the well-oiled popular industry focused on the Bangladesh Film Development Corporation, which is a part of the Ministry of Information, as the Censor Board is. Both filmmakers have participated centrally in the spaces of high cultural life so prized in the middle-class and bourgeois circles of Dhaka. One is a well-regarded poet and maker of short films, Kamruzzaman Kamu; the other, Jean-Nesar Osman, the scion of a literary family and established documentary filmmaker. Both can be seen as part of a cultural avant-garde or, at the least, not a part of the popular film industry. Both failed to get their first feature films certified by the Bangladesh Film Censor Board.

Taking up the censorship journeys of these two films, I will show that in both cases the tussle between the filmmakers and the Censor Board hinged on a comparative film criticism and practice of film appreciation that became part of the films' production processes. In both cases, the question of how to make a proper film, an aspect of film appreciation, animated members of the Censor Board as they were confronted with these two nontraditional films. The Censor Code in Bangladesh does not include any headings for artistic competence or aesthetic considerations but instead focuses on things such as morality and questions of law and order. These things are regularly and predictably invoked to demand cuts and withhold certification from films. In the case of these two films it is the question of an inadequate story or the lack of skill on the part of the director to make a proper film that appears in their censorship files and that interests me here. It is at this point that censorship becomes a part of the film production process (a site in the industrial process of making a film) as well as a critical reflection on that process (How well or adequately does this filmmaker use the production process?). Exploring how these critiques are articulated and how they are understood both on the part of filmmakers and on the part of members of the Censor Board will illustrate that censorship is crucially part of, rather than subsequent to, the film production process. While I have argued this previously with regard to the question of preemptive excision of scenes and shots in popular cinema by editors (Hoek 2014), here I approach this problem from the vantage point of the Censor Board, and filmmakers' entanglement with it, to show how censorship is imagined as part of the process by which proper films are produced.

The questions I seek to answer in this chapter are how film criticism can come to act as censorship; how film criticism is premised on an understanding of industrial filmmaking practices; and whether we should therefore understand censorship as a part of film production processes and even the film industry. Using the examples of *The Director* by Kamruzzaman Kamu and *Dekh Tamasha* by Jean-Nesar Osman, I look at the practices of aesthetic evaluation at the heart of their censorship cases. In both cases, censorship took the shape of legally binding film criticism that resulted in exceptionally intractable battles over certification. It shows that censorship can be focused on the formal qualities of a film and that film appreciation and criticism can act as a mode of censorship. Ultimately, this chapter illustrates that certain expectations about industrial film production processes and the shape of its outputs are embedded within censorship practices. With this, I respond to the call by Nitin Govil to "broaden the range of practices that count as industrial" and to use a "more dynamic sense of industries as social and textual arrangements, sites of enactment, and other dramaturgies of interaction, reflection, and reflexivity" (2013, 176).

In linking state censorship practices to modes of film appreciation, I understand film criticism as a set of practices by which films are evaluated on the basis of personally held theories about the nature of cinema, exercised with implicit and explicit reference to, and comparison between, films. The practice of film appreciation that is at play in this form of film criticism can be understood parallel to how Noël Carroll describes art appreciation. He suggests we see it as a heuristic by which "in order to appreciate a work of art, one must 1) identify its intended purpose or purposes and 2) determine the adequacy or appropriateness of form—its formal choices—to the realization or articulation of its intended purpose" (Carroll 2016, 5). The case studies in this chapter show members of the Censor Board evaluating whether an appropriate form has been found to articulate the ideas animating a cinematic work. This practice can be understood in terms of an "administration of aesthetics," the regulatory practice around cultural production that "prompts one to wonder whether regulating aesthetic production (state censorship) and regulating aesthetic consumption (criticism) can be opposed" (Burt 1994, xvi). In this chapter I show that such regulatory practices are embedded within film production processes and the industry understood in an expanded sense. I show that the critical evaluations made by members of the Censor Board proceeded on the basis of assumptions about the type of product that ought to be delivered through established film production processes in the first place. Taking seriously the film criticism at the heart of these two cases allows me to address the question of cinematic discernment that is often central to film censorship but is rarely explicated within the formal censorship regulations that focus on morality or law-and-order questions.

The arguments in this chapter are based on data collected through the use of anthropological methods. I undertook fieldwork at the Bangladesh Film Censor Board in Dhaka during 2013–2014 while working on a larger project about the film society movement in Bangladesh. There, I talked to and visited with the film inspectors, peons, and the vice chairman of the board at their offices in Eskaton in Dhaka, spending long days there. They very kindly facilitated archival work I was doing, and I spent a significant amount of time looking at the files relating to film societies as well as particularly long-drawn-out censorship cases such as the ones under discussion in this chapter. Drawing on their censorship files, which include handwritten examination reports by individual Censor Board members, as well as the letters exchanged between the board and filmmakers, and informed by many casual conversations with the officers at the board, the case studies presented here illustrate how Censor Board members struggle with the question of form in their evaluation of films, rather than with the question of the content of a film. This chapter illustrates the value of doing long-term anthropological fieldwork as part of a study of the cinema and its production processes. Media anthropology explores the everyday social contexts of media production and consumption through long-term, immersive, slow, and incremental fieldwork practices (Ginsburg, Abu-Lughod, and Larkin 2002; Larkin 2008). Such methods open up the possibility of reexamining mundane aspects of well-oiled industrial processes for analytical reconsideration.

The scholarly literature on censorship, in South Asia and elsewhere, and irrespective of theoretical orientation, has tended to focus on the relationship between certain types of content and their publics (Kuhn 1988; Robertson 1993; Vasudev 1978). In part, this is because of the ways in which the relationship between certain images and audiences came to be imagined as one of effects (especially the effect on vulnerable spectators of all sorts) by early legislators and theorists alike and how this understanding has been written into censorship legislation to police disruptive, imperiling, or dangerous images (Brooker and Jermyn 2003; Mazzarella 2013; Schaefer 1999). The emphasis in legislation in South Asia, drawing on its colonial form, is similarly on content or representation, what William Mazzarella calls in this context "the image-object"

(2013, 17). The image-objects that censorship legislation in South Asia is concerned with are circumscribed: representations of the police, of religion, of the nation-state, et cetera. The censorship legislation, then, speaks of content but remains silent on form because of the ways in which cinematic harm has come to be understood: the immediate disruption of susceptible audiences caused by certain types of audiovisual representations. Discontent with artistic form has instead been relegated to other sorts of public vocabularies. This often comes in the form of a rejection on the basis of lack of skill, described by Partha Mitter (2007) as the Picasso manqué syndrome, leveled against artists outside the centers of Western art practice. Such criticism was and continues to be frequently used across South Asia to discredit filmmakers, memorably articulated early on by Satyajit Ray ([1976] 2005) in his 1948 essay "What's Wrong with Indian Cinema," and a recurring trope in debate on film (Dass 2015). Such critiques are echoed in rejections of films and filmmakers in Bangladesh today; they express themselves in a general disregard for popular action films and extend to discontent with certain types and styles of telefilm. The academic literature on film censorship in South Asia tends to focus on the images and representations that get caught up in censorship battles while discussions of form are imagined to be reserved for critics, connoisseurs, and artists.

Anthropological and ethnographic research in the field of film censorship in South Asia has repeatedly shown that there is no necessary overlap between the wording of a censorship code that animates a legal process and the image objects that the legislation is applied to (Hoek 2014; Kaur and Mazzarella 2009; Mazzarella 2013; Mehta 2011). This gap between the wording of the code and the images against which it is wielded also provides the space in which film criticism can come to operate as censorship, as I show in this chapter. The question whether the meaning of a film or work of art has found its appropriate form as a principle of art appreciation appears in the working of the Bangladesh Film Censor Board despite the fact that it is entirely outside the wording of the code. And this is not surprising: to come to any form of judgment about a film, members of the board need to read the film, and its content is inevitably merged with its form. Nonetheless, the scholarly literature on censorship tends to focus on the meaning of images, located at the level of representation, rather than considering how censorship is concerned with formal strategies and choices inherent in filmmaking practices: that is, the formal characteristics of the film. This is in part due to the assumption of a clear division of labor between art and law that scholars such as Lawrence Liang have tried to undo in the context of Indian film studies. He notes that "we often hear the complaint that lawyers and judges should not play art critics, and while there is something intuitively agreeable to this sentiment, it recycles the assumption that the world of law resides in the domain of reason and rationality, while the province of aesthetics lies in affective states and sensorial experiences" (Liang 2011, 26). My ethnographic fieldwork with filmmakers and with the Censor Board in Dhaka underscores the imbrication of these domains. This chapter extends debates on film censorship in South Asia by suggesting the place of formal aesthetic procedures within censorship practice. Taking this as my central focus, it also allows me to move the discussion of censorship in South Asia away from religious sensibilities, which have, for historical reasons, been consolidated as the means to understand censorship in Muslim South Asia (Ahmad 2010; Ahmed 2009; Qureshi 2010; Rashiduzzaman 1994).

The Director Freedom Movement

A small group had gathered outside the Bangladesh National Museum in Shahbag, central Dhaka, one morning in February 2014. Three young men busied themselves with unfolding a large banner while a fourth took pictures of the process. Once unfolded, the banner laid out their demands: "We want the release/freedom of The Director" (*The Director Mukti Chay*) and "We want change to the Censor Code" (*Censor Protha Shongskar Chay*). Their name was at the bottom of the banner: "*The Director* Freedom Movement" (*The Director Mukti Andolon*). The movement had gathered young poets and journalists on symbolic ground: the Shahbag square has historically been associated with political protest (Sabur 2013). The small group stood awkwardly in front of the museum, amid the rush of traffic that clogs this major intersection. Within twenty minutes it was decided that this display at Shahbag sufficed; now they would proceed to their true destination: the Bangladesh Film Censor Board.

Setting off in a small procession, the young men held their banner aloft as they walked through the heavy traffic to the nearby offices of the Censor Board. There they were joined by more of their friends, all holding placards stating their demands. The media too had appeared by now, with camera crews from Bangladesh's many television channels recording the slogans hollered by the young men who had lined up on the pavement across from the Censor Board. "The censorship act needs to be abolished," said one of the protestors to me. "It dates from 1963!" When I asked different protesters why they had come, most said that they knew the film director personally, that they felt that the arts should be left without government interference, or that they felt that his case illustrated the antiquated nature of the Code for Censorship of Films in Bangladesh.

The television cameras zoomed in on a graying man and his *lungi*-wearing bearded companion at the heart of the small crowd. They were the poet-turned-film-director Kamruzzaman Kamu, whose film had been denied certification by the board, and his friend, a left-wing intellectual and folk heavy metal singer.

The Director was Kamu's second film. Having established himself as a poet, he then turned to filmmaking. His first film, *Scriptwriter* (2007), was a short film that was screened on television and at a few international film festivals. The film had the stamp of artistic approval not only due to its success at these festivals but also due to the casting of one of the most recognizable contemporary alternative filmmakers in Bangladesh, Nurul Alam Atique (who also trained at FTII). Having done well with his short film, Kamu decided to make a second short film, this time centered on the director. Sitting down with his footage, he explained to me in a subsequent interview, he felt that the narrative really warranted feature length. He decided to center the longer film on his main character, a film director loosely based on himself. Finding producers willing to invest in his project to convert his short film into the feature film *The Director*, he completed the film in a self-described ad hoc manner. Once complete, he submitted the film to the Censor Board to certify it for general release. To his astonishment, the board refused to certify his film, leaving him effectively without the means to screen his film in theaters and recoup his, and his producers', investment.

As the protest wound up with tea and excited conversation about the state of cinema today, I crossed the road into the fourteen-story building housing the Censor Board. Taking the elevator to the ninth floor, I went up to talk to the vice chairman and the senior film inspector at the board about the protest. The vice chairman was out, but the inspector was behind his desk. "What protest?" he asked as his colleagues handed him files to sign. Having all reached the office by 10 a.m., none of the officials staffing the board had any need to go down to ground level until the much-awaited 5 p.m. end of the working day. No one had noticed the protest by *The Director* Freedom Movement. I asked whether the inspector thought the movement would have any influence on the board's decision. "It is no longer in our hands," said the inspector. "The film has gone for appeal at the ministry. We are no longer involved." The appeal board had upheld the ban on public screening of *The Director*. *The Director* Freedom Movement, gathered at the wrong time, in the wrong place, seemed at a great distance from the everyday workings of the Censor Board.

The Director and the Inadequate Story

A few weeks after the protests outside the Censor Board offices, I met up with Kamu to discuss his film and the movement. Describing to me the way in which the film came into being, organically developing from a short film into a feature-length movie, he said that the process hadn't been entirely planned. This had a direct impact on the final form of the film. "My story is made up of many different stories. Characters appear and get connected in different ways," he said. He added that because of this, "not all of it is based on a narrative structure."

Still indignant a year after the film was rejected by the Censor Board, he showed me the letter he had received from them. In it, they listed the reasons why the film was deemed unsuitable for public screening. This included the predictable charge of indecency. But the first objection listed in the letter was that "the main story in the film is inadequate" (*cholochitrite mul kahini oporyapto*). The Code for Censorship of Films in Bangladesh does not have a category under which a film might be rejected on the grounds of a filmmaker's incompetence or a film's incoherence. There is, however, the ability to justify cuts or withhold certification on the grounds of an "inadequate story." This option features in the Code for Censorship under the first general principle, Security/Law and Order, subheading (k): "Has an inadequate story intended to cover up sequences predominantly consisting of lawlessness, violence, crimes, spying etc. likely to affect adversely the average audience" ("The Code for Censorship of Films in Bangladesh" 1985). The letter to Kamu, however, did not suggest that the story line was inadequate due to its intention to cover up sequences damaging to law and order in Bangladesh or that would impact negatively on an average audience. Instead, the letter just stated that the story was inadequate.

Kamu was agitated by the suggestion that his film had an inadequate story line. I asked him to tell me what he thought they meant by this. He said,

> My film doesn't match their experience. I think that they couldn't understand the film. Why? . . . The films that they are used to, those films are so straightforward [*ora ye shob chobi bhitor diye asche, she chobigulo eto shorolrekhi*]: an actress holding a water vessel [*kulshi*], an actor behind her. When someone gets put there [on the board] after seeing films with nearly all the same images, then that person has no connection with more diverse art forms [*aro bichitro dhoroner shilpo*]. That person doesn't know that in this field, there is so much to do, so much freedom for people.

Kamu accused the members of the Censor Board of being inexperienced film viewers, who lacked the understanding that would derive from familiarity with a range of art forms and cinematic experiences. Ridiculing the common image of the village belle in popular Bangladeshi cinema, holding her kulshi on her hip, Kamu suggested that the problem with the board members was that their expectations were formed exclusively by popular cinema. In Kamu's view, the Censor Board's evaluation of his film as inadequate was borne of their familiarity with the films produced within the film industry, based in the Bangladesh Film Development Corporation, through which genre films were made. Genre films, in which narratives and pleasures depend exactly on the audience's familiarity with certain cinematic conventions (Braudy 2004; Gopalan 2003), are the mainstay of popular cinema in Bangladesh. In the industrial process of filmmaking in Dhaka, staffed by industry hands, elements of the production process, such as action or song sequences, set building, or sound recording, overlay generic narrative elements found in the script with familiar aesthetic forms (see Hoek 2014). These films are comparable with genre films from elsewhere in South Asia which "display a set of features that are akin to pre-classical cinema, especially several extra-diegetic sequences or sequences of attractions" (Gopalan 2001, 367). The mainstream commercial genre film in Bangladesh similarly involves standardized narrative elements and visual and aural conventions that include extradiegetic aspects, including six or seven song sequences, fight or action sequences that thrash out a moral conflict, and comedic subplots tangentially linked to the main narrative built around a central romance that is initially thwarted but ultimately victorious. The execution of such conventions was not uniformly successful, but the mainstream genre film in general stuck to these broad patterns across the majority of mainstream film output in Dhaka. It was this that Kamu imagined as the background against which the members of the Censor Board failed to understand his film *The Director*.

Film scholars have demonstrated the significant relationship between the organization of the film industry as a site for film production and the conventions and ideologies of the cinema produced within these industrial structures (Bordwell, Staiger, and Thompson 2003; Prasad 1998) as well as the ways in which audience expectations and appreciation of genre are linked to industrial formations of production and distribution in South Asia (Gopalan 2003; Govil 2015b; Thomas 2013; Vasudevan 2010). It is the industrial context of production and the conventional nature of commercial genre films that have generated criticism and disdain for the genre film, because genre films "outrage [people's] inherited and unexamined sense of what art *should* be [rather] than because the films are offensive in theme, characterisation, style, or other artistic quality" (Braudy 2004, 665). Zakir Raju (2013) has explored how a discourse of disdain sets off commercial from alternative cinema in Bangladesh (see also Rahman 2017). Kamu rehearsed exactly such a perspective when he disregarded the

Censor Board's evaluation of his film based on their familiarity with unsophisticated and predictable genre films. The problem was not with his film and its fragmented narrative structure, shot with modes of improvisation at its heart, but rather with the incapacity of the board members to recognize the diversity of form and imagination that cinema as an art allows, steeped as they were in the domain of commercial genre film.

As Kamu explicitly linked the cinematic imagination to artistic freedom, I asked him about this freedom. "This freedom is the freedom of the artist, of the poet," he said. "When I practice my art, when I see it as a personal expression of my art, then that needs to be given total freedom. God's level of freedom [*Ishwar-er level-er shadinota*]." Kamu attributed a divine level of freedom to the personal practice of the arts. Kamu here echoes a long-standing trope, articulated by Satyajit Ray in his 1958 essay "Problems of a Bengali Film Maker" when he notes that "the *avant-garde* experimentalist . . . is essentially a free artist, being responsible only to his own artistic conscience" ([1976] 2005, 38). The cinema was one of the spaces Kamu saw for the exercise of his artistic practice: "Within this space, I can imagine what I like." While the imaginations of the members of the Censor Board were tied down by convention, a shared and repetitive form of cultural production, Kamu saw his artistic imagination as free and rooted within his own thought. That is, his was a truly autonomous artistic practice. That this could be deemed ineligible for public screening was an outrage to him.

"If it was a foreign film, they probably wouldn't have blocked the film," said Kamu, "but because I am Bangladeshi, they are messing with me. [They're saying,] 'Who is this guy?!'" Kamu said this was something he and his colleagues had faced before. He described a gap between those in the industry, those who knew only popular filmmaking, and his friends and colleagues who made short films, films produced by television stations, or TV dramas. Imitating the line of thought of the members of the board, he suggested that they would ask, "'Who are they? What sort of filmmakers are they?! Let them make television! What sort of filmmakers are *they*? *We* are filmmakers.'" He said, "That is what they think. It is a very patronizing tendency [*Khubi moroli tendency*]." Kamu felt the gatekeeping around the industry acutely, and the difficulties faced by film directors were in fact a central, and often comedic, plot line in *The Director*.

The distinction that Kamu invoked here goes to the heart of his conflict with the board. It is about the question of who can rightfully call themselves a filmmaker. Kamu considered himself an artist with an autonomous artistic practice that included poetry, lyric writing, and filmmaking. He considered the members of the board as uninformed, their understanding of cinema narrowed by an exclusive engagement with mainstream Bangladeshi cinema. Kamu felt that their reliance on the familiarity of film conventions as shaped by the production process within the mainstream industry blinkered them to the possibilities of other forms of films resulting from different types of production processes. He considered those forms equally and importantly part of the cinema. He thought that the Censor Board was blinkered and could only accommodate these types of film products by placing them in other production contexts, such as those of television.

The case of *The Director* shows how through the question of whether a film has narrative coherence—which is a formal evaluation—film criticism acts directly as a form of censorship. The wording of the code is used piecemeal to allow members of the Censor Board to say something about the inadequacy of the formal properties of the film ("inadequate story line") and to accommodate that evaluation as a legally binding judgment. Kamu counters this with even more emphasis on the formal qualities of the film ("it is nonlinear," "not all based on a narrative structure"). Kamu does not consider the board capable of making aesthetic evaluations because he feels that its members are not trained to do so, nor does the law positively articulate formal qualities as domains of censorship intervention. Kamu and the board struggle over who can make appropriate cinematic distinctions, who has the capacity for cinematic appreciation and critique. Their conflict pivots on who can be the judge, both in the aesthetic sense and in the legal sense, which in this case are entirely intertwined. It describes exactly the tussle over the grounds for the censor's judgment that William Mazzarella (2013, 78) identifies as a source of conflict in the context of Indian film censorship.

In response to my questions, Kamu sketched his standoff with the board in the most elevated registers. He juxtaposed the uninformed and petty judgments generated by the Censor Board's film appreciation model of evaluating films with the sorts of critical practice animated by a divine artistic freedom that he practiced himself and which interrogated the very boundaries of the board's mode of film appreciation. Kamu wanted the board to recognize that the practice of filmmaking and film viewing should be about opening up categories and expectations, not about closing them down. It doesn't need to be pointed out that his idea of the divine freedom of a creative practitioner is highly modernist (Krauss 1986), and that this idea has been particularly entrenched in audiovisual production, where the director has remained a key authorial site (Caldwell 2008, 17) despite its waning in other fields of creative production. It is also significant that it has been exactly in the face of genre cinema, understood as conventional and without an autonomous maker or auteur (Braudy 2004), that these unexamined assumptions about the autonomous nature of art and artistic practice are most sharply articulated.

Kamu had run into trouble with the Censor Board not because he had aspired to create a film on the basis of his autonomous artistic vision but because he had wanted it to be publicly screened in theaters. It is important to note that Kamu's first film, *Script Writer*, was made as a short film, not screened in theaters. In that form, the film had not required certification by the Bangladesh Film Censor Board. Only when a film is destined for release in theaters (and certain specified festivals) is certification required. This means that conflicts between self-described "art" or "good" filmmakers are relatively rare in Bangladesh, compared to the endless, nearly daily but often very pragmatic, negotiations between commercial filmmakers and the board. Short films, television dramas, telefilms or documentaries (often described by film industry insiders as "media" rather than cinema) can circulate within spaces that are outside the domain of the film censors. In those formats, autonomous artistic practice or formal experimentation can be indulged in largely at arm's length from the Film Censor Board. But once you do put your film forward for certification, desiring a particular type of exhibition and, importantly, financial reward, the Film Censor Board becomes involved. At the Censor Board, this makes your work into a *film*. And this is where they have the final say.

Dekh Tamasha and Incompetent Filmmaking

The Director was caught up in the process of censoring and certification between early 2013 and 2015. But its time at the Censor Board was nothing compared to the fate of the film *Dekh Tamasha* (Jean-Nesar Osman, dir.; the film's title is satirical, literally meaning "See the commotion" but implying a cynical and clear-eyed view of the act put on). This film has shuttled back and forth between its director and the various branches of the Ministry of Information since 1995. Between 1995 and 2013, the film was submitted to the Censor Board five times, and decisions about the film were appealed to the Ministry of Information's appeal board four times. Like *The Director*, the film has been deemed unsuitable for public screening, and it was refused certification on many separate occasions. This is the film that the vice chairman of the Censor Board said didn't have a proper story and that the filmmaker wasn't able to make a film.

The fraying file for *Dekh Tamasha* at the Censor Board hardly held together the more than 250 pages of documents that constituted the official records of the progress of the film through the Ministry of Information. Handwritten notes and forms documented the communications between a changing cast of bureaucrats tasked with keeping track of the film as well as recording the opinions of individual board members about the film through two decades of censoring. Typed and printed material tracked the correspondence between the board and the filmmaker, documenting objections, demanding excisions, and requesting the return or transfer of reels of celluloid. Here, I'm not focused on the thick account of the bureaucratic progress of film censorship mediated by its paper artifacts (Hull 2012) but on the reasons given on the forms filled out by the members of the various boards that watched and rejected *Dekh Tamasha* for public screening. To show how film criticism operated as a means of censorship in the case of *Dekh Tamasha*, in this section I go through the notes made on the forms filled in by individual Censor Board members upon examining the film.

Two central themes run through each of the rounds of examination that the film endured: filmmaking incompetence and lack of taste. In 1998, one of the members of the board writes on the form that *Dekh Tamasha* is "absolutely unsuitable for screening and of unrefined taste [*sthulo ruchipurno*]. Presentation is ugly [*kodorjo*]." Part of *Dekh Tamasha*'s problem of taste was its obscenity and violence, to which the Censor Code is well equipped to respond and which the members could easily invoke to block the film's certification. What is remarkable, however, is that while the film's obscenity and violence are mentioned here and there in the forms, over the years the board members repeatedly suggest that the central problem with the thing they are watching is that it is not, in fact, a proper film. During the examination of the film in 2000, one of the members of the board wrote that "this has not become a film [*eti chobi hoy ni*]. A film is not made by merely adding some obscene images and dialogues to create a *tamasha*." A colleague in the same round wrote that "this isn't what can be understood as a film [*chayachobi bolte ya bujhay eti ta hoy nei*]."

But *Dekh Tamasha*'s fortunes did fluctuate over the two decades of its censorship progress. By March 2005, the board (always changing in composition) was more favorably inclined toward *Dekh Tamasha*. Although the film had by that point been refused certification four times, and three appeals had been rejected, the March 2005 board now decided that the film was suitable for public viewing after all, as long as two scenes were modified: the image of a dead child next to a dustbin had to be removed, and the view of a woman's breasts while she bathes needed to be excised. On a form from that round, one of the board members did bring up the film's inadequacies again: "The film's print is very bad. The story is incomplete [*osompurno*]. The film has been cut so many times, it doesn't stand alone as a film any more. It cannot be evaluated." Nonetheless, the letter sent to Jean-Nesar Osman suggested that with the two cuts and a submission to the board of all previously cut celluloid, the film could be certified for public screening.

This could have been the end of the saga of *Dekh Tamasha*. But something happened. The file does not record where the problem emerged (and it might very well be a problem that cannot be articulated within the formal documentation of the censorship process), but on reexamination in December 2005, the board found lots of problems with the film, including the fact that it has no positive message. The concerns were so urgent that the Ministry of Information demanded the confiscation of the censor copy of the film. The forms from this examination round all stress the inadequacy of the film as a film. One of the members wrote on the form, "The story and the screenplay, dialogue and cinematography, everything is very weak [*durbol*], in comparison to what is necessary for a feature film. That is why it is unacceptable for public screening." Another suggests, "There is no way this film can be considered a feature film. The story, dialogue, screenplay, cinematography, sound recording are despicable [*jogonnotomo*], of such low grade [*nimno man*] that it is unsuitable for public screening. Under the censor board law, this film can never be resubmitted to the censor board." The signature on the form suggests the comment may have come from a well-established popular filmmaker. One of his colleagues, a famous actress who defined Bangladeshi melodrama in the 1970s, wrote on her form, "There is no way this film can be considered a feature film. The screenplay, dialogue, cinematography and sound are of low grade. This is unsuitable for public screening." Yet another member writes on their form, "The story, script writing and dialogue have not added up to become a screenable film [*prodorshonyoggo chayachobi hoy nei*]. The problem with *Dekh Tamasha*, according to these examination forms, was the inadequate quality of the film as a film.

The handwritten forms recording the viewing experiences of individual members of the Censor Board over the years provide a rich source of empirical data that highlight how evaluations in terms of film appreciation come to ground censorship judgments. The notes focus on the director's lack of skills to execute the film as a material object. Sound, editing, and cinematography, in the opinion of various members of the board, have not come together in such a way as to make the object recognizable as a film. While the board members did not explicitly state what would conform to their expectations, in the different files, the cinematic elements under their consideration are explicitly named: dialogue, script writing, cinematography, sound, print quality. What is also clear is that they don't want a spectacle or *tamasha*, turning the tables on Osman's title. Instead, they are looking for something that is recognizably a film and is executed according to their expectations of what a film looks and sounds like and has a properly realized story or narrative. As Kamruzzaman Kamu had sensed in his own confrontation with the Censor Board, the members had certain expectations of a film's proper realization, and when these were not met, they refused to certify the film. But, unlike Kamu's suspicions, the board members viewing *Dekh Tamasha* did not attribute their frustrated expectations to their own incomprehension of the film in front of them. Instead, they transcribed their experience as the filmmaker's incompetence, his lack of skill and taste, rather than their own incapacity to read the film before them.

In December 2005, the members of the Censor Board, including its vice chairman, were clearly unwilling to allow the film the certification that seemed to be offered only nine months earlier. Nonetheless, on their forms, the members do not note the obscenity and violence of the film, both of which could easily be attributed to any film while simultaneously being easily defensible grounds for rejection by the board under the Censor Code. Instead, they all continued to cite the technical and filmic inadequacies of the film.

Both *The Director* and *Dekh Tamasha* failed to be certified for public screening on the grounds of inadequate filmmaking skills. The referents in these two censorship cases were the integrity of the film as a cinematic object, not the representational content itself. That is, the Censor Code, with its emphasis on the representation of the police, or morality, or the state, was hardly invoked. Instead, a vocabulary of film criticism played a central role in the censoring of both these films. This significantly shifts the contours of how we might understand censorship. It places censorship within the process of film production, not just because of the way in which it may ask for cuts to a film but because of the ways the censor's imagination is situated within the production process of a film. Film criticism as censorship asks: has this film been realized according to our expectations of what makes for a coherent filmic object? Bureaucrats and film industry insiders on the Censor Board thus make binding statements about how the production process for filmmaking ought to proceed when they refuse to certify a film because of its formal or technical inadequacies. This places censorship within the process of film production and shapes it from the outside in. Besides a politics of the state, censorship here is also a politics of the film industry.

Censorship as Film Criticism in the Context of Bangladesh

Why do questions of aesthetic value and filmmaking skill appear to be subject to censorship beyond the wording of the Censor Code in Bangladesh? The criticism that a film is not a film can act effectively as a means of censorship because of the particularities of the historical, social, and political contexts of the film landscape and cinematic public in South Asia in general, and Bangladesh in particular. Film as an object, an experience, and a commodity has, since the first half of the twentieth century in South Asia, been shaped within distinct discourses about publics and audience preference, as well as within legislative, economic, and technological contexts (Hughes 2000; Jaikumar 2006; Srinivas 2000; Vasudevan 2010). All these have shaped a cinematic culture that encompasses structuring factors ranging from ideas about types of theaters and their audiences to import regimes and financial structure. In his classic text *Ideology of the Hindi Cinema*, M. Madhava Prasad (1998) has shown that the formal particularities of Hindi cinema during much of the twentieth century were significantly determined by the modes of industrial production within Bombay that have emerged out of these broader structuring contexts. The cinematic conventions thus shaped were widely understood and played with by directors and audiences alike, and this continues to be the case for the Hindi cinema as much as most of the other regional and national cinemas of South Asia. Cultures of film viewing are shaped within these conditions (Srinivas 2016), and in Bangladesh, audiences in movie theaters respond to generic conventions not through some involuntary triggering or deep cultural proclivity, but as part of a profound familiarity and engagement with film as a recognizably organized structure of storytelling, display, and circulation (Hoek 2010). The studied knowledge of how to watch and discuss films has further been made widely available within South Asia through film societies that have produced both film critical skills and "a culture of debate" associated with cinema (Mazumdar 2009, 105; see also Dass 2015; Majumdar 2012). This longer history and culture of the cinema in South Asia means that everyday modes of film appreciation and criticism are widely available as discursive and experiential registers that shape encounters between cinema and its subjects. Mazzarella (2013) has shown that these modes of viewing and debating film inform the thinking of members of censorship boards in India. In this, they are not unlike the members of the Bangladesh Film Censor Board who wielded their own expectations of the structure and form of a film as grounds for their censorship.

In his fight to gain certification for *The Director*, Kamu and his allies made liberal use of these everyday registers of film appreciation. At the same time, however, he situated his film within a tradition of repressed artistic freedoms that is particular to the history of Bangladesh. Artists and intellectuals played a central role in the production of the affective formations for which the War of Independence (*Muktijuddho*) was fought (Ahmed 2014; Mookherjee 2007). The affective qualities of these forms are derived from the fine arts, nationalized folklore, and literature (Chakrabarty 1999, 31; Samaddar 2002). These forms have produced a hegemonic national aesthetic in which the idea of autonomous art is also associated with freedom. Such art is recognized as a relevant aspect of national character while its forms are tightly circumscribed by the modernist thrust of those art forms that express this freedom (*mukti*) of Bangladesh (the freedom to paint in the styles of modernist painters such as Zainul Abedin, Quamrul Hasan, and Murtaza Basheer, or to build in the modernist tradition of architect Muzharul Islam). Modernist ideals around both the independence of the autonomous artist and the freedom of form come together in this national aesthetic associated with the independence and freedom of Bangladesh. Kamu used this notion of freedom in an extremely effective rhetorical manner in *The Director* Freedom Movement. The slogan and its form (the procession, the banners) imported the historical and political resonances of the terms *mukti* and *andolon*, freedom and movement, respectively, not only to mean "freedom struggle" but also to indicate the modernist national aesthetic it is associated with. It simultaneously demands the release of the film, with *mukti* meaning "release" in the context of film production (as in the release of a film). In this instance, then, the conflict over cultural sophistication and powers of discernment between the filmmakers who consider themselves autonomous artists and the guardians of Bangladesh's official artistic landscape, in this case the film censors, played out on a national artistic terrain that was both deeply felt personally and highly significant politically. In these public registers, high art must be defended, and the artist must be free to create. The understanding that the Censor Code operating in Bangladesh inherits its wording almost entirely unchanged from the colonial and repressive British and Pakistani periods of rule exacerbates these tensions. It added to the resonance of the campaign for *The Director*.

Within this field of highly charged artistic production, the cinema comes to take up a political position in the 1970s and 1980s. Film societies, organizing the screening of films, running film appreciation courses, and eventually mediating the emergence of independent or short or art filmmakers (Mokammel 2013), were increasingly seen as potential threats to the military rule in Bangladesh throughout much of the late 1970s and throughout the 1980s. This is the source of what has become known among film activists as the Black Law (Kalo Kanun): the Film Clubs (Registration and Regulation) Act of 1980. At this point, the conflict around aesthetic discernment and filmmaking capacity, and its political implications, became consolidated as the film industry radically fractured into a nonindustrial avant-garde that avoided theaters on ideological and practical grounds, and a government-backed mainstream industry that fully occupied movie theaters due to the continuing limitations placed on screening foreign films there. Film appreciation thus became the domain of an avant-garde housed in film societies that screened (often foreign) art cinema outside the theaters (see Hoek 2019). Shunned from and shunning the mainstream theaters, younger filmmakers started in the late 1980s to move from 16 mm to video, which, over the long run, put them in increasing proximity to new types of funders and producers: television stations and nongovernmental organizations. Questions of what sort of cinema has become appropriate for what type of exhibition, and what sort of production context and finance, have since become a source of great contention between self-acclaimed art filmmakers and those who operate within the government-sponsored industry. It is at this point that the very question of what truly constitutes a film that is screenable in public comes to be a major cause of conflict between the Censor Board and filmmakers. Films screened at the public library or foreign cultural missions, films made with money from TV producers, may be invested with significant financial or cultural capital and perhaps extensive film theoretical knowledge, yet these do not quite constitute cinema in the ways that films screened within movie theaters do, irrespective of their generic aesthetic and apparent disregard for the latest technologies or theories of cinema. Instead, it is the contours of the film as an outcome of a particular industrial process of production that can predetermine whether the Censor Board will be receptive to the idea of a particular film as a film. This is the context in which film criticism comes to constitute film censorship.

The final fate of Kamu's film *The Director* illustrates how limiting the industrial contexts of production can be for a film's chance of theatrical exhibition. After extensive campaigning and negotiations with the Censor Board, *The Director* was finally certified for public exhibition in 2015. However, while now officially recognized as a film suitable for public screening in theaters, the film failed repeatedly to find a theater willing to screen the film. Distributors and theater owners are notorious in independent circles for refusing to take on or exhibit certain types of films, effectively killing off such films. And so, during Eid in 2019, Kamu released his first feature film on YouTube instead. When first made available online, the film opened with a solemn, and much aged, Kamu speaking directly to the viewer in what can only be described as the most formal of Bengali. He explained that in the making of a film, an eon of a person's life gets lost. He then greeted all the supporters of *The Director* Freedom Movement. He noted that this was the first time a feature-length Bangladeshi film was released on YouTube, and he asked the YouTube audience to support his next feature film through a crowdfunding donation. Despite receiving certification, then, *The Director* had in fact failed to become a film in the sense used by the Censor Board. It failed to move into the theaters and instead remains caught in the realm of what industry insiders call "media." While this may be a blow for Kamu now, it is not unimaginable that in the near future this will be the fate of cinema at large, as theaters close down and audiences move online. At that point, the link between what constitutes a film and theatrical exhibition, so strenuously upheld by the Censor Board in the two cases explored here, will inevitably fade.

Film Criticism as Censorship

The two cases of film censorship I have laid out in this chapter present a tussle between filmmakers and members of the Censor Board over the nature of filmmaking and the proper ways of producing an artifact that can be understood as a film. While this concern does not feature anywhere in the Code for Censorship of Films in Bangladesh, it appears in informal conversation with officials and on official documentation in the files of the board as well as in discussions with filmmakers. While questions of obscenity or law and order are official categories in which films can be denied certification, the problem of inadequate filmmaking skills cannot be articulated with reference to the code. Instead, such a judgment relies on the deeply felt capacity for cinematic judgment on the part of censors and filmmakers. Within this domain of formal discernment, a central conflict plays out between filmmakers and the board: what constitutes the right forms of a film to be recognizable as cinema and who has the capacity for this discernment? This is censorship that is not about content or modes of representation within a film. Rather, the censoring judgments in these two cases are about form, and the appropriateness, suitability, and adequacy of the forms of these films to warrant being labeled a film at all. Here censorship as a practice relies on modes of film criticism that then produce a particular type of censorship.

Of course, the parameters within which film criticism can act as censorship are industry specific, to the extent that the industry is embedded within particular contexts, histories, and networks by which ideas of cinematic form have come to be articulated and set in motion through film culture. In Bangladesh, these parameters include the history of cinema in South Asia more broadly, as well as the place of artists and the fine arts in the history of the Liberation War and its politics of remembrance more particularly. These have resulted in a delimited set of industrial production processes and certain types of aesthetic outcomes as well as a wider discursive context in which the question of film form and purpose are widely debated, and the terms of this debate are widely distributed within society.

The way in which these structuring contexts produce censorship practice is of course also related to the types of censorship legislation in place. In the case of the two films discussed in this chapter, I have highlighted where the board struggled to frame its anxieties over aesthetic and formal qualities of the film within the existing legal framework of the Censor Code. In Kamruzzaman Kamu's case, concerns about his film became articulated as a problem of incoherence of the narrative, while in the case of Jean-Nesar Osman's film, these concerns came to be described as a lack of filmmaking skills. Both are aesthetic judgments that make use of the existing legislation to express discontent with a type of filmic product that sits awkwardly within existing industrial production processes. It illustrates the dispositions of both filmmakers and censors with regard to their unarticulated sense of cinema and the ways in which this informs their engagement with censorship legislation and its formalized processes.

Note

1 All translations are the author's.

5. "THIS MOST RELUCTANT OF ROMANTIC CITIES"
Dis-location Film Shooting in the Old City of Sana'a

STEVEN C. CATON

The Arab poet and traveler—Amin al-Rayhani—
    had seen half of the modern cities
        of the world
but when Sana'a loomed before his eyelids, he cried out:
"Sana'a!
History reports that you are the Queen of Time,
Science reveals you as the Lady of Knowledge,
Fables sing of you, Mistress of Human and Jinn.
These are your towering houses!
       These are your sighing palaces!
History doesn't lie.
Your untouched beauty and Arab splendor!
Poetry doesn't lie."
Every morning the sparrows get up early
Just to say: "al-Rayhani doesn't lie either!"
—ABD AL-AZIZ AL-MAQALIH, *The Book of Sana'a*

The Road to Hell Is Paved with Good (or Is It Bad?) Intentions

On November 20, 2005, I attended the Ninth European Film Festival, held in Sana'a, Yemen, November 20–27 and again in Aden, Yemen, December 3–12. It had been held annually in Yemen since 1997 and was sponsored by the German and British embassies as well as the Yemeni government. Of course, film festivals are ways by which film industries promote themselves and their products, and this festival was no exception. As in years past, there were film entries from all over the world, but this year it featured the first Yemeni feature-length film, *A New Day in Old Sana'a* (2005), made by a Yemeni British director, Bader Ben

Hirsi. Anticipation around Yemen's film entry was keen, so I came early to secure good seats for myself and my friends in the Exhibition Hall of the Yemen Cultural Center where the film was shown. It was a beautiful sleek auditorium with a large stage and screen and state-of-the-art projection equipment and audio facilities. We settled into our plush, comfortable seats to enjoy the show.

Few among us, myself included, had any inkling that the ambitions of both the director and the highest echelons of the Yemeni government that supported him went beyond the making of this film. Their hopes were to create a Yemeni film industry that this film was supposed to launch. None of what is described in this volume's introduction as (1) through (3) in film industries existed in Yemen when on-location shooting for *A New Day in Old Sana'a* began in 2004. Nothing existed comparable to the infrastructure described for Abu Dhabi or Johannesburg, let alone postproduction facilities such as editing, sound mixing, color printing, and so on. All films shot in Yemen up to that time were completed entirely in postproduction studios in Paris, London, Prague, and elsewhere. Of course, this was the case for most film industries at the time, with the exception of Hollywood, Bollywood, China, Hong Kong, and a few other megafilm industries. Ramyar Rossoukh, in chapter 2, talks about how groundbreaking it was that a digital editing machine was imported to Iran for postproduction editing of Majid Majidi's *The Willow Tree* (2005), after which it became a staple technology within the Iranian film industry.

It was Ben Hirsi's hope, shared by the Yemeni government, that a film industry (model 1) could be nurtured in the country to the point where Yemeni film directors would work with Yemeni crew, Yemeni scriptwriters, and Yemeni actors to tell Yemeni stories. To that end, Ben Hirsi included local actors wherever possible (mainly from Yemen's theater and television industry but also some untrained novices) and brought Yemenis into the production to learn hands-on tasks of filming such as lighting and sound, to become the foundation of a future film industry in the country. If that industry was to shoot films with Yemen as their backdrop, it could draw on its visually stunning landscape and cities as well as its culturally distinctive people to do so. Why couldn't its scenic mountain vistas and beautiful, historic cities like Sana'a, Zabid, and Shibam become the Monument Valley and New York City of a burgeoning Yemeni film industry? But there was also the question of a national cinema, which we argue is analytically distinct from a national film industry (see the introduction), and we might ask, "What would a national Yemeni cinema look like?" By focusing on a Yemeni story, the film *A New Day in Old Sana'a* might also become (along with documentaries shot to date on other Yemeni subjects) the seed of a national cinema project.

The organizers of that year's festival welcomed the audience and then introduced the two main speakers for the opening remarks, the British ambassador (because Britain headed the European Union that year, it was deemed appropriate for Britain to organize and sponsor the festival) and the vice minister of Culture and Tourism (the main governmental agency that sponsored the film).

The British ambassador explained that what we would see that night was a preexhibition cut of the film, and we should therefore expect small technical flaws that the director was hard at work rectifying in postproduction studios outside the country. Ben Hirsi's hope was to finish the final cut in time for a showing at the upcoming Dubai and Oman film festivals, not to mention Cannes later in the year. Unfortunately, that meant he was too busy to attend the film's debut, for which he was truly sorry. (Audible gasps of dismay could be heard in the audience at this announcement.) The ambassador went on to explain that, although the director couldn't attend in person, he wanted the audience to know his artistic intentions, which, besides capturing the beauty of Sana'a's Old City, were to show the difficulties of love and communication across ethnic and class divisions within Yemeni society. He did not expect everyone to agree with his interpretation, but he hoped they would at least appreciate a film about a Yemeni subject by a Yemeni British filmmaker. Perhaps it would inspire young people in the audience, men and women, to aspire to do the same and become the next generation of Yemeni filmmakers to make their own images inside their country and tell their own stories of their beautiful land and its people.

Next, the Yemeni vice minister of culture stepped onto the podium to deliver his remarks. They were spoken in Arabic but not translated into English. It is, of course, common in high-profile international events like this one for multiple languages to be spoken, and for simultaneous translation to be the rule rather than the exception. The fact that the vice minister gave the official remarks rather than the minister himself—who figures prominently in our story about the film production, as we shall see—was telling, and it amounted to a snub. As the vice minister spoke, it became clearer why there was no translation, his remarks being a scathing indictment of Ben Hirsi and his film. It was explained that the government of Yemen had agreed to filming inside Sana'a only if certain conditions were met: that no women be shown on-screen unveiled; that certain scenes in the script be removed from the film (especially scenes showing mosques and a controversial scene in which a foreign male character has an elaborate design drawn on his back by a low-status Yemeni woman); and that the daily footage be shown to Yemeni censors before shooting could continue, to make sure their content complied with these conditions. The vice minister sternly reported that all these conditions had been violated, thereby breaking the trust the government had placed in Ben Hirsi and his project. He ended by saying that he wished the director had come to Sana'a for this exhibition, to answer questions not only about his film but also about his reprehensible conduct during on-location filming. It was clear that Ben Hirsi would not be welcome back to Yemen to make a film anytime soon.

If the ambassador's remarks constructed an image of Ben Hirsi as the consummate film professional, the government's remarks constructed him as a hypocritical, two-faced opportunist. It was alleged that it was not professionalism that kept him from attending the film festival but fear of prosecution by the government on charges of misrepresentation and fraud. The audience's reactions were now shock and disbelief. How could a native son with laudable intentions of portraying Yemen in a positive light have behaved so duplicitously when it came to directing his film? The ambassador's remarks, combined with those of the vice minister of culture, presented us with a Jekyll and Hyde or, if that is too extreme, then at least a Janus-faced figure, one in whom professionalism and moral turpitude made up two sides of the same coin. But it was not only Ben Hirsi's reputation that was at stake; the very possibility of building a film industry in Yemen was in the balance. Something in the vice minister's remarks hinted at problems that ran deeper than the director's character and had to do with the idea and practices of the film industry itself. Before *A New Day in Old Sana'a* was even exhibited at the festival, the ambition to build a Yemeni film industry was on the rocks.

It was at the film festival that I realized what was to be my anthropological project and the research questions I would be asking of it. I had come to watch a film simply out of curiosity about how it would represent Yemen and its people, and what its production standards would be. Then it became clear to me that the controversies surrounding the film went far beyond its representations of females on the screen but extended to conflicts between the filmmaker and the state regarding the very process by which the film was made. Were these conflicts specific to the film? Or were they about the very idea and act of filmmaking itself, which would have wider implications for the creation of a national film industry in Yemen? Why did such conflicts exist?

On-Location Shooting as Dis-location Shooting

What this ethnography will reveal is the challenges of making a film that go beyond finance, infrastructure, or logistics (as daunting as these were, in fact, for *A New Day in Old Sana'a*). There are two ethnographic sections in this chapter, which are kept separate to underscore this point. One ethnography pertains to the production, and as such is in line with what production studies thinks of as ethnography (see the introduction to this volume). But there are broader questions of cultural politics surrounding not only what is represented on the screen in story and image (the filmic text) but filmmaking like on-location shooting and its emplacement in gendered and religiously coded spaces within the Old City of Sana'a. Answering those questions will require a second ethnography in roughly the second half of the chapter. That second ethnography will help us understand that, while perfectly standard in terms of film production practices, Ben Hirsi's filming of *A New Day in Old Sana'a* was nonetheless anything but value neutral, or merely a technical matter, where the local culture was concerned.

Though on-location shooting was fraught, of greater concern to the Yemeni government (specifically parliament) was what would happen to the footage from daily on-location shooting. Parliament passed an edict saying that it was to be handed over to state authorities for review, to make sure what was actually shot did not contravene the agreement Ben Hirsi had signed with the government. Here, the director balked not only for reasons of artistic freedom. He feared he might never see the footage again, or would see it too late to complete the picture in time for film festival submission, so he kept the footage to himself and in the end smuggled it out of the country, as was revealed at the Sana'ani film festival. Lotte Hoek (chapter 4, this volume) argues that state censorship is not only about images that may or may not appear in a film, which is the usual way in which film censorship is understood, but also a metanarrative about what a film should be, not to mention standards of filmmaking that a film should achieve. Drawing from her insight, I would argue that what was at stake was not only the censorship of specific images and dialogue in *A New Day in Old Sana'a* but the very idea of what filmmaking should be in Yemen, a metanarrative about filmmaking and state control.

Finally, this chapter makes the argument that the notion of indexicality, adopted from semiotics by film studies to talk about the filmic text and the ways in which it gestures to the spaces in which the filming occurred (the way New York is indexed in the films of Woody Allen, for example, to become the place of action for the diegesis), ought to be extended to on-location shooting itself and done so in two senses. The first sense is how the *filmic text* indexes the way it was made, or on-location shooting. *A New Day in Old Sana'a* is not only indexical of the city (as is argued in film studies literature on indexicality and the film image) but a complex index of its on-location shooting in the city itself, in ways I reveal below. But I wish to push the sense of indexicality beyond the analysis of the filmic text to include on-location shooting. Contrary to some of the myths propagated by film industries themselves, on-location shooting is not a matter of parachuting actors and crew into a particular space, taking the required footage, and flying out again, with little or no disturbance to the space around it, let alone to the production. A set has to be constituted that minimally cordons off the scene of filming from the rest of the real-world space that might inadvertently intrude on it. That requires signs indexing the scene as a "set," signs that indicate to the people observing the filming how to behave ("quiet on the set"), and members of the film crew who direct pedestrian and vehicular traffic around the set with hand gestures or traffic signs indicating the direction of flow. Drawing attention to the indexically mediated way in which a set is constituted allows us to understand more precisely how "dislocating" on-location filming is. Add to this the fact that the spaces around the set are themselves saturated with cultural meanings, some of which presuppose their own codes of seeing and being seen that may run in opposition to the codes of the film company and on-location shooting, and one has another power-ful force for dis-location. My ethnography of on-location shooting will analyze this problem in depth.

A Note on Fieldwork

The film was shot in early 2004, before I was in Yemen, and so I could not do fieldwork on the film's location shooting in Sana'a's Old City. Upon my ar-rival in 2005, I did archival research in the Yemeni newspapers representing a range of different political views, from the religious conservative Islah Party to the socialists, that reported and commented on both the film script and the film's shooting in the Old City. That research gave me a sense of how the film became politicized and a subject of intense debate in the public sphere. There were also a number of press interviews (a self-reflexive film industry practice; see Caldwell 2008) conducted in Arabic and English with the director, Ben Hirsi, and two of the stars, Dania Hammoud (Ines) and Nabil Saber (Tariq), that gave one a sense of how the filmmakers wanted the film to come across to the public and how the director responded to criticisms of his production that were mounting in the press. I also interviewed some of the below-the-line crew members (Mayer 2011) such as low-level Yemeni technicians and one Yemeni character actor, Yahya Ibrahim, who played the police chief. (Several other ac-tors I tried to contact were either unavailable at the time or did not respond.) Most important was a chance meeting with a Yemen-based, Spanish freelance photographer, Marcos Puig-Abs, who had been hired by the film company to

FIGURE 5.1. Ines, Henna artist. Photo: Marcos Abbs.

take still photographs on the set, one of whose images was used in the poster to promote the film. He kindly let me see the hundreds of images he took on that assignment and sat down with me to explain them. With his permission, I made an audio recording of our discussion and then a transcription. On the basis of his photos and commentary, I was able to reconstruct the day-by-day chronology of the shoot and what transpired on it. Later, I had the opportunity to see the film with specific Yemeni audiences to gauge its more popular reception. One of these was a group of students, male and female, on Sana'a University's campus. I tried to follow up with private conversations about the film with some of the students, knowing that individual reactions might be quite different from crowd responses, especially for such a controversial film, but all of them shied away from the invitation. Finally, I wanted to get a sense of what Old Sana'a looked like independent of the images of it on the screen. Having rented an apartment in the Old City, I got a feel for what an old neighborhood was like and the organization of public space more generally. I walked down the streets and alleys where the film was shot to sense those spaces, and then compared my impressions with how these spaces became places in the film. This comparison gave me a rough idea as to why certain aesthetic decisions were made about on-location selection, image framing, angle, depth of field, lighting, and so forth.

Film Production Ethnography and an Emergent Film Industry: Hierarchies of Nationalism, Gender, Class, and Race

Let us now do an ethnography of the film's production, more or less following the lead of production studies (see introduction). It will be shown how the production was meant to foster an emergent film industry. First, the personnel.

The Director, Bader Ben Hirsi

The director had deep cultural roots in Yemen that from one point of view made him seem authentic, but from another deeply problematical, as would be the first to admit. Bader Ben Hirsi is a British citizen of Yemeni parentage but a relative by marriage through one of his sisters to the last Yemeni imam, Bader, who went into exile in Britain when the 1962 revolution ousted the theocracy that had ruled Yemen for a thousand years, and of which he was the last representative. Bader's father, Yahya ben Hirsi Al-Ban, followed the imam into exile in London, where his son, Bader (named after this imam), was born in 1968. Lest one conclude that such a distinguished pedigree would give Ben Hirsi a leg up in the estimation of Yemeni society, one has to bear in mind that the former religious elite to which he was related were no longer powerful or that well liked, for that matter. His reception based on his genealogy alone would have been ambivalent at best. Having grown up in Britain and not gone back to Yemen after his birth (because of his father's connections to the former imam, it was impossible for a long time to get a visa), he didn't have any firsthand experience of the country, and his contact with its people and cultures was by way of the Yemeni diasporic community in London. He was alienated from his ancestral homeland in other ways. He grew up tending to fall prey to the same negative stereotyping about Yemenis harbored by British society at large. They were backward, they were primitive, they were violent.

Realizing that his views of the country were biased, he traveled to Yemen to learn about it firsthand, once the travel ban on the religious elite connected with the former imamate was lifted. In an early film (*The English Sheikh and the Yemeni Gentleman*, 2000) Ben Hirsi meets up in Yemen with the travel writer Tim Mackintosh-Smith, who resided in the country year-round, and asks him to show him the Yemen he knows and loves. Ben Hirsi may have gone back to look for his roots, so to speak, but the irony is that he does so through the mediation of an Englishman, though to be sure, not just any Englishman but one who is fluent in Sana'ani Arabic, has a profound understanding of Yemen's history, and is utterly familiar with and comfortable in contemporary Yemeni society. The film has many scenes of Ben Hirsi with camera in hand filming Mackintosh-Smith striding through the Yemeni countryside or strolling through Sana'a's streets, and Ben Hirsi is shown to be reluctant to get too close to aspects of Yemeni culture he finds distasteful (chewing qat, a daily pastime in Yemen) or unnerving (joining a group of male tribal dancers wielding daggers aloft and brandishing rifles, all for symbolic effect), preferring to let the English sheikh perform his culture in his stead.

It is important to realize that Ben Hirsi is a highly trained film professional and that his film was made according to demanding film industry standards. This was to reassure the authorities that he had the chops to deliver on his promise to make a film that would win prizes and garner favorable attention for Yemen, as well as to lay a solid foundation for the creation of a Yemeni film industry. He studied drama at Goldsmith College (University of London), and three of his plays were performed at Edinburgh Festival Fringe (Edinburgh, Scotland) before he turned to filmmaking. He established a film production company, Felix Films Ltd., in London in 1998 whose emphasis is on "high quality projects of international appeal that focus [on] the rich culture and history of the Arab and Islamic World. . . . Our target audience is the international market" (Anonymous n.d., 1). According to the production company's brochure, Felix Films was committed to promoting film industries in the Arab world, and in Yemen especially, where it had ambitions of establishing a Yemen Film Institute to help train fledgling filmmakers, including technical crews. Encouraging the growth of film industries within Yemen was seen as a priority not only for Ben Hirsi but for the Yemeni government at the time. To put this in context, one has to bear in mind that there have been other distinguished Yemeni documentarians (interestingly, all of them women) who have created films about their country, ones that are, in fact, much more politically engaged than Ben Hirsi's. For example, there are Khadija Al-Salami (*The Scream*, 2012, about women's conditions in Yemen) and the Scottish Yemeni director Sara Ishaq (*Karama Has No Walls*, 2013, and *The Mulberry House*, 2014, both of which are about Yemen's Arab Spring and the former of which was nominated for an Academy Award for Best Documentary, Short Subject). But they produced their films using technical resources mainly from outside Yemen, whereas Ben Hirsi's film employed local people and was shot entirely in the country. Its success was supposed to jump-start the local film industry.

The Cinematographer, Muriel Aboul-Rous

The cinematographer was Muriel Aboul-Rous, who is sometimes credited with being the first female cinematographer in the Arab world. Before teaming up with Ben Hirsi, she had been the cinematographer on several award-winning films. Like nearly everyone else who has been to Sana'a, the cinematographer was enchanted by its light. Indeed, Ben Hirsi chose her because she was famous for her ability to create light. The predominant hue of the Old City in the film is orange, while the light itself is made to appear diffuse. Special lenses were created to produce this orange tinge; dust was mechanically blown through the air to create the diffuse effect. The production photographer, Marcos Puig-Abs, was supposed to reproduce this effect with a grainy look in his still photographs that were incorporated into the film as Federico's photographs of the Old City.

Hiring a renowned female cinematographer along with female assistants sent a message about gender equality in the film production, which was no accident, for Ben Hirsi is a committed feminist. Yet the message backfired when these women started to film on location in the Old City, for reasons we have hinted at but have yet to explain in depth.

The Rest of the Film Crew

The film crew was notably international. They were British (two were in charge of sound), Lebanese (lighting and cinematography), and Yemeni. The more sizable crew were the Lebanese because of the many assistants to the cinematographer for her lighting effects: the focus puller, who measures the distance between the actor and the camera to make sure the image is in focus and then adjusts the focus as the actor moves on the set; another to look through the viewfinder; someone else in charge of lights; someone reading the light meter; assistants to hold the light reflectors; other assistants to hold the light diffusers; and so on.

Yemeni participation in the film production was mandated by the Ministry of Culture, which saw the production as a way to help train Yemeni counterparts and build a Yemeni film industry, but being untrained, they took positions subordinate to the foreign technical staff, who looked down on them as unprofessional. Unfortunately, they ordered them around on the set. The Yemenis naturally resented this treatment, though it is not unusual in film industries for higher-level technical crews to treat below-the-line production members with disdain by withholding information or telling them only the minimum of what they need to know to get work done (Caldwell 2008, 132; and see also chapter 6, this volume, which talks about directors concealing the risks of filming stolen shots from actors and crew alike). In other words, a national mandate to train crew on the set to build a local film industry ran afoul of standard industry practices. In the end, most low-level Yemeni technicians were consigned to be "runners" (i.e., running errands), and while such jobs were presumed to be inferior to the more technical ones, they turned out in fact to be essential when it came to certain visual effects in the on-location shooting module. For example, Maran Al-Saaʻi, a Yemeni who was hired to assist in the art department, worked on decor and costuming and helped invent the jinn costume the director wore in a cameo appearance at the end of the film. He also strung traditional Yemeni lanterns outside the houses in the Old City to produce a special romantic glow at night. He admitted these lanterns were not realistic but said they added a special dreamlike effect (the film crew's comments come from interviews with the author, Sanaʼa, Yemen, June 29, 2006).

The sense of segregation between the Yemeni and non-Yemeni crews was reinforced off the set when they took their lunch breaks. The more important technical crew would eat first, followed by the Yemenis, who complained of getting "leftovers." They also complained about the "chaotic working conditions" on the set. They didn't mind working hard, but they kept being asked to do different things, often unexpectedly; or they would be left with nothing to do and hang idly around, and then be called "lazy" by the non-Yemeni crew. To them, quite understandably, this did not seem "rational" or "efficient," even though the film production was constantly representing itself as such. If they tried to take initiative, they would be criticized for not knowing what they were doing and told to stop meddling. Out of curiosity, the Yemenis would ask the film

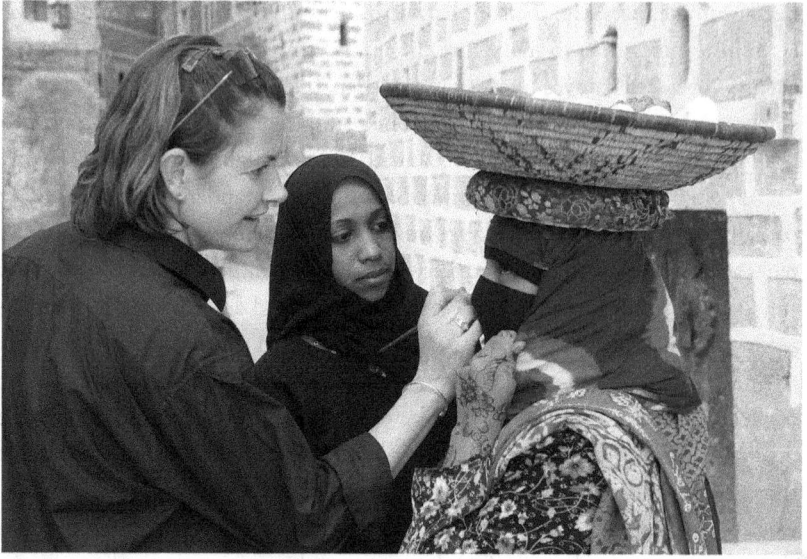

FIGURE 5.2. On-set training in makeup. Photo: Marcos Abbs.

crew about why things were done one way and not another, or how certain equipment worked, which irritated some of the foreign below-the-line crew. One of the Lebanese lighting crew apparently told one of the Yemenis, "Just shut the fuck up! Your job is to move equipment around, that's all!" When another Lebanese crew member felt sorry for the Yemeni and explained the function of the equipment, he told the Yemeni to keep what he said a secret and not tell anyone, fearing retaliation from his Lebanese counterpart. The Yemenis also found Ben Hirsi's high-handed directorial manner on the set offensive. They understood that the director was under pressure to complete the film quickly, for both budgetary and political reasons, but his ordering people around in a loud voice offended them (interviews of Yemeni film crew with the author, June 29, 2006). They felt shamed because of his treatment of them and suffered loss of face.

Adding to the Yemeni crew's grievances was the fact that Felix Films ended up with less money than it had anticipated to pay expenses, including salaries, and of course being the least important on the set, the Yemeni crew were paid the lowest wages (the equivalent of $40 per day). The Yemenis said they stuck with the production because of the "valuable work experience" they gained on the set, which they hoped would make them employable in the future film industry; but in truth this was the only work they could find, and sadly they were unemployed when I interviewed them a year after the film's completion.

Actors

The main actors were for the most part Yemeni, with the exception of the Italian Paolo Romano, who played Federico, the photographer and narrator, and the Lebanese actress Dania Hammoud, who played the female lead, the servant girl and henna tattooist Ines.[1] The egg seller Amal and the police chief were played by professional Yemeni actors who were well known in Adeni television and theater. This crossover between industries such as television, theater, and film is not unusual, of course, though in the Yemeni case there was little choice on the part of the producers but to tap into these media, given that no film industry existed at the time. The women shown unveiled in some of the scenes, such as Bilquis's wedding celebration, were Somali. This was no accident, given the strictures about showing Yemeni women unveiled on the screen.[2] The only Yemeni woman who appears unveiled before the camera is the actress who portrays Tariq's fiery sister (who was married to an American expatriate at the time and was considered unconventional to begin with). Thus, the Somali women were not just extras but were crucial to indoor scenes where Yemeni women would be expected to appear unveiled in front of each other when no males were present. Without these Somali women, these scenes never could have been shot. In that sense, these women were like the Yemeni runners on the set—low-status, unheralded, and underpaid, yet crucial to the very possibility of the film's production, with the addition that they were culturally classified as black African (and socially inferior to Arab Yemenis). Because of their marked racial difference and social inferiority, they would have no social honor to protect and thus could appear unveiled before the camera without loss of face. In other words, all the way down the production line there was an implicit hierarchy of differences consisting of nationalism, gender, race, and class, and while these differences created tensions in the production, they also enabled filming in the Old City and made gender visible within its precincts. Hierarchy and exclusion made possible the film's realist project.

If the foreign actors had to immerse themselves in Yemeni culture, and in particular Sana'ani Arabic, the Yemeni actors who had no previous acting experience in front of the camera had to be coached in film acting. The lead protagonist, Nabil Saber, playing Tariq, was a complete novice, having been cast primarily for his looks, and required quite a bit of coaching. The non-professional Yemeni actors were unused to film industry work schedules and routines. They had to get up early to prepare for shooting, arrive punctually on the set, sit patiently all day if need be before their turn came to act, and accept the fact that when their time came, the whole scene might only take two minutes to shoot. On the other hand, the Arabic dialogue as written in the script was not very colloquial or conversational, and the actors often improvised their lines to make them sound more Sana'ani. A scene was often the result of a collaboration between the Yemeni and non-Yemeni actors and not just the execution of the director's commands (interviews of Yemeni film crew by the author, June 29, 2006).

The Filmic Text: Icon, Index, and Symbol

In this volume's introduction, it was argued that textual analysis, as deployed, for example, in literature and film studies, should also be considered a methodological tool for anthropological analysis. This is obviously so in a film's representations of another culture, offering a so-called window onto its world, which more often than not is formed of stereotypes that feed into one ideological agenda or another (Caton 1999, 2000). But suppose the world of the Other is not simply inert or passive to the gaze of the Western camera, and that it has its own codes of visual representation, including what can or cannot be seen, that clash with and even resist the realist project of Western film: it is argued here that this clash will leave its traces in the film's production history and even the filmic text. This gets us to the bottom of seeing as something made or produced, not only in terms of the camera apparatus but the wider space within which that apparatus operates, a space that contains competing visual regimes.

The introduction to this volume discusses what film studies has meant by the "filmic text," which is not the script per se but what is seen and heard onscreen in a particular film (which greatly exceeds what is in the script, which is by and large written before shooting begins and is focused on scenes and what characters say in them, with often only minimal pictorial direction). In an article by anthropologists Constantine Nakassis and Amanda Weidman (2018), the notion of the filmic text as taken from critical film theory is reinterpreted to analyze the sound (voice)-and-image nexus in Tamil film. The presence of the female on the screen is a morally charged representation, or performative, as the authors put it, but the effects of this anxiety-inducing performative can be mitigated through the disruption of the unity of sound and image (by dubbing the lead actress's voice with the instantly recognizable voices of famous dubbing artists), so that the audience is always aware that the female presence on the screen is just that, a presence and not reality, an artifice and not an authenticity. To make the point in terms familiar to Peircean semiotics, the discordant voicing in the filmic text indexes something important about the film's production, namely, that it is now not the actual screen actress who is singing but a film industry double or stand-in, and it is her voice from the wings, as it were, that permits the actress's performance on-screen.

An interesting theoretical question, or so it seems to me, that follows from this observation is whether most, if not all, filmic texts metareferentially signify the conditions of their own making. My analysis of the filmic text of *A New Day in Old Sana'a* shows the film iconically indexing the struggle over realism that the production faced in on-location shooting. By way of telling the story of a tragic romance, the icon is the camera as wielded by the Italian photographer in the story, vainly attempting to "penetrate" the gendered and religious spaces of the Old City, just as Ben Hirsi's film crew struggled to assert its right to shoot in certain places and with certain people, as granted to it by the Yemeni state. I would argue that probably all films metareferentially come back to the history of their production, the traumas of their birth, the triumphs of maturation.

So let us now examine the filmic text of *A New Day in Old Sana'a* and determine how, through its tragic love story of Tariq, a handsome son of a leading *qadhi* (Islamic jurist), and Ines, a beautiful low-status servant woman (*muzayyinah*), it indexes the film's production. Their ill-fated romance is told through the eyes of an Italian photographer, Federico, though his knowledge of what is going on is necessarily partial, given that he knows little Arabic and has never been to the Arab world before, let alone to Yemen, and therefore is dependent upon Yemeni friends to explain things he doesn't understand. The story of his problems in shooting female subjects is an indexical reference to the problems the film production ran into while shooting in those same urban spaces. It might be worth analyzing the filmic text in some detail to see how this referentiality of the film's production works semiotically.

Federico has come to the Old City of Sana'a to penetrate its mysteries (and wields a phallic camera to that end). But he gets into trouble, as any photography-obsessed tourist in this part of the world does, and he has to be taught what he can and, more importantly, what he cannot film (that is, where his gaze must be averted) due to cultural conventions which he does not know and, when they are explained to him, cannot quite accept. These strictures are obvious from what the characters tell Federico about photographing women in public. But there is a deeper signification in the text that has to do with the ethical dilemmas the filmmakers faced while filming their story in Old Sana'a, again due to strictures that limited what the camera could record and, concomitantly, what the audience could see on the screen. In short, Federico's travails are an iconic indexical of filmmaking in a culturally charged space such as Sana's Old City. They are iconic because they resemble the operations of cinematography, and they are indexical because they refer back to what was happening at the very time in which Federico was being filmed "stealing" pictures (to borrow from Sylvia J. Martin's formulation from chapter 6 in this volume) of his forbidden subject, women in the streets of Sana'a.

One night Tariq sees a beautiful young woman in a white dress, which he recognizes as a wedding present he gave to his fiancée, Bilquis, the daughter of a powerful and wealthy sheikh. Because he has not seen his fiancée before (due to modesty codes), Tariq mistakes the beautiful Ines for Bilquis and falls madly in love with her. Meanwhile, Federico has hired Tariq as his assistant, who learns the art of his trade (a deeper allusion to the apprentice relationship between this film's more skilled production members and its Yemeni crew). Tariq explains to Federico that, even though women are veiled, it is still shameful to photograph them in public. Federico expresses his frustration with these strictures to a female egg seller he befriends in the Old City, and in an uncanny way this substory again mirrors the difficulties the filmmakers faced in the Old City of Sana'a, especially in its gender-marked spaces (streets outside residential homes, urban vegetable gardens that women cultivate and tend, and neighborhood spaces in general). As in the film production (as we shall see in a moment), so in the filmic text, Yemenis act as cultural translators or brokers for the realist project.

He then notices the henna designs on the egg seller's hands and asks if he can have them drawn on his back. She laughs, explaining that only women have such designs painted on their bodies. In short, it is a uniquely female art, in terms of both who is the artist and who is the canvas. But she finally relents and arranges to have Federico's back hennaed by a skilled *munaaqishah* (a woman who draws the henna designs on women's hands and feet, especially for special occasions such as weddings) and agrees to let Tariq photograph the procedure. It turns out that Ines is that woman, but Tariq doesn't recognize her because she is wearing black and is heavily veiled. It is a contrived and highly convoluted plot device, but interpreted metareferentially it is a not-uninteresting commentary on the ironies of gender and representation in the film. The macho Italian Federico is feminized by having done to him what, according to the culture, can only be done to women, that is, having himself hennaed, while the young woman Ines, now in the dominant position because she wields the instrument of artistic creation, the quill (a thinly veiled phallic symbol), draws her brilliant design upon his back. She is the artist, Federico merely the canvas. Tariq, who is now finally doing the photographing rather than Federico, is unaware that the woman before him is the same one with whom he has fallen in love. Of course, Ines can be photographed only because of her low social status. It may be shameful for women to be photographed in public, but that shame is not evenly distributed across the social stratification system. Looked at one way, of course, the scene is utterly absurd or even banal; yet looked at another way—as a parable about the powers of seeing, being seen, and artistic creation—the scene is all about on-location shooting in the production.

The rest of the film's story unfolds in the course of that day, and the details of the melodrama/farce need not detain us here. Suffice it to say that Tariq eventually learns the identity of the woman he saw in the street and fell in love with and proposes to break his engagement with Bilquis, the tribal sheikh's daughter, to elope with her. He tells her to meet him at midnight on one of the bridges that span a riverbed separating the Old City from the rest of Sana'a. As midnight approaches, Ines goes to the appointed meeting place to await her lover. Meanwhile, Tariq has had a change of heart, due to enormous family pressure placed upon him to "do the right thing" and marry within his own social class, and we see him praying in his room, seeking Allah's forgiveness for having strayed from his family duty and crying for having to give up his true love in the process.

But there is a witness to Ines's suffering, the photographer Federico, who takes snapshots of her standing alone on the bridge. He sees her only from behind and photographs her back. If women are to be photographed in public, it must be through subterfuge. In one sense, this is perfectly in accord with the gendered codes of seeing and being seen discussed earlier, but it is also an ironic nod to an earlier scene where Ines was in charge of creating her art on Federico's back and he was in a submissive posture. Federico then tells the audience that she stood on the bridge every night thereafter in the hope of meeting up with her erstwhile lover, though to no avail. There might be a new day in Old Sana'a for Tariq when he marries Bilquis, but there is none for Ines, who is condemned to an eternal night of lovelessness and forlornness.

However complex and subtle the filmic text might be in iconically indexing the visual codes surrounding gender that impacted the production, it has practically nothing to say about religious codes that also affected it. One can only glean them through the film's production history. In the next section I examine that history, but I also show that anthropological ethnography is indispensable for understanding the religious structuring of urban space; without it, one may know that certain imams, say, clashed with the filmmakers and the government authorities over filmmaking in Sana'a, but one cannot really understand the grounds for their objections without considering the question of how urban space is religious space.

FIGURE 5.3. Ines on the bridge. Photo: Marcos Abbs.

On-Location Shooting: Icon, Index, and Symbol

Let us turn now to the module of on-location shooting, the subject of this chapter, and bring it into alignment with scholarly work on film indexicality. Film studies has for some time been concerned with on-location shooting (Gleich and Webb 2019; Rhodes and Gorfinkel 2011), and has framed its discussion in terms of an analytical distinction between space (the ground in which the shot took place, rendered visible through technological means in the photographic negative or the film stock) and place (or that "out there" which appears as the context for the action of the drama within the film's diegetic). Within place, both landscapes (Harper and Rayner 2010) and cityscapes (Clarke 1997) have been examined in film. The other theoretical framing, which is often intertwined with the analysis of space and place, has to do with the Peircean notion of indexicality and the claim that a photographic or filmic image necessarily indexes the space in which it was shot, a point that becomes especially salient in the case of on-location shooting where that space is then turned into a place by the film apparatus. For example, the images of a cityscape like New York—or in the case study at hand, the Old City of Sana'a—are indexed in their respective films as the authentic locales of on-location shooting.[3] But they necessarily are also iconic of New York (invoking a resemblance or familiarity with images of the city that viewers already harbor in their memory). And in terms of their occurrence in the movie's scenes, these iconic indexicals of New York become symbolic of some other meaning related to the narrative; for example, the dystopia of urban life.

None of the film literature on indexicals to date touches upon the indexicality of the film production per se, and in particular the indexicality of on-location shooting. This is an indexicality that denotes not only the urban landscape in the filmic text but the actual film apparatus and its semiotic powers within that space. The act of filming (and not just the film exhibition) is, after all, an act of semiosis, and thus has its own indexical, iconic, and symbolic modes of signification. These are connected to its power to ground itself in a particular space and to take it over for its own visual purposes.

The actual semiotic operations of the film apparatus in shooting locales has only infrequently been analyzed in film studies literature, even in archival research into film production histories. One of the most interesting of the latter, to my mind at least, is Joshua Gleich's (2019) essay "'Good Oriental Setting': Negotiating San Francisco Locations," an analysis of the production of Sam Peckinpah's *The Killer Elite* (1975), which was set in San Francisco. One of this essay's main points is that the choices directors make (even directors as powerful as Peckinpah) are often influenced less by aesthetics than by budgets and logistics, or matters of film industry, a point that obviously resonates with this volume's theme. Gleich talks about indexicality, but again it is the indexicality of the final filmic text vis-à-vis certain San Francisco cityscapes and not necessarily the film production in those locales that he is at pains to reconstruct. For example, the filmmakers discussed among themselves whether this or that shot was iconic (or iconic enough) of San Francisco (i.e., would conform to viewers' presuppositions of what the city looks like) and at the same time be symbolic of "oriental" and "seedy or shady" stereotypes the filmmakers wanted for the film's atmosphere.

How does the indexicality of on-location shooting work? For example, setting up a camera, crew, and actors in a specific locale is a powerful indexical act, signifying this locale as something filmable and presupposing the film company's power and right to possess it for its visual project. This indexical act makes the locale into a movie set, an infrastructure iconic of other forms of territorialization and occupation such as planting a flag and building a fort, or putting up a fence and building a barn. No wonder Felix Films was symbolic of neocolonialism to its Yemeni detractors.

To understand the power of a production's indexicality, it is helpful to return to one of indexicality's most perspicacious theoreticians, the linguist Emile

FIGURE 5.4. On-location shooting in Old Sana'a. Photo: Marcos Abbs.

FIGURE 5.5. The cinematographer. Photo: Marcos Abbs.

Benveniste. In a famous essay, "The Nature of Pronouns," Benveniste (1971) distinguished between the *énoncé* (the utterance) and the *énonciation* (the situation of speaking), the latter of which corresponds to the set in on-location shooting. Benveniste made the point that first- and second-person pronouns (I/we and you) denote persons in the situation of speaking (denoting the speakers and addresses, respectively) and that the specific person referred to changes with each new speaker. Third-person pronouns (he/she/it and they), on the other hand, do not denote persons in the situation of speaking but rather outside it (they may very well be in the larger context surrounding the situation of speaking but not in the latter itself). On the set, actors and crew are indexed as "we" or "desirable persons" who are crucial to the filmic enunciation. Infrastructure of various sorts will also index a space within the location—a particular street, a particular park, a particular storefront or building façade—as part of the set. By contrast, there are people, objects, and events that are denoted as "them" because they are outside the situation of filming. Indexical signs may have to be put up such as "No unauthorized personnel past this point" or "Quiet on the set" to secure the *cordon imaginaire* around the set. They are equivalent to the personal pronoun "them." In other words, filming is not simply a matter of planting a film apparatus, crew, actors, and infrastructure in a space; it is a matter of semiotically marking that space as territory that belongs, if only temporarily, to a production company for its specific purposes and demarcates who is and who is not part of the filmic enunciation.

To grasp those powers requires an ethnography of those places prior to the ethnography of the film production in them. What if one were to ask, What is the sense of the city from the perspective of its diverse dwellers and inhabitants? In other words, how do they view (literally) their city? And more importantly for film analysis, What are their ways of seeing that the film might co-opt, occlude, or even threaten and vice versa? The Old City of Sana'a is a complexly coded space of seeing and being scene (pun intended), and on-location shooting there encountered a very different "sense of the city" than the production's sense of what the "city is really like." In short, the achievement of cinematic realism is a political struggle, one that is grounded in the on-location shoot in complexly coded visual spaces, though this struggle may already begin before the shoot in controversies swirling around the production and continue in the editing of the film footage that make up the filmic text and the final exhibition. *A New Day in Old Sana'a* was certainly mired in this politics, as we will now see.

An Ethnography of the Old City of Sana'a as an Urban Space

An ethnography of urban space, especially in relation to what can or cannot be culturally filmed (or photographed) in it, is crucial for understanding the possibilities or impossibilities of on-location shooting. It brings to light codes of visibility and invisibility within urban spaces (what is desirable to show, what is permissible to show, what must remain in the shadows, and what must be excluded altogether), public dress and conduct, and places of gathering and mobility—all of which pertain to cultural questions of gender, race and ethnicity, class and religion.

Politics of Cultural Representation: Sana'a, the 2004 Arab Capital

So let us now seek the senses of the city of Sana'a ethnographically. There are two parts to this exploration. The first has to do with the politics of cultural representation of the Old City. The second has to do with an ethnography of gendered and religiously coded spaces in the Old City of Sana'a. This part then concerns the politics of cultural representation.

The production was launched in a year, 2004, when the politics of culture heated up around two other more contemporary events. The first of these concerns the Arab League, which, acting under the auspices of UNESCO's Capital Cultures Program, announced that Sana'a would be the Arab "cultural capital" of 2004. This event was to be marked by various exhibitions and festivities celebrating Sana'a's splendid architecture and historical greatness, and Ben Hirsi naturally assumed that his film would fit nicely into the occasion, at once representing the city in its best light and conveniently promoting the film production to the Yemeni public.

Preceding this announcement of Sana'a as Arab capital of 2004, however, was an earlier event and its political reverberations, the building in 2003 by the Ministry of Culture (headed by Khaled Al-Royshan) of an amphitheater in the Old City's Sa'ila (or flood plain) with the city's beautiful tower houses, dramatically lit at night, for its backdrop. Different dramatic and musical events were to be held there, Arab and non-Arab, to celebrate multiculturalism, but the initiative backfired badly. For instance, when a German orchestra played classical music in the amphitheater in 2004, attendance was by invitation only and restricted to Yemeni officials and high-profile Westerners while the residents of the Old City had to watch and listen from the sidelines. "The shadows of young Yemeni men seated along the wall created a disturbing, pseudo-colonial scene, with the natives excluded from their own territory" (Lamprakos 2015, 102). The amphitheater was strenuously objected to by the Majlis Al-Tansiq, a religious student organization that declared it blasphemous because of the Western music heard there, let alone unveiled women seen in theater productions, in the middle of what was a traditional space. What the conservative religious segments wanted to do was to secure Sana'a as a sacred space, and so "traditional" in this sense meant Islamic. And it was not just modernity or liberal secularism that was threatening; it was the colonial encroachment of Western culture in this Arab space. Thus, the playing of Beethoven in Old Sana'a was anything but an innocent gesture on the part of well-meaning if naive Western actors. The newspaper *Al-Sahwa*, of the Islah Party (the religious conservative party), denounced the amphitheater, and a parliamentary inquiry was called for. In the end, it was taken down.

When it became known that Felix Films was to film in the Old City, it took little time or effort to mobilize a campaign against it, and the same objections that had been raised against the amphitheater now were mobilized against the film production. Complaints went out to Ruqeihi, imam of the Grand Mosque, arguably the most venerable religious space in Yemen. Ruqeihi requested a meeting between himself, the filmmaker, and the minister of culture to discuss the script. He argued that it would be better for the film to focus on the learned religious elite of Sana'a rather than banal lovers, if something of genuine importance to Yemen's culture and its religious standing in the world were of concern to the film company. Ben Hirsi replied that the script had been approved by the president and it was too late to change the story. After being pressed, though, he agreed to consider some minor alterations.

The dangers represented by both the amphitheater and the film production were given expression in a fiery Friday sermon by Al-Sheikh Hizaa' Al-Maswari (2004) in a mosque in the Al-Hadda district (now modern Sana'a). It was delivered just as filming began in the Old City. It is worth quoting almost in full.

> For the last few days our country has celebrated the announcement that Sana'a has become the cultural capital of the Arab world. But I regret that in the name of culture we disobey God. In the name of culture we declare war against God. . . . The Sana'a of today complains, O Yemenis; the Sana'a of today cries out. The Sana'a of today, O Yemenis, complains that in the name of culture a stage has been built for art, song, and dance. Do you know where? In the garden whose owner endowed it as *waqf* land [i.e., intended only for the most religious of purposes], so that it could become a farm belonging to one of the righteous houses [of the city]. So that the people of Sana'a could inhale its fresh air, so that the people of Sana'a could breathe in its [fresh] air and fragrance. And if the Ministry

of Culture—it's not a ministry of culture but of simple-mindedness—has allowed a stage to be built in this waqf garden, a stage that has been made morally permissible through the sacred status of the waqf, then male and female lovers can meet on that stage and on its surface male and female artists from different places in the world can meet in the name of culture. But that's not permissible because it's waqf land. It's not permissible to transform waqf into a stage for singing, dancing, and theater, for Allah says, "He who exchanges Him after he has heard about Him, that is a sin."

Sana'a of today, today Sana'a cries out that these days they are filming in Sana'a a cinematic film by the name of *A New Day in Old Sana'a*. Do you know what that means, a film photographed in the Sana'a of Goodness, the Sana'a of Ritual Purity, the Sana'a of Faith, the Sana'a of Ethical Being, the Sana'a of Moral Excellence, a film that disfigures modesty and does away with moral worth, that laughs at religion, that ridicules ethics and destroys values and traditions? . . . We don't want Sana'a to be the capital for the culture of cheap art. The capital of slavish culture. The capital of dance and impudence. We don't want Sana'a to be the capital of artistic and cultural rottenness.

The sermon's biting irony is that an irreligious cultural space (a theatrical stage) has been built on sacred land or waqf, a garden that was donated by its original owner to the local mosque (the Qubbah Al-Mahdi). A parallel is then drawn between the presence of the stage and the filming of *A New Day in Old Sana'a*, a film that "disfigures modesty." This is a telling trope. Modesty is attached particularly to the female body and behavior, with women being required to veil in public and keep their interactions with nonkin males businesslike and to a minimum. The implication is that the film disgraces the female body not only in the way it represents that body on the screen but also in the way on-location filming attempts to penetrate a deeply gendered space. The public act of filming in the Old City was thus criticized as culturally insensitive and quasi-colonial.[4]

Ethnography of Religious and Gender-Coded Space in Old Sana'a

Some understanding of the cultural politics of urban space is needed to grasp the depth and vehemence of the objections to filming in Old Sana'a, but so too is the spatial organization of the city and the architecture of its buildings, which reinforce certain religious and gender codes of visibility, seeing, and interaction within its spaces.

Like other traditional cities, Old Sana'a's space is complexly coded as inside and outside: as that which is sacred and that which is profane; as that which is intimate or private versus that which is outside and public; as that which is old or traditional and that which is new or modern; as that which is female and that which is male. Old Sana'a is regarded by many Yemenis as the oldest city in the Arab world. According to local legend, after the Flood, Noah's Ark touched land on the highest peak just outside what would become Sana'a and was settled by his son Shem. Added to its mytho-historical significance is the fact that the Old City is considered in Zaydi Islam (the predominant sect in northern Yemen) a *hijrah* (a protected enclave), a settlement where descendants of the Prophet Muhammad are protected to practice their faith as well as to promulgate it in the purest manner possible in the mosques in which they preach and the madrassas in which they teach.

Though the whole Old City is technically sacred, there are gradations of sacredness within it as well: the Grand Mosque is the epicenter of sacred space; and the dozens of other mosques dotting the individual neighborhoods are more sacred than their surrounding neighborhoods, consisting of local *souq*s and residential houses. However, even souqs are quasi-religious spaces, in which violence is off limits. Also considered sacred are the many privately owned houses and gardens that have been donated to local mosques, which come to be known as waqf and cannot be alienated from the possession of the mosque. These holdings are maintained by the mosque for the benefit of God-fearing Muslims, though it is usually its neighbors who use it. Waqf is distinguished from privately owned houses and gardens that are not associated with a mosque, nor are they open to the public, though even these homes are marked by relative degrees of sacredness (such as the protected space of the women's quarters).

Now let us consider how this sacred space is overlain by gender codes. Neighborhoods are a self-contained warren of passageways in which strangers can easily get lost, which is why they can also be confronted and then ejected if they are perceived as threatening. Such spaces are said to be *harām* or forbidden to strangers, at the same time that they are said to be protected spaces for women and children. Women (and children) have to be protected by their kinfolk, which is considered a sacred duty. While the souq and the mosque might be the preserve of the males (though females frequent these places as well, chaperoned by males), the neighborhood in many respects is the domain of women and children (though men pass through on their way to and from work). It is incumbent upon women to visit their neighbors as both a social and religious obligation, whether it be to help out in time of need or to socialize, which requires them to move up and down the street. The street must thus be protected from the presence of strangers and their unwanted gaze. Women also congregate in the shade of the mosque vegetable gardens to seek relief from the heat, pass the time, and gossip. As these are waqf, women are protected by the religious mantle conferred on this land by Islam. Gendered spaces are, in short, protected and legitimated by Islamic notions of sacredness.

The affront to this coded space is this: the film company, a profane or secular and modern enterprise, proposed to film entirely on location in Old Sana'a, and specifically in streets and gardens that are culturally coded as female and sacred. The production penetrated, as it were, not only a sacred space but also a female space by putting its cameras and crews in protected streets, neighborhoods, and gardens. Mosques were avoided after objections were raised by the imam of the Grand Mosque; instead, filming took place in public squares where several narrow streets converge, in back alleys, in the central floodplain (*sāyilah*) and the bridges crossing it, and in beautiful small communal vegetable gardens that dot the Old City. As for interior spaces, Ben Hirsi managed to get permission to film inside a couple of private houses in the Old City, those traditional tower houses with their glistening white-plaster interior rooms and stained glass windows so greatly admired by visitors to the country. These houses are, of course, also the preserve of women and children and therefore harām, except for the public sitting room (*mafraj*) where the men of the house gather with their male companions. Interestingly, that male space is never shown in the film; instead, we see a female sitting room in which the wedding reception for Bilquis is held, and it is filled with unveiled Somali women, a problematic representation in that the film makes them visible to the public and violates the gender norm of modesty or privacy.

This embedding of the film production in the Old City was essential to the film company's claims of authenticity within the film industry, and yet at the same time it made the film politically threatening. To its critics, the filming was analogous to the installation of the amphitheater on waqf land in the Old City, that is, a neocolonial domination of Western cultural apparatuses (a stage, a film production) over a non-Western cultural and religious space. It is inconceivable that Ben Hirsi wasn't aware of how potentially threatening the prying camera lens would be in such a charged cultural space (this, after all, is one of the film's subplots involving the photographer, Federico), though perhaps the director thought he could mitigate that threat by having women wielding that lens in the roles of cinematographer and assistant.

The film industry's idea of a set (a technical, largely esthetic and secular space) operated inside a deeply sacred and gendered space of the Old City, and the end result could only have been fraught with ambiguities and outright conflicts. For conservative, religious Yemenis, there is no distinction between the technical/aesthetic and the moral where the film set was concerned; the presence of women on the set (whether as actors or as crew) was ipso facto religious pollution. For that crew to operate in the urban spaces it did only compounded the grievance.

Ethnography of On-Location Shooting

If a film production's presence in an urban milieu like New York City can seem strange, unsettling, and peremptory, think how much more that would be the case when filming takes place in a city like Sana'a with almost no history of filmmaking in its midst. Add to the above adjectives "illegitimate," as was heard in many of the denunciations of *A New Day in Old Sana'a*'s production.[5]

The film set became a particularly fraught space. Army soldiers were on hand to guard the set in case of armed assault. Although unrelated to the criticisms of the production, weeks before there had been a knife attack in public on the lead actor (who dropped out and was replaced by Paolo Romano), and the fear of copycat attacks prompted heightened security precautions. But the soldiers also indexed that the set had the state's authorization and backing, which gave its presence in the Old City legitimacy. There were attempts by curious onlookers gathered around the set to stop the shoot through public protest. Yemeni runners (essentially errand boys) played important roles as cultural brokers on the set, explaining to bystanders what the filming was about and thereby allaying their fears. One such Yemeni crew member, Muhammad Al-Matari, a good-looking young man with a good sense of humor and a strong personality, was approached on the street by a young girl and asked if he was not ashamed to work on a film that presented a bad picture of Yemen, like others before it. He told her what the film was about and assured her that it would represent Yemen in a good light. The minister of culture showed up on the first day of filming, and when confronted by the imam of the Grand Mosque and other religious conservatives about his decision to allow filming to proceed even though the script was still under scrutiny by parliament, he essentially passed the buck up the chain of command to the president. It would be the last time that Al-Royshan, the minister of culture at the time, appeared on the set. Ben Hirsi was warned by the imam about filming mosques and reminded that his film crew's presence in the Old City threatened its religious sanctity. The fact that a government minister retreated in the face of Yemen's most respected religious cleric indexed which authority—that of religion versus that of the state—was actually paramount in the urban space in which the film production operated, regardless of the presence of army soldiers.

FIGURE 5.6. Hostile crowd surrounding the director, Ben Hirsi, on the first day of shooting. Photo: Marcos Abbs.

Filming proceeded, but it was not long before the Yemeni crew pointed out to Ben Hirsi that the female cinematographic crew showed up in tight-fitting jeans and blouses that showed their midriffs, hardly fitting attire for women in a traditional public space such as the Old City; so on the following days, they dressed more modestly in long-sleeved shirts and head scarves.

Al-Matari meanwhile met with the *'aqal* (head) of the neighborhood to get his cooperation and then worked with the police to empty the streets of traffic and parked cars on every day of the shoot. Besides meeting with neighbors to explain the film and reassure them about it, he also met with homeowners to negotiate the rental of their homes for the interior shots. There is no doubt that Al-Matari played a crucial role in making on-location shooting possible, yet only the technical side of his labor was recognized in the film credits, when what he did in the lighting or sound department may have been of secondary importance to his informal interventions with the public on the set's periphery. The tumult of the first few days on the set eventually subsided, thanks to Al-Matari and others, and the filming proceeded unimpeded, perhaps because

FIGURE 5.7. Imam confronting the director, Ben Hirsi, on the first day of shooting.
Photo: Marcos Abbs.

people got used to the presence of the set in the urban space. The army's presence diminished, though traffic police were still on hand to clear the streets.

Anxieties about filming were not confined to people outside the film production but extended to the Yemeni film crew itself. Some of the Yemeni crew's families were unhappy about their participation in the production, fearing public criticism and censure, and Al-Matari talked to them as well. Then their worst fears about being involved in what was characterized by certain members of the Yemeni public as an immoral, even obscene, undertaking seemed to come true on the day the scene was to be filmed in which Federico has his back hennaed. The Yemeni film crew was told to take the day off, though they weren't told why. Rumors circulated that the filming of this scene was clandestine because it had pornographic content, a not unreasonable fear given the history of the Pasolini film (author's interview with crew member, June 26, 2006). Given that he was asked by the Ministry of Culture not to film this scene, the director feared the Yemeni crew would report back to the ministry if they were present at the filming, and the footage would be confiscated by the government and not released until many months later, when it would be too late to edit the film in time for a release on the festival circuit. Eventually, he had the footage smuggled out of the country. Unsurprisingly, this would be a sore point when the film debuted at the film festival in Sana'a in 2005.

In spite of the aggravation he experienced over the filming of this scene and many more, Ben Hirsi may have had the last laugh after all. At the very end of *A New Day in Old Sana'a* we see a figure dashing down a street, who then stops to turn around and look at the camera. He has cloven hooves, hairy legs, and a human torso but with horns on the head, in other words a jinn. The jinn is played by the director, who is laughing at the camera. Here's an iconic index, if there ever was one, in the filmic text of the trickster role of the director in the film's shooting in the streets of Old Sana'a.

Conclusion

This chapter has examined the module of on-location shooting for the first Yemeni feature film, *A New Day in Old Sana'a*, to show how it became entangled in local cultural politics about space, specifically the Old City of Sana'a, that not only threatened to derail the production but thwarted the director's ambitions of creating a Yemeni film industry.[6] The ill-fated romance between Tariq and Ines is told through the eyes of an Italian photographer, Federico, who is stymied from taking pictures of women in the Old City. I have argued that the photographer's predicament is an allusion to the film's on-location shooting in

FIGURE 5.8. The director, Ben Hirsi, as a jinn. Photo: Marcos Abbs.

Old Sana'a, broadening our understanding of semiosis in the filmic text beyond the modality of indexicality in which sense it is usually discussed to include iconicity, specifically of the filmic text being an iconic indexical of the film production. As this essay is also an ethnography of the film's production, I also argue that we consider on-location filming as a semiotic act, one with its own indexical, iconic, and symbolic modes of signification that have as their effects the constitution of the set as a place in which filming takes place. While these signs are intended to secure the smooth operation of the shoot, a production ethnography of *A New Day in Old Sana'a* shows how threatening the set can be in highly charged symbolic spaces marked as gendered and religious spaces, which the presence of the filmmakers disturbs.

But one cannot fully grasp the reasons for this, I argue, unless ethnography goes beyond the production and its history to include the lived spaces in which filming takes place, specifically how those spaces already have their own visual codes that may challenge or resist the film's ways of seeing and representing. An ethnography of the cultural discourse surrounding the film production of *A New Day in Old Sana'a* reveals the religious and gendered tensions over filming. In addition to examining popular cultural discourse, however, an ethnography of urban space and the conditions of visibility within that space give one the deeper understanding necessary for grasping the reasons actual filming in those spaces competed with and threatened local visual codes.

To capture the instabilities in filming that arise from such entanglements, I speak of on-location shooting as dis-location shooting. There were attempts to halt the film on the very first day of on-location shooting, and then to disturb it after that, which could only be overcome by tact and persuasion on the part of the Yemeni crew, who acted as cultural brokers with locals. They became an indispensable part of the production's success, for without their cultural translation work, the production would arguably never have succeeded. Yet film industries rarely if ever acknowledge this kind of intercultural work because it belies the idea of the set as merely a technical, logistical, or artistic space, not one with deep moral and political entanglements.

Perhaps after the current war in Yemen (2015–present) is over, another film company will come to Yemen to film its scenery and cities, and perhaps the initiative to build a local film industry will be revived and eventually realized. If so, it should go back to the production annals of *A New Day in Old Sana'a* as well as the broader ethnographic contexts in which the company and the emergent industry operated, and learn from its mistakes. But for now, sadly, that seems to be an ever-receding possibility. Like Ines waiting for her erstwhile lover on the bridge in the Old City—to suggest a final filmic index to film production—the Yemeni film industry might not have a new day in the end after all.

Notes

The quote in the title is said of Sana'a by Federico, narrator in the film, *A New Day in Old Sana'a*.

1   The actor who was originally cast to portray Federico was stabbed and had to withdraw from the production. It was determined that the assailant was mad and his motives had nothing to do with objections to the filming that had mounted in the press at the time shooting began.

2   The actress playing Bilquis is seen unveiled in several scenes, but it is unclear to me whether she is a Yemeni national.

3   As with the space and place framing, so with indexicality; there has been much critical discussion of how Peirce's original tripartite scheme has been used in film studies, and to my mind the best of these critical overviews is by Martin Lefebvre and Marc Furstenau (2002). One of their points is that indexicality, as Peirce understood it, was a mode of signification and not an ontological entity, for the reason that any empirical sign-entity is always already an indexical as well as an icon and a symbol, if in different strengths or emphases.

4   This often happens. For example, the filming of *Lawrence of Arabia* in Jordan was denounced by the Arab press as a colonial maneuver (see Caton 1999).

5   As I was not present at the filming, this ethnography is based on oral testimonies provided by some of the crew, in addition to the photographs of Marcos Abbs of the daily progress of the shooting.

6   "Entanglement" has become a term used in anthropological literature to talk about global industries such as oil, which, though they may think they are immune to local political protests, in the end provoke them or become embroiled in them (see Appel 2012).

6. STEALING SHOTS

The Ethics and Edgework of Industrial Filmmaking

Since October 2017, many accounts of sexual harassment and assault in the Hollywood entertainment industry have been reported in the news and posted on social media, culminating in the #MeToo movement. Similar allegations have emerged from film industries around the world. Recognition is long over-due, yet all manner of exploitation is not new in such industries (see Martin 2017; Miller et al. 2005). A Hollywood insider account such as Shirley Temple's autobiography, *Child Star*, provides an instance of abuse on a film set from nearly a century ago (Black 1988). Temple filmed *Kid "in" Africa*, one of the *Baby Burlesk* series, in 1933, when she was five years old. The one-reel short contains sexualizing and racist imagery; cast as Madam Cradlebait, Temple is dressed in a diaper with an oversized safety pin, and described as being on a "cannibal taming mission." Temple recounts that some of the black child actors, who were about her age, were for one of the scenes supposed to be chased and "felled by a barrage of arrows" (Black 1988, 26). However, the children apparently did not provide a convincing enough reaction for the director. So, as Temple tells it, "a thin piano wire was secretly rigged shin-high across the trail," and when the little boys tripped over the wire, their cries were genuine as they were bleeding (26). Temple explains that she burst into tears of sympathy for the other children, but that the director, Charles Lamont, "was laughing above the wailed chorus of pain" (26).[1] Temple then states, "By then I had begun to suspect how powerful and purposeful the people were who ran things on the set" (26). Temple's account serves to contextualize the formation of a white "male gaze" in the production process (Mulvey 1975) and reveal the conditions in which performers who were particularly vulnerable, such as black child actors, worked. The mothers of child actors were typically banished from the set by the production as they were told their presence could instigate "divided authority," and, as Temple recounts, the child welfare supervisor assigned to that set was dispatched to a dressing room, leaving the child actors at the hands of the production management (Black 1988, 22). Temple's graphic recollections make it clear that filmed entertainment, while often dismissed as offering mere escapism to its viewers, nevertheless has its roots in very serious exploitative conditions shaped by racist and gendered dynamics. So how should anthropologists understand the production of mass-media images in contemporary contexts?

Again, a look back proves instructive. *Kid "in" Africa* was filmed just two decades after the early cinema that film historian and theorist Tom Gunning refers to as a "cinema of attractions": pre-1906 American and French filmmaking that featured a series of stunning images intended to evoke shock and awe. Gunning explains that the "cinema of attraction directly solicits spectator attention, inciting visual curiosity, and supplying pleasure through an exciting spectacle" (2006, 384). The cinema of attraction emphasized showing over telling, offering images such as train crashes, stripteases, and magic tricks in which a magician, for instance, would gesture directly at the camera, hailing the audience. Nor was such spectacle restricted to Europe or America; Chris Berry and Mary Farquhar (2005, 28) locate the emergence of a "Chinese cinema of attractions" in the first several decades of twentieth-century Chinese film. Decades later, Gunning claims, despite the turn to narrative film with its carefully plotted and "self-enclosed diegetic universe . . . the system of attraction remains an essential part of popular filmmaking" (2006, 386). "In some sense recent spectacle cinema has reaffirmed its roots in stimulus and carnival rides, in what might be called the Spielberg-Lucas-Coppola cinema of effects" (387). The system of attraction, with its focus on image over intricate narrative, is also evident in popular Hong Kong cinema, which, as David Bordwell points out regarding kung fu and gunplay films, offers "expressive amplification"—a style of physical choreography (such as "pause-burst-pause" and "pose-strike-pose" for 1970s kung fu films) and filming that, as he describes of the 1988 gunplay film *The Big Heat*, "add up virtually to a circus act" (Bordwell 2001, 88). He explains, "By American standards, many Hong Kong films (of all genres) look broadly played, perhaps seeming closer to silent film conventions than to those of post-Method Hollywood" (88). Bordwell suggests that expressive amplification is "part of a distinct aesthetic" which is key to "the performance of actor and ensemble" (88), an aesthetic which I suggest recalls the cinema of attraction's style of display and spirit of the fairground. An anthropology of film industries will provide an enriched analysis of media representations and evocative visuals if the processes by which they are created as a legacy of such attractions and live entertainment are acknowledged and explored (see Martin 2017).

In their quest to achieve memorable images and effects, filmmakers have been known to steal a shot. "Stealing shots" is Hollywood industry jargon for quickly filming in outdoor locations without permission or a permit from the appropriate authority, perhaps on a busy street or in an off-limits area. Sometimes stealing a shot involves little harm to the participants and to unknowing members of the public. Stealing shots is often understood by filmmakers as an expedient practice, even a "creative solution" to problems of access (Rossoukh and Caton, introduction, this volume). But in some cases—action sequences in particular—it comes with the risk of being shut down by the police, fined, and possibly hurting people and property. The precariousness that especially characterizes contemporary film labor means that contracted cast and crew members may not feel secure enough to challenge or resist if they feel that their safety or their dignity is being taken from them in the rush of filming on a tight budget and, more broadly, in the name of what is frequently lauded as creative freedom. Stealing shots may entail filmmakers impulsively transgressing ethical practices, especially if directors (and producers) film people without their full and informed consent, not alerting them to possible repercussions.

In this chapter, I examine two contemporary instances of stealing shots, one in the Hollywood film industry and one in the Hong Kong film industry—both of which are highly commercial and hypercompetitive production sites where I have conducted comparative research since 2003. I explore the industrial impulses that animate these acts of what some may consider to be thievery. I argue that stealing shots represents a potential theft from the vulnerable bodies and psyches of actors, stunt workers, and crew members who may not be fully informed about, or empowered to resist, this activity. An ethos often embraced in the pursuit of cinematic affect, stealing shots (*tau paak* in Cantonese) is, I suggest, a form of edgework for the individuals involved—an exhilarating risk taking and rule breaking that have come to be seen as a necessary, even desirable, element of filmmaking. Sociologist Stephen Lyng posits that edgework illustrates the intentional pursuit of not only perilous hobbies (such as extreme sports or extreme selfies) but also "dangerous occupations such as firefighting, combat soldiering and *movie stunt work*" (1990, 857, emphasis added). Given its mix of physical, spiritual, and emotional risks, I would add movie work in general (see Martin 2012a; Martin 2012b). Edgework means laboring at the edges of order and disorder, legality and illegality (Lyng 1990, 857). The high-risk occupations mentioned also tend to be highly gendered, and on film sets in both Hollywood and Hong Kong, it was mostly men that I observed between 2003 and 2007 performing the majority of direction, camera work, and stunt coordinating. These accounts of stealing shots in Hollywood and Hong Kong contribute to a richer understanding of the anthropology of film industries by revealing the culture of masculinist media production and its contemporary pursuit of attractions and professed aspirations of creative freedom amid precarious labor conditions.

Ethics and Edgework

The practice of stealing shots is occasionally documented in industry interviews, memoirs, behind-the-scenes footage, and gossip; its results may sometimes be celebrated with awards and accolades. American director William Friedkin's street and train scenes in the famous car chase in *The French Connection*, for which the director won an Academy Award in 1972, includes stolen shots. As Friedkin discloses in his memoir about that sequence, one evening over drinks during filming he chastised the film's stunt driver, Bill Hickman, for not dazzling him with his efforts. According to Friedkin, in response, Hickman dared him to get in the car with him the next morning "if you've got the balls!" (Friedkin 2014, 178). The next morning Friedkin and Hickman filmed from inside a car for twenty-six blocks at ninety miles an hour, "through red lights, with no traffic control, no permits, no safeguards of any kind, only Hickman's chutzpah, his skills behind the wheel, and 'the grace of God'" (179). Friedkin himself operated the camera over the shoulder of his stunt driver; he claims that his cinematographer and his camera operator declined to shoot that sequence as "they each had families and knew what we were about to do was dangerous" (179). It is doubtful that they drove ninety miles an hour the entire time, bragging being a part of production culture (Caldwell 2008, 54), but certainly they took enormous risks in filming without permits, protections, or informing members of the public. The processes by which visceral stolen shots are created, and their potential costs to film labor, are often not made publicly visible unless they are praised, after the fact, in professional circles as artistic achievements accomplished against the odds, or if they result in accidents and investigations reported in the media.

The French Connection would also win the Oscar for Best Picture, and although Friedkin describes his pride in filming this part of the chase, he concedes, "I put people's lives at risk. . . . I say this more out of shame than pride; no film is worth it" (2014, 179). Friedkin also admits that for his next film, *The Exorcist*, he secretly filmed a "hospital ward of mentally ill female patients" with hidden cameras. In these and other stolen shots, in what may be an unsafe or unsecured setting—and often without the fully informed consent of those involved—the director may potentially rob those members of the cast, crew, and public of their well-being and their dignity.

The practice of stealing shots in Hollywood and Hong Kong has emerged as a behind-the-camera and mostly male-directed heroics over the physical environment and legal bureaucracy (recall Hickman's reference to male anatomy). I specify "mostly male" as, for Hollywood, USC's Annenberg Inclusion Initiative's 2018 findings on directors revealed that for the one hundred top domestic films released in the U.S. between 2007 and 2017 (totaling eleven years and 1,100 movies), 95.7 percent of all directors were male and 4.3 percent were female (Smith, Choueiti, and Pieper 2018, 6). That means that twenty-two male directors were hired for every one female director. Of those women, the majority were white; four were black, two Asian (one of whom directed multiple films), and one Latina. Tellingly, in the action genre, there was a gender ratio of sixty male directors to every one female director. For historical perspective, the Women's Steering Committee of the Directors Guild of America found in 1979 that only 0.5 percent of all film and TV directing assignments over several years in that era went to women (Directors Guild of America n.d.). In her *2017 Celluloid Ceiling* report on employment for the Center for the Study of Women in Television and Film, Martha Lauzen (2018, 2–3) found that women accounted for 4 percent of cinematographers for the top 250 domestic grossing films. It was the same number in 1998, with minimal variation in the years between. A few similar studies have been carried out in Hong Kong, and based on research, interviews, and available production records, the majority of commercial, theatrically released films over the past century have been directed by men (notable exceptions include Ann Hui, Mabel Cheung, Sylvia Chang, Barbara Wong Chun-chun, Ivy Ho, and Heiward Mak) and shot by male cinematographers. According to a member, the Hong Kong Director's Guild, as of August 2020, includes 308 current members, with only 27 women members. Nevertheless, there are women directors in both Hollywood and Hong Kong who have insisted on stealing a shot, and in male-directed films, there are women assistant directors and producers in both sites who participate in those shots, for various reasons discussed below. The gender norms of location filmmaking in both sites, however, have long been shaped by industry ideals of conquering terrain and taming bodies.

During my fieldwork on film and television sets in Hollywood and Hong Kong, I observed an explosion stunt in Hollywood and a car crash stunt in Hong Kong, and saw that both scenarios provided excitement for many of the cast and crew involved, enlivening a sometimes mundane process, despite the potential dangers and issues of set safety. On the Hollywood production in particular, members of the crew hollered, high-fived, and back-slapped one another after safely filming an explosion on a studio backlot. However, filming does not always occur in such a controlled space as a studio lot. Location filming, in which exterior shots such as the chase scene for *The French Connection* are filmed, is less structured, allowing for more improvisational methods for capturing images. The concept of edgework is particularly apt in helping to understand these often unscripted and spontaneous decisions and events. Sociologists claim that people pursue high-risk hobbies and jobs for a pleasurable, sometimes even liberatory, experience (see Lyng 1990). In doing so, they draw upon a combination of skilled control and chance, in which one's physical or mental stamina is tested and aspirations to self-actualization are achieved, understood by some as bringing forth their authentic self (Lyng 2004, 6; see also Martin 2012). Edgework entails boundary negotiation, between the edges of order and disorder, sanity and insanity, legality and illegality, even life and death—the often intoxicating experience of skirting those boundaries described as "seductive" (Lyng 2004, 5). These edges correspond neatly with tropes about filming in rough climes and conditions, recalling filmmaker Robert Flaherty's foundational excursion into exterior filming, most notably in northern Canada. Cultural criminologists have also adopted the concept of edgework to account for the "adrenaline rush" of graffiti writing in their efforts to understand what they consider to be an "irrational" act that "emerges from the intersection of creativity and illegality" (Ferrell 1993, 172; see also Lyng 2004). Sociologists further develop the concept to understand resistance to societal norms (see Kong 2015). Yet risk taking, even in its most extreme form, is not only sometimes rewarded across societies, markets, and institutions; it is also required (see Zaloom 2004), making its voluntary character in the workplace debatable, especially for people who experience pervasive job insecurity.

The precarious labor conditions within film industries—precarious in terms of fewer and fewer short-term jobs, with decreased pay and reduced protections—exacerbates the dangers of stealing shots and contributes to the sense and stakes of edgework. Downsizing in locally based productions for both the Hollywood and Hong Kong film industries, which also entailed having to shoot on faster schedules with less turnaround time, was a common complaint from film workers in both sites, especially those working below the line. In their volume on media workers in six continents (*Precarious Creativity: Global Media, Local Labor*), Michael Curtin and Kevin Sansom state that "what is perhaps most remarkable about these precarious labor conditions is that the pattern repeats itself in many parts of the world" (2016, 4). Currently, despite the differing sizes of Hollywood and Hong Kong film markets, film workers in both sites share similar concerns about reduced locally based production jobs since the late 1990s; Hollywood productions have been moving out of Southern California and out of the country to film in cheaper locations that also offer tax incentives and, often, less union oversight. Hong Kong productions started to drop in number in the late 1990s, but some film workers found work across the border in China on coproductions, coordinated by the 2003 Closer Economic Partnership Arrangement with the mainland, a trade agreement that provides Hong Kong producers and directors greater access to the mainland market. However, the pay and regularity of jobs for below-the-line workers within Hong Kong decreased while, across the border, they found themselves increasingly competing with cheaper labor for Chinese coproductions.

The overall precarious work conditions in both sites also mean that there is even less motivation for film workers to resist or report labor abuses and generally exploitative conditions when they do find work (see also Szeto and Chen 2013). The fear of being labeled a complainer or poor team member for film workers in either place is paramount, as speaking out can often result in not being rehired. Physical set safety is generally well maintained on Hollywood union productions filmed within Los Angeles, with safety manuals and representatives as well as anonymous hotlines to call, but the rush to meet deadlines for each shooting day and a masculinist ideal of rugged determination to complete tasks at hand means that corners are sometimes cut and the best judgment does not always prevail. In Hong Kong, the pressure not to speak up is compounded by weak unions and a lack of collective bargaining rights, first under the British colonial and later the Special Administrative Region governments. In these largely post-Fordist work conditions, "states of anxiety, desperation, unbelonging, and risk experienced by temporary and irregularly employed workers" were at times discernible, especially among nonunion members in Hollywood and below-the-line workers in Hong Kong, similar to "irregularly employed" workers across industries in other parts of the world (Millar 2014). The situation is exacerbated for performers and production personnel having to work long hours, sometimes filming in difficult locales or weather, leaving workers physically and emotionally vulnerable. This is part of the context for understanding stolen shots, in which there may be consequences for film workers who often feel they are expected to meet spontaneous demands from directors (although, like William Friedkin's cinematographer and camera assistant, some do resist). Films with themes of violence or loss, which call for shock-and-awe images, are especially the kinds of films in which directors steal shots, therefore intensifying risks for workers.

In fact, while very different in scale and enjoying vastly different levels of state support, both Hollywood and Hong Kong share an industrial history of a Fordist studio system that shifted to a flexible production system, with specific features that reflect their local environment. Indeed, these industries do not exist in isolation, but rather operate as linked nodes within a global media network, with a long history of interaction between the two. Material links between the two production centers over the last several decades include Hollywood productions made with Hong Kong talent, Hollywood studio offices opened in Hong Kong–based offices, and coproductions with each other and with companies in China. Some of the connections go back nearly a century. For instance, Moon Kwan-ching, the founder of Hong Kong film production company Grandview Film Company, worked as an extra in Hollywood in the 1910s and later as a consultant for "Chinese culture" for D. W. Griffith's production of *Broken Blossoms* as well as a Lon Chaney film. Decades later, U.S.-born, Hong Kong–raised Bruce Lee would also work in both Hollywood and Hong Kong, taking his film knowledge and stunt practices back and forth across the Pacific with him.[2] It is actually in the context of a contemporary (and casual) interaction between members of the Hollywood and Hong Kong film industries that I introduce the fatal accident of assistant camera operator Sarah Jones on a "runaway production" that occurred in the U.S.

"We Make Movies by Our Own Rules"

In the summer of 2014, I was invited to a meeting between two Hong Kong filmmakers and visiting Hollywood entertainment lawyers. The topic of American camera assistant Sarah Jones came up, and one of the lawyers mentioned that the shot in which Jones lost her life was a stolen shot. The details of the accident are as follows: While filming a biopic based on the life of musician Gregg Allman called *Midnight Rider*, on location in Georgia in 2014, Jones, a twenty-seven-year-old female second camera assistant, was killed and six production members were injured in a train accident. The LA-based director and cowriter, Randall Miller, and his producer and wife, Jody Savin, filmed in Savannah, Georgia, and surrounding locations. While they filmed in Georgia partly because of Allman's professional ties to the state, Georgia was also the site for Miller and Savin's earlier runaway production of *CBGB*. Georgia is one of several popular destinations for filming outside of Southern California in order to reduce production costs; the production of both film and television have, since the late 1990s, like much American factory labor, increasingly moved to cheaper and less regulated locations, including right-to-work states.

Some location shooting, and runaway productions in particular, is intended to save costs by taking advantage of larger subsidies and tax credits offered by other states. These productions (even union ones, as *Midnight Rider* was) may also cut costs by working on a faster, cheaper schedule with less turnaround time and less professionally trained crew than if they were in LA's studio zone where union reps are closer at hand. More recently, in 2017, stuntman John Bernecker for the TV show *The Walking Dead* was killed in a fatal fall on the set in Georgia. "This would never have happened in LA," the Hollywood-based lawyers kept repeating during our conversation.

On February 20, 2014, in Wayne County, Georgia, Randall Miller brought his film crew to a live train track, the Doctortown train trestle, which is located twenty-five feet above the Altamaha River. He did so without permission from the railroad owner, CSX. Miller wanted to film a dream sequence of actor William Hurt on a metal hospital bed on the train track. Hurt would disclose later that the first assistant director told them that if a train was spotted, they would have a full sixty seconds to clear the track (Szklarski 2015); in actuality, they only had twenty-six. What neither Miller, his first assistant director, nor his executive producer did not tell the rest of the crew was that they were not allowed to be on the live train track.

Crew members such as hair stylist Joyce Gilliard recall the unease they felt while setting up the shot (Johnson 2014b). The hospital bed was laid across the tracks. As they started to film, a train was sighted. Members of the crew tried to move the bed quickly, but then ran or, like Gilliard, clung to a girder on the trestle. Survivors recall yelling at Sarah Jones to leave the camera equipment. A part of the bed lay across the tracks, and, when hit by the train, pushed Jones in front of the train, which killed her immediately. Gilliard's left arm was flung into the path of the train by its force, and she was badly injured. Miller was sentenced to two years in jail for criminal trespassing and the involuntary manslaughter of Sarah Jones—apparently the first such jail sentence for a Hollywood director. He issued a statement from his jail cell: "It was a horrible tragedy that will haunt me forever. Although I relied on my team, it is ultimately my responsibility and was my decision to shoot the scripted scene that caused this tragedy" (Busch 2015). The production could have filmed on other, inactive train tracks in the area. Released early from jail in 2016 after serving one year (due to a technicality in his plea), Miller is currently under a nine-year probation in which he is not allowed to serve as director, first assistant director, or supervisor responsible for safety in any film production.

With these events, a trespass was committed that culminated in the taking of a life. Sarah Jones's death is especially tragic given the dearth of women working and moving up within camera departments. Jones's father told a Hollywood publication that the night before the shoot, "She did make some comments about it being low-budget, and she was a little nervous about a few things. . . . She made a comment that some of the people asking her questions should have known more than her and she thought that was odd" (Johnson 2014a). According to court testimony during the civil trial, there was no safety meeting nor medical staff on the bridge. Ironically, in the silent era, Hollywood representations of women included them as damsels in distress on train tracks as a kind of attraction and a way to raise the stakes for spectators. One such film is 1917's Keystone Studios and Mack Sennett comedy short *Teddy at the Throttle* (Badger 1917), starring Gloria Swanson. It includes a scene of Swanson chained to a train track by the film's villain as the train chugs toward her. Swanson herself actually performed the stunt of dropping into a hole underneath the track, the train missing her head by seconds as it rushed past. While a stunt man dressed up as Swanson was prepared to double for her, according to her biographer Tricia Welsch (2013, 32), Swanson felt "challenged" to impulsively offer to do the stunt herself by the laughter from the cast and crew at the discrepancy between her small frame and her male stunt double's larger frame. After safely accomplishing the stunt, Swanson was applauded by the crew and kissed by the director. Jones's death is especially disturbing viewed in light of the popularity of this century-old gendered gag with its very real dangers.

It is important to note that Miller's producer and wife, Jody Savin, the executive producer and unit production manager Jay Sedrish, and the first assistant director Hillary Schwartz also bear responsibility. In the 2015 criminal trial, Sedrish and Schwartz were found guilty of criminal trespass and involuntary manslaughter, fined, and sentenced to ten years of probation. Like Randall Miller, they are prohibited from similar jobs, but they were not sentenced to jail time. Charges against Jody Savin were dropped as part of a plea deal with her husband. Sedrish and Schwartz were also found partially guilty in the 2017 civil trial, in which jurors ruled that the train company, CSX, was also liable for Jones's death, as conductors on trains earlier in the day had seen the crew on the tracks and not reported them, as per company rules. First assistant directors are in charge of communicating and implementing safety measures on a film set; based on my observations on other sets, there was likely substantial pressure on Schwartz from her superiors to participate in the stolen shot; project-based work in a hypercompetitive industry that underpays people in increasingly rough conditions can help lead to very poor judgments in the field. The location manager, Charley Baxter, had refused to show up at the train track that day and testified that before the crew left for the shot, another crew member mocked him for being cowardly by not participating (Busch 2017b). Several heads of departments had worked with Miller and Savin before and, according to some, reportedly trusted them. Actor William Hurt, who was supposed to lie on the bed on the train track, told the Canadian Press news agency that when he challenged the first assistant director's claim that sixty seconds was enough time to get everyone and all the equipment off the track if a train came, no one else said anything because they seemed to trust her (having worked with her on previous projects), and he didn't want to be seen to "throw his weight around" (Szklarski 2015).

Tellingly, according to members of the local Savannah, Georgia, Women in Film group, just days before the shoot, the producer, Jody Savin, claimed of the production company and their guerilla methods, "We make movies by our own rules"—a sentiment that the Savannah Women in Film group reported after the accident as having left "a negative impact on the entire group" (Yamato 2014). Yet although other crew members were also involved in choosing to film on the train track, it was Miller, as director, who made the final decision. It is also important to note that he chose to be on the live train track himself, with the crew, when the train came barreling through; he wasn't safely removed from the action. As he testified in court, "I was in the middle of the track, and I almost died." But when Miller stumbled on the train track while trying to escape, the film's still photographer, a woman named Beau Giannakopoulos, helped him get back on his feet and off the track, unscathed. Giannakopoulos would later testify in court that she felt "deceived by her superiors" (Busch 2017b).

Since Jones's death, Hollywood industry members have rallied to raise awareness about set safety and to commemorate Jones. Described as hardworking, talented, and sweet, and often seen smiling in photos, Jones has been invoked and inserted into multiple Hollywood filming rituals at a time when Hollywood has only recently started to publicly come to terms with its lack of female representation in cinematography, as seen in the 2017 first-ever Oscar nomination for a woman cinematographer (Rachel Morrison), after the uproar of #MeToo and renewed calls for gender parity in hiring such as the 50/50 by 2020 initiative and inclusion riders. Slates for Sarah is a popular initiative in which camera slates (clapperboards) are dedicated to Jones on film and television sets. Jones's whiteness also likely lends itself to the embrace from film and TV crews, which tend to be predominantly white (Caldwell 2008). Jones's parents have also created the Safety for Sarah Agreement, a letter of intent for productions and studios that establishes the Sarah Timeout, a procedure in which anyone on set can call out, without reprisals, should they feel concerned about a safety issue (Safety for Sarah n.d.b). The agreement also stipulates calling the first shot of the day "the Jonesy" to remind the cast and crew of safety standards (the last shot of a typical shooting day is generally referred to as "the Martini"). The website for the Safety for Sarah nonprofit started by Jones's parents links to an app that her guild, the International Cinematographers Guild, created and which provides safety measures and bulletins, and allows members to report violations and harassment.

"The Reality of Shooting Reality Was So Difficult"

I turn next to the experience of a Hong Kong interlocutor, named Lee. This stolen shot occurred during location filming in Hong Kong and involves a child actor on the set of a film that Lee worked on. In the film's story line, the adult characters decide that a boy must be cleaned up. One of the actors was directed to hose down the child and scrub his face and body. Bound and gagged, the child actor was directed not to actively resist. As Lee described it:

> He was tied up and his mouth was taped shut, so he couldn't really control how the soapy water was coming down. . . . It was painful. He was really crying. After the first scene I was so relieved, I was ready to untie the kid. But then the producer, who had been watching, said to me, "Let's push it further, with the way he is now." Now the kid is really crying. This is one of the horrible things you really have to do, the lengths to which you go. . . . I was most worried that the detergent would blind the kid. And then he'd lose his sight. And nothing is worth that, no movie.[3]

Lee explained to me that the producer, who was his boss and a powerful figure in the industry, wanted to capture the boy's "authentic" agitation. The boy's mother, who, according to Lee, was in another room in the apartment in which they were filming, apparently appeared to them not to be upset, but one wonders what she really thought or knew. As Lee described to me, he decided to leave the room in which the filming was occurring; he chose, in his own words, "to hide," overcome by the actual labor process. Even though the boy's sight was (thankfully) not taken from him, according to Lee's account, his temporary well-being was. The theme of visuality here also emerges: the film production was creating an attraction intended, Lee had explained to me, to "shock" people; the boy's vision was potentially threatened in the filmmakers' efforts to create shocking imagery; Lee turned his own eyes away from the spectacle of managerial power.

Filmmakers such as Lee and his boss strive to create story lines and cinematic worlds to which audiences are transported, yet Lee was confronted by the human vulnerability involved. He had helped develop the film with the intention of creating what he described as a "mad film." Yet, perhaps more than any future audience member, Lee was the spectator most affected by the crafted image, demonstrating how filming environments can be highly immersive for those working within them. This episode also illustrates how the authenticating process takes the filmmaker and his subjects to a dangerous edge. The boy's grueling experience gave pause to Lee and his boss's goal of thrilling anonymous audiences with the graphic and what Lee described as a "gritty" style of filming. As he pronounced to me, "The reality of shooting reality was so difficult." The efforts to which the filmmakers went to capture this attraction reveal a slippery sense of managerial accountability. With his own projects, Lee has been extremely cautious and respectful toward the filmmaking process. Upon hearing about Sarah Jones's death, he was surprised and remarked that it was worse than any filming experience he'd heard about in Hong Kong or mainland China.

Borrowing from the industry's own description of stealing, both cases illustrate a kind of theft of workplace rights and personal dignity in the name of spectacular storytelling. From Sarah Jones and her crew members to the crying boy and his mother, the quality of consent from these people is in question. What makes a team of producers and a director steal a shot on a live train track? Is it to get the shots needed for the day's schedule and to keep one's job? For many personnel, yes. Is it to dazzle one's peers and superiors in a high-stakes, hypercompetitive industry? As Jonathan Simon (2005, 217) asserts in his edgework study of Victorian lawyers and their "Alpine adventures" in mountaineering, in our modern world, "edgework is increasingly what institutions expect of people," even as those institutions retain much of their bureaucratic rationality. Is it to tantalize audiences with dark visions and display filmmaker heroics at playing creator and destroyer? Is it for their own thrill seeking and aspirations to creativity? Edgework entails rule breaking, and in navigating the boundaries of categories, there is the opportunity to unsettle the regularity of an "ordered existence," which initially appealed to Lee. William Friedkin offers his own mythologizing reason for his continual risk taking in his memoir: "Why did I do it? Why did I take things so far? You'd have to ask Ahab, Kurtz, or Popeye [the lead in *The French Connection*, based on real-life detective Eddie Egan, who helped bust an international drug ring]. If the film works, one reason may be that I shared their obsession" (2014, 182). Over the years of research, informants attest that filmmakers and their personnel such as cinematographers, lead actors, first assistant directors, and stunt directors at times become taken over by the energy and intensity of their work, particularly in the moment of filming. A few have even suggested that, despite their transgressions, the results of stolen shots ultimately contribute to the art of filmmaking. Claims of creative freedom coming at a cost, which are cited by filmmakers in both Hollywood and Hong Kong, recall Lewis Hyde's trickster figure. Hyde (2010, 13) celebrates the trickster as an individual who advances their culture in some way, sometimes through an act of thievery, unsettling received categories and thereby innovating the world around them. Filmmaker Robert Flaherty, renowned as much for artistic expression as for contested authenticity, recorded his attitude toward the well-being of the Inuit men he filmed for *Nanook of the North* (see also Rony 1996, 114). During their famous struggle in the water for the walrus hunt that he filmed, Flaherty was "pretending," in his own words, not to understand their cries for help; "the camera crank was my only interest then" (Flaherty 1922, 632–640). Surely this qualifies as a kind of trespass, the "white master" (Rony 1996, 317) seizing an opportunity from his trusting Inuit hosts. In his own uncompromising pursuit of an evocative story and images that have become legendary and lionized, at the expense of the possible well-being of his indigenous subjects/participants, Flaherty established himself as a kind of founding father to Randall Miller, Lee's colleague, and even Shirley Temple's director, Charles Lamont. To be sure, these filmmakers' actions were not those of a heroic trickster, but their trespasses are condoned, not always fully detected, at crucial moments in the production process, spurred by the momentum they largely control to create spectacle for a story, and often celebrated. Throughout years of fieldwork, I heard numerous accounts of stealing shots on location: of camera operators urged by directors to run in and grab a shot in an unpermitted location; of filming near the water in Hong Kong during typhoon conditions, which people are strongly cautioned against. As another director told me, "You have to get 'that shot,' no matter what. And sometimes you have to break the rules."

Yet understanding the lure of stolen shots and filming attractions as a form of edgework avoids reducing commercially oriented filmmaking to an activity solely geared to profit potential. While recouping production costs and pursuing profit can normalize the labor of working at the edge for variously positioned players, in the day-to-day of filming, some film personnel, even those below the line, deliberately seek out that journey of traversing the edge in order to create images of shock and awe that are so embedded in film industries. How a story is filmed, even when it is scripted and storyboarded ahead of time, may develop through spontaneous and even daredevil inspiration and intuition. Pursuing the "passions" that Michael Hardt (2007, xi) and others have noted that entertainment industries evoke, the composition of affect and intended authenticity cultivate a high-risk environment. Film workers in both locations were embedded in genres such as crime, action, war, and horror—themes that highlight the threats and challenges of the actual human experience. And that is in fact the appeal for some film workers, who get to (re)create crises and catastrophes (attractions) that bring audiences—and themselves—closer to the edge. Some of the perils that come with telling visual stories (such as gun violence, explosions, floods, and car crashes) provide a release from the rationalized, mechanized world, spurring edgework's sense of immunity and omnipotence, similar, Stephen Lyng claims, to the adrenaline rush of crime and its "anarchistic nature" (2004, 27).

Conclusion

"In order to understand the complexities of media production," Tejaswini Ganti argues in her analysis of Bollywood producers, studies of "commercially oriented mass media productions must examine issues of social relations and subjectivity" (2012b, 7). Edgework highlights the role of ethics in the attractions and provocations that filmmakers and film workers pursue, particularly when stealing shots. The concept's prevalence in criminological scholarship to explain thrill-seeking behaviors makes it a productive lens through which to view cinematic transgressions and trespasses on this scale. As *Midnight Rider*'s injured hairstylist Joyce Gilliard told reporters, the producers "wanted to get the shot, so whatever it took to get the shot is what they did. . . . The entire crew was put in a situation where we all had to basically run for our lives" (Dorian, Putrino, and Valiente 2014). In these various examples of stealing shots, of *tau paak*—be that thieving from a physical location or a body—we see how ethical concerns are sometimes cast aside. Gilliard has spoken of waking at night because of pain in her arm and nightmares of Sarah Jones's death. Discussion and debate exploded among Hollywood industry members about the risky practice of stealing shots after she was killed, compounded by the concern that low-budget productions film in other parts of the country, away from the studio zone of Hollywood, with less experienced local crews, and are prone to increased negligence and risk taking. Jones's parents continue to meet with Hollywood members to help ensure other professionals are protected. As their site says, "We expect our sets to be safe. But often times people's focus on safety can get lost in the collective rush to 'get the shot' or 'make the day'" (Safety for Sarah n.d.a).

The pattern that emerges from conversations with informants is that the standard for cinematic art, especially in Hollywood, remains largely defined by a history of masculine accomplishments (especially in direction and cinematography) that privilege a decisive manner, a stoic attitude toward physical hardship, a military-like ability to motivate and mobilize the troops (crew). Long-standing dynamics of gender disparity in leadership positions and institutionalized sexism in both film industries result in dynamics wherein women in support positions or even in parity with men in key decision-making roles on film sets often feel pressure to participate in these edgework activities, even to initiate them. Scholars such as Jennifer Lois (2001) have also examined the gendered expectations of other edgeworkers such as female search-and-rescue workers—for instance, that they are expected to be protected from grisly remains or dangerous terrain. A similar sentiment is also present in the production culture of both Hollywood and Hong Kong, in which on the set, the dirty work and heavy lifting are often still presumed to be men's work, especially for jobs with camera and lighting equipment. At the same time, however, for those working in front of the camera, women actors and women stunt workers are exposed to the particular challenges that come specifically with being the object of the heteronormative male gaze, such as having to run in high heels for damsel-in-distress story lines or wearing less protective padding under their costumes for stunts because the female characters may be more skimpily dressed than their male counterparts (see Martin 2012).

Why is looking at extreme filmmaking as edgework relevant? As anthropologists of film industries, we need to better grasp the fast-moving contexts of power in which meaningful media representations are produced. We should understand the various stakes for film workers below and above the line in dealing with contingencies and creating risk-filled conditions. As calls for ethical sourcing and ethical consumption grow louder around industries such as agriculture, coffee, and mobile phones, and as there is increased global attention to sexual misconduct and abuse in media industries with demands for greater accountability, we need to reconsider how filmmaker assumptions about creative freedom actually play out in the capitalist workplace amid precarious labor conditions, especially in industries whose leading filmmakers have been expected to be highly competitive in the global marketplace. For such visible film industries with transnational audiences, rivalry in spectacle making is not surprising.

Revealing attitudes toward the ethics and enchantments embedded in industrial filmmaking can also provide context for exploring broader social relations around cameras such as the rise in "extreme selfies" taken by people all over the world and resulting campaigns to promote "selfie safety." But unlike the (largely) individual pursuit of extreme selfies, industry standards for safe storytelling practices can be more publicly and consistently monitored and regulated, as the Safety for Sarah foundation has sought to do, alongside renewed efforts of unions and guilds in both Hollywood and Hong Kong. We must also think about imagery that consumers demand (or are perceived to demand by commercial markets) and the thrill of watching racially and sexually charged danger and violence: escapism comes at considerable cost to some of its creators. Should consumers inquire about the labor conditions that go into producing such spectacle—should we resist it?

Finally, the practice of stealing shots is thought provoking to anthropology because both anthropologists and filmmakers are in the profession of crafting narratives and amplifying images drawn from work conducted in the field. Like film work, fieldwork often occurs some distance from our institutional base, and we experience a form of immersion in our attempt to fashion perspectives. As many anthropologists have noted, we take great precautions in trying to uphold our disciplinary ethic of "do no harm," and trying to foster enduring collaborations with the communities we study, yet vexed issues of trespass and truly informed consent may linger.

Notes

1 Although in the screen credits of *Kid "in" Africa* the producer Jack Hays is listed as its director, Temple refers to Lamont as the film's director in her book, as do other sources (see Drew 2013, 30).

2 Cantonese opera troupes performed on the West Coast for overseas Chinese workers and incorporated elements of Hollywood films into their opera, including, according to film historian Law Kar (2000, 60–61), "special effects, makeup techniques, settings, costumes, and mise-en-scene," as well as Western musical instruments. Opera performers would also work in Hong Kong films, so those elements would surface there as well. Later Hong Kong talents such as John Woo, Chow Yun Fat, Yuen Woo Ping, and Sammo Hung were among those working in front of and behind the camera in Hollywood while also working in Hong Kong and China.

3 Interview with Lee, Hong Kong, January 31, 2005.

7. MAKING VIRTUAL REALITY FILM

An Untimely View of Film Futures from (South) Africa

JESSICA DICKSON

My first encounter with virtual reality (VR) was in Johannesburg in 2015. While in the early days of research on South Africa's coproduction economy, wherein local filmmakers partner with foreign production companies to access certain tax incentives and international markets, I was told by a prominent South African producer that VR was about to take off in the film scene. Steven Markovitz—a member of the Academy of Motion Picture Arts and Sciences, and known for producing features and short films with artists from across the African continent—had recently seen VR exhibitions at prestigious film festivals like Tribeca and Sundance.[1] He was eager to explore what the medium could mean for film and wanted to see African perspectives involved early on in its development. So when asked to showcase a series of short films for an upcoming interdisciplinary festival on the theme African Futures, he decided to organize a VR exhibition and production workshop instead. In an article promoting the event some months later, Markovitz was quoted about this choice in terms that echoed our conversation: "I thought, here's a new platform in its infancy and a chance for African filmmakers to get involved at ground level. . . . The VR I'd seen of Africa was generally of wildlife or, in one instance, Ebola, and the work I do is about challenging precisely that sort of dominant narrative. This isn't about Africa as safari destination or as basket case, nor is it about 'Africa rising.' Instead, it's about everything in between" (quoted in Wilson 2015). To coincide with the exhibition, which would feature VR short films made by early adopters (predominantly based in North America and Europe), Markovitz invited artists working in various mediums and hailing from different African countries to participate in a workshop intended to launch multiple new VR projects on the continent. "The idea [is] to bring this mixed group together, run a workshop and then commission them to produce new work so that by this time next year there'll be a selection of fresh material to show" (quoted in Wilson 2015). Taking his enthusiasm seriously, I booked a ticket to the event, hosted by the Goethe Institute of Johannesburg in October 2015. In addition to its VR program—aptly titled "New Dimensions"—the African Futures Interdisciplinary Festival would feature keynote presentations, panel discussions, film screenings, art talks, and performances by prominent academics, artists, and curators from across Africa and the diaspora (Goethe-Institut South Africa 2015). The event also happened to coincide with the first wave of student protests that would become the largest youth-led movement in South Africa since the 1976 Soweto Uprising.

Nearly two years later to the day, the #FeesMustFall movement—an ongoing call to decrease or eliminate university fees in South Africa, and to decolonize education and knowledge production more broadly—remained the backdrop of another conversation I had about VR. "It's not film—it's something else," insisted Riaan Hendricks, an established filmmaker based in Cape Town. We spoke in a sports club in late 2017 at the University of Cape Town, where he had recently enrolled in a program to explore VR academically. A crowd of nearly thirty police officers in riot gear chatted nonchalantly near the entrance of the building, visible through the windows just above our table, their presence intended to deter protestors from interrupting an exam taking place nearby. I had seen the premiere of Hendricks's latest (non-VR) film, a moving documentary that follows a Rastafarian fisherman for one evening of penetrating conversations about politics, economics, and imperial history. In our meeting, he spoke intuitively from his experience as a filmmaker, now studying what he felt was a very different medium. "How do you tell a story based on experience? Because with VR it's not film-language that gives you that moment to take the audience on a journey. . . . It's a kind of madness."[2]

This chapter draws on just over two years of attention to VR filmmaking with a particular view from Africa at the point when the medium and its implications were only beginning to emerge globally. Starting with my own introduction to VR at the African Futures festival, I proceeded to follow the work of VR producers, filmmakers, and artists who participated in its program, as well as others with an interest in VR that I came to know through film industry events that followed. This inquiry into VR's significance to film and its industries therefore takes as its entry point a particular conjunction of artists, academics, and film industry stakeholders at a moment in South Africa that might be broadly characterized by an ethos of technological, economic, and political disruption, as well as anticipation. Because my attention to VR was an unexpected detour taken while conducting fieldwork on more traditional (as in framed, or nonimmersive) film economies in the Western Cape province of South Africa specifically, a comment as to the slippery and awkward scales concerning the invocation of an entire continent in the analysis offered here is necessary. The ethnography from industry events is limited to those which took place in South African cities between 2015 and 2017, and my introductions to many of the emerging VR practitioners and other interlocutors cited below came through a Cape Town–based production company with international funding and aspirations for Pan-African reach.[3] By 2017, this organization had supported VR filmmakers in the Democratic Republic of Congo, Ghana, Kenya, Nigeria, Malawi, Senegal, South Africa, Uganda, and Zimbabwe.

Below I offer insights from early endeavors in VR filmmaking undertaken by several artists and producers working from South Africa, Ghana, Kenya, and Senegal, respectively. The views expressed here come from conversations with VR filmmakers and stakeholders either in person or via Skype; attendance at VR exhibitions, industry talks, and panel discussions held in Cape Town, Johannesburg, and Durban; as well as my own interpretations of the VR films that emerged from the Johannesburg workshop. I also followed online news articles and blog posts either authored by, or about, these creatives and their institutional supports. I cannot, therefore, claim to speak to all VR content production on the continent at large, or even in South Africa alone. The invocation here of "Africa" rather reflects its discursive use by film industry stakeholders—including filmmakers, producers, festival organizers, and funding bodies—based in different countries both within and outside of Africa. These stakeholders professed an interest in promoting VR-narrative media across the continent at large, but with only particular institutional infrastructures and networks in certain cities for doing so.[4] I understand this gloss of parts for an imagined whole as a conscious acknowledgment of the continent's historic and too-often persistent positioning within a U.S.-European imaginary as the shadow of, or foil to, Western progress and technological advancement, a damaging sentiment that was reiterated, and not for the last time, by the president of the United States just a few months after this fieldwork concluded (Vitali, Hunt, and Thorp 2018).

At the risk of reproducing the grossly generalizing tendency to address Africa as if it were a country (and not fifty-four countries and additional territories[5]) with a single story (see Adichie 2009), I follow and share my interlocutors' desires to proliferate an image of Africa that stands in singular contradiction to the entire continent's misrepresentation in media as backward, premodern, and perpetually underdeveloped. The results involve admittedly hasty moves between scales of ethnographic particularity, postcolonial theory, and reference to the Global South broadly, the pivots from which I have tried to signal clearly below. I had set out to explore the stakes perceived in harnessing VR for Africa, assuming after my introduction to the medium at the African Futures festival that VR's iconic association with the future would be a driving discourse in its development. I was to find that, in many ways, VR-content production was indeed touted as a sign of Africa's imminent futurity, or its unique position to leapfrog presumed stages of development using tools of the Fourth Industrial Revolution. The VR filmmakers I followed, however, tended to resist fetishizing VR as some kind of arrival and instead focused on the medium's potential for modes of storytelling that might challenge the very assumptions underlying temporalities of so-called development, industry imaginaries of the future, and Africa's positionality within it.

In the sections that follow, I draw on one burgeoning field of anthropological inquiry, described here as African futures, to explore another: the anthropology of film industries (this volume).[6] I endeavor to show how different perspectives concerning VR's emergence in Africa elucidate contested yet entangled temporal orientations toward visual culture, technology, and decoloniality in one part of the Global South. Following scholars who have worked to unsettle entrenched Euro-modern orientations toward time by mobilizing notions of "untimeliness," I explore two interrelated tendencies.[7] The first concerns the fact that VR, as a filmic technology and object, gathers varying affective orientations toward time and the future around it. Namely, many industry stakeholders both inside and outside Africa have tended to anticipate VR film as a technological and economic disruption already transforming cinema into its unknowable, but inevitable, future form(s). The second is that many of the VR filmmakers I spoke to emphasized, at one time or another, the opportunities presented by VR to disrupt teleological narratives about Africa that placed it either ahead of or behind persistent Euro-modern measures of progress. What follows is therefore an untimely account of a particular, yet transnational context in which filmmakers and industry stakeholders worked both pragmatically and discursively to make VR into film. And to rethink what film is, and what it could be, in doing so.

A Brief Note on VR's Past and "Present." Virtual reality is a visual technology that, in the few years preceding this research, moved from being an outmoded fantasy of late twentieth-century science fiction (SF) to a very real and burgeoning sector of the media industry, inspiring a mix of enthusiasm, skepticism,

FIGURE 7.1. African Futures. Photo: © Goethe-Institut/Lerato Maduna.

and technosocial prophecies. Holding a prominent position in the technological imagination of the 1980s and '90s—especially in iconic film and television such as *Tron*, *The Matrix*, and *Star Trek*—real-world consumer VR prototypes that drew from developments in military and aerospace engineering stirred both excitement and anxiety for artists and academics alike (Manovich 2001; Pinney 1992; Rheingold 1991). Interest had fizzled by the early 2000s, however, as the hardware consistently failed to live up to its hype. It took until the 2012 debut of a new head-mounted display, designed by an eighteen-year-old Californian in his parents' garage, for VR to be reintroduced into popular conversation (Rubin 2014).[8] The question of VR now seems to be less a matter of how and when than "as what?" or "which kind?," and increasingly, "for whom?" (Bielskyte 2017; Kopp 2017; Sinclair 2017).

A brief description of the different modes of VR-related content currently being produced is useful, if only to better signal for the future reader what kinds of equipment and capabilities the practitioners at the time of this writing are working with. New vocabularies have emerged to describe the various forms of VR under development, including augmented reality (AR), which is the digital overlay of figures or infographics onto a view of the real world.[9] In contrast, VR more specifically refers to the total replacement of a user's visual field with a new one. This most often involves a head-mounted display, some of which are tethered to a computer or game console for the strongest processing power. Some VR systems allow room-scale experiences, which require small sensors that track handheld controls, allowing movement within, and interactivity with, the virtual space. The most affordable consumer options are portable head mounts with an attachment for a smartphone to be inserted and act as the display screen. Google released a US$15 version of a smartphone-compatible head mount made of cardboard in 2014 along with an open-source design available online so users could construct their own. These smartphone VR applications only allow stationary or seated experiences, however, where interaction is limited to moving one's head to view 360 degrees of immersive virtual space.[10]

As with the platforms available for viewing VR, there are also different formats for making VR content that require different kinds of equipment and production processes, some versions of which are, again, more affordable and accessible than others. While wholly computer-generated VR environments can be made with 3D modeling software and open-source video game engines, 360-degree video rather captures moving images of real-world space on a 360-degree camera, or on a rig of multiple GoPro cameras, that are then stitched together using an algorithm application to form an immersive field of vision. Debates continue over whether 360-video and smartphone-compatible applications can include enough interactivity to count as VR as much as wholly computer-generated imagery.[11] For reasons that will become clear, I focus here exclusively on immersive 360-video production (referred to from here on as simply VR film), which was the predominant form of narrative VR content being made by the artists and producers I spoke with over the course of this research.

* * *

A dancer in a white dress alternates between jarring and elegant movements. The stage is the interior of a polygonal sculpture lined with fluorescent lights, which stands in a courtyard surrounded by crumbling concrete walls covered in colorful artwork. Your attention is divided between the artist and the audience.[12] Some record the performance with cell phones. Children play in a corner. A spectator leans against a mural-adorned wall so that the wings of a giant butterfly appear as if belonging to him. The dancer steps through the geometric structure and continues through the crowd as the scene fades to black. Text appears in bright graffiti bubble letters: "Spirit Robot." A subtitle appears in a different typeface, reminiscent of the opening credits to Star Trek: The Next Generation: "Renaissance on the Streets of Accra." (Author's viewing notes)

FIGURE 7.2. *Spirit Robot*. Photo: Electric South/Jonathan Dotse.

VR Film Title: Spirit Robot *(Ghana)*
Creator: Jonathan Dotse
"A VR documentary which explores the Chale Wote Street Art Festival" (En-
counters Film Festival, 2017)
"Jonathan Dotse is a Ghanaian science-fiction writer and Afrofuturist. As
well as creating the first ever African VR experience, [Pandora,] Dotse also
runs the AfroCyberPunk blog where he discusses the future of Africa and how
new technologies will affect the continent" (de Klee 2016).
Watch it here: https://youtu.be/PGWsZMzc5eM

African Futures

The African Futures Interdisciplinary Festival was hosted by the Goethe Institute in October 2015, and held simultaneously in Nairobi, Lagos, and Johannesburg. Each venue featured panel discussions, keynotes, and performances by
prominent academics and artists from the continent. The VR film exhibition
was supported in part by Markovitz's production company and curated by fellow South African and consultant for the Tribeca Film Institute's Interactive
department, Ingrid Kopp. The event took place at the Johannesburg venue
and was titled "New Dimensions." Free and open to the public, its curators invited Jo'burgers to "discover this exciting new medium and get to know new

languages of expression, storytelling, and audience experience." Emphasizing that VR space "is still in an expansive, experimental stage," it posed its anchoring question as, "What might VR for an *African Future* look like?" (African Futures 2015).

The exhibition space was equipped with swivel stools and computers, with a team of volunteers on hand ready to assist visitors. Festival participants and the public at large casually came and went in between talks to view thirteen short VR films, each chosen to showcase different forms explored by early VR filmmakers. The featured African VR film was Jonathan Dotse and Kabiru Seidu's *Pandora*, a reimagining of the Greek myth in "the dreamscape of virtual Accra" (quoted from the program). In the film, the viewer moves from spaces indicative of modern travel—train tracks crossing a highway, a bus station, a bustling harbor, and a curio shop—to a lush forest where Pandora offers up her gourd. The viewer encounters an Accra characterized by connectivity and a suggested caveat: that such gifts come with a price. This intent was confirmed for me when I interviewed Dotse about his next VR film, *Spirit Robot*. "The central idea behind *Pandora* was that we were on a threshold of a new paradigm. . . . I wanted to highlight the elements of unpredictability and the kind of power that VR was about to unleash on the world. To try and encourage people to think in the optimistic sense that VR could be amazing, but also to think about all the other implications."[13]

In Greek mythology, Pandora was created by Zeus as punishment for humankind for stealing Prometheus's fire—a common metaphor for technology. By removing a stopper from her jar (represented in Dotse and Seidu's film as a gourd), she unleashed evil into the world. Yet Pandora has also been associated with how humans have shaped the world around them, suggesting ambivalence more than a curse (Chan 2014, 146). Dotse and Seidu's *Pandora* expresses optimism in the utopian impulse to shape the world, as well as a subtle warning about the dystopian consequences of industrial production readily visible in Ghana's landscape, home to one of the world's most publicized electronic waste dumps.[14] If a VR revolution is on the horizon, massive amounts of outdated hardware and e-waste will follow.

The conversations that took place at the African Futures festival also rarely conveyed an uncritical optimism toward emerging technologies or their promises of dramatically transformed futures. Speakers rather pointed out the continent's complicated relationship to claims for the future and voiced suspicion around its sudden thematic attention concerning Africa. As curator Bonaventure Soh Bejeng Ndikung asked in one panel, "What is this sudden interest in futurism . . . what are we trying to skip in not talking about the present, and not talking about the past?" (quoted in Heidenreich-Seleme and O'Toole 2016, 131). Acclaimed artist and VR filmmaker Jim Chuchu also asked, "Why do so many Afrofuturistic images involve Africans appropriating junk and remixing waste? Is there no room for the new in the future? Does the too-easy, broad-stroke application of the term Afrofuturism eclipse other irreverent or subversive urges that have nothing to do with futurism?" (95). And as curator Adrienne Edwards explained, "The entire apparatus that determines that there is such a thing as blackness is built on the system of modernity. We cannot afford this sweep from past, present, to future. . . . In order for me to proceed on a future position, I claim everything that preceded it" (151). Or, as artist Wangechi Mutu stated simply, "But Africa has always been a place of future" (171).[15]

Skepticism over rhetorical trends about Africa's position in time, or place in history, are not surprising. In the dominant discourses of colonialism and its neocolonial sequels, the continent has persistently been positioned relative to the Western world as out(side) of time, as lacking or lagging behind modernity; a dark continent still encumbered by superstitions and disorder while the light of reason points the rest of the globe forward.[16] Particularly around the millennial turn, the troubling resilience of this narrative reframed as apocalyptic forecasts, coming pandemics, or perpetual states of crisis (Kaplan 1994) seemed to indicate a mere reorientation from visions of a dark past to a degenerate future. More recently, however, this brand of speculation has provoked counternarratives of Afro-optimism, such as calls for an African Renaissance (Mbeki 1998; Ngũgĩ 2009), or an "Africa Rising," as the often-quoted 2011 issue of the *Economist* suggests. Yet, as evidenced in South Africa by the #FeesMust-Fall student movement, in many countries the postindependence promise of socioeconomic transformation extending beyond a rising elite class is yet to be realized. Moreover, widening gaps in wealth, the accumulation of debt, the increasing precariousness and outsourcing of work, aggressive exploitation of new and speculative markets, and even xenophobic sentiments, are in fact global trends.[17] The diverse entanglements of various African countries and subjectivities with these dynamics cannot be reduced to polemic judgments of pessimism or optimism (Makhulu, Buggenhagen, and Jackson 2010).

These rhetorical trends have resulted, however, in a body of scholarship on the subject of Africa's futurity. Significant among these in anthropology are Jane Guyer's (2007) attention to prophecy in Nigeria and "the near-future," Janet Roitman's (2013) interrogation of "crisis" in Cameroon, Jean Comaroff and John Comaroff's (2011) provocation that Euro-America is in fact emerging toward Africa, and Achille Mbembe's (2016b) centering of Africa in modern criticism. These texts draw from earlier critiques of Africa's prescribed temporality, or lack thereof, made by theorists like Frantz Fanon (1967), Chinua Achebe (1977), and V. Y. Mudimbe (1988). Academic interests in Africa's future have been paralleled by a growing canon of African SF, with a scholarly following of its own.[18] Moreover, celebrated literary works by authors like Kojo Laing, Ben Okri, Wole Soyinka, and Amos Tutuola (often categorized as magical realism) and the myth-histories of Vusamazulu Credo Mutwa are increasingly being counted among what many argue is a rich history of African SF (*Chimurenga Chronic* 2016; Sunstrum 2013; Thompson 2018).[19] What these new, and not-so-new, bodies of literature share is a rigorous critique of Western-conceived, so-called universal propositions of personhood, liberal humanism, rationality, and temporality. Rather than seeking recognition as possessing some equivalence to the posited timeliness of Euro-modern subjecthood, African SF authors and artists embrace a postcolonial and ostensibly post- or even "unmodern" outlook. One in which representations of African cosmologies and mythologies are taken up anew, technology and magic are given equal footing, and Western claims to scientific authority are decentered by Indigenous knowledge. These works seek to unsettle persistent hegemonic logics of temporality as a linear model—a consequence of Imperialist Enlightenment thought. They challenge contemporary narratives in which terms like "tradition" still relegate certain practices to the past, and what counts as innovation is reserved only for certain visions of the future (see Mavhunga 2017), denying their coexistence and multivalence in the present. As one speaker reflected at African Futures, "I know more people today becoming *sangomas* (traditional healers), not as a return to traditions, but as a way forward."[20]

It was in this interdisciplinary and international context, and as part of the African Futures program, that an experimental VR film production workshop for African visual artists convened. Experimental because no standardized processes or workflows for making VR films yet existed. Out of this endeavor, its organizers formed Electric South, a Cape Town–based nonprofit organization dedicated to the development, production, and exhibition of the VR projects conceived at the "New Dimensions" workshop. With their support, four of these original workshop participants had completed VR films by 2016.[21]

In light of these theory-driven beginnings at the African Futures festival, which happened to coincide with the start of the largest student movement in South Africa since 1976, I loosely frame the making of the VR films discussed here after what Kodwo Eshun (2004) has described as an "untimely" meditation and critical filmic practice.[22] A stance of untimeliness is one that remains purposefully out of step with notions of temporality that were made normative under European imperialism, which discursively positioned Africa as behind the times while phenomenologically colonizing the very temporal rhythms of life under industrial capitalism (Comaroff and Comaroff 1991; Nanni 2012; Thompson 1967).[23] An untimely ethic, explains Wendy Brown, involves an effort to "grasp the times by thinking against the times" (2005, 4). Methods of untimeliness, I argue, are made visible in the experimental, immersive visual practices of these trailblazing VR filmmakers in the postcolony. And because to be untimely is to resist linear modalities of sense making, and so-called rationalized forms associated with Euro-modern aesthetics, the results may very well constitute, as Riaan Hendricks put it, "a kind of madness"—or a disruption of the normative tempos, scales, and dimensions that have come to frame what counts as reality, or realism. Below I describe how the filmic strategies and production processes of virtual reality, utilized by the VR filmmakers discussed here, constitute an unframing of conventional film language—itself with origins in European Renaissance painting. But first I wish to make more explicit how VR's iconic association with the future, as an object first conceived in the popular technosocial imaginaries of SF, have incited some to enthusiastically reaffirm what are in fact normative conceptions of linear progress while inspiring others—namely, visual artists in Africa—to creatively subvert the very same temporal presuppositions.

By thinking with untimeliness, however, I also wish to avoid delineating simplified counterposing timescales. More complex than temporalities of the so-called "West and the Rest," VR was being discursively made into film at the time of this research through industry imaginaries of the future, emerging at the intersections of global media markets, international investment and philanthropic support for the arts, and visual culture production in different African countries and cities. Rather than delineating abstract "time zones" according to the presumed positionality of various stakeholders, I look to describe "the flow of social and political worlds as they are actually composed and decomposed . . . dreamt up and desired, in the multiple times they may inhabit" (Goldstone and Obarrio 2016, 18). Attention to forums where VR's status—as a new filmic medium, an economic disruptor, and a sign of things to come—was being rigorously negotiated afforded a rich ethnographic field from which to do so.[24]

* * *

You find yourself in a desert. Infographics for oxygen level and temperature appear before you. A computerized voice informs you that your suit is damaged: "Mobility and speech modules are offline. You are unable to move." Figures on the horizon approach from every direction, wielding weapons. "Identify yourself!" someone commands. A weapon is fired. Everything goes dark. . . . Text appears: "REBOOTING." *You are inside a large room or warehouse. Five people in military-style dress enter the room and surround you. A woman looks you over. Walking a slow circle around*

FIGURE 7.3. *Let This Be a Warning*. Photo: Electric South/The Nest.

you, she says they've read about your kind; a people obsessed with consuming every-
thing, that abused her ancestors. She tells you they are sending you back, but as a
warning. . . . Text appears: "If black worlds exist(ed), would you be welcome in
them?" (Author's viewing notes)

> VR *Film Title:* Let This Be a Warning *(Kenya)*
> *Creators: Jim Chuchu and the Nest Collective*
> *"A group of Africans have left the Earth to create a colony on a distant planet.*
> *They respond with disquiet to the arrival of an uninvited guest" (Encounters*
> *2017).*
> *Watch it here: https://youtu.be/AreWCYoqofE*

Industry Futures

For the purposes of this volume, early endeavors in VR filmmaking, and the
discourse surrounding its purportedly imminent proliferation from the major
media centers of the Global North, offer useful insights into traditional (or
frame-oriented) film industries more broadly during a period of supposedly
acute disruption. With the rise of premium TV series and "digital-native"
platforms like Netflix and Amazon, entertainment journalists from *Vanity Fair*
to the *Wall Street Journal* argued "why Hollywood as we know it is already over"
(Bilton 2017), and went so far as to declare "the end of the feature film" (Fritz
2017). Headlines proclaiming the death of the movies in 2017 may say more

about hyperbole in news media than the state of film industries themselves, however. At the time, movie theater market statistics were rather showing a modest growth, particularly outside of the U.S. and Canada, and people were consuming more visual content than ever before. Yet there was an overwhelming consensus that the practices of film consumption had dramatically changed over the last decade (MPAA 2016). As cinemas became more immersive, offering panoramic screens with 3D and 4D viewing experiences, and film technologies increasingly merged with gaming, communications, and data industries, VR existed at a nexus where anxieties over technological disruption and anticipation of social and economic transformations came to a head for traditional film industries.

The anticipation and anxiety that surrounded VR should therefore be considered alongside broader questions concerning the future of film. And popular industry news was quick to point out how speculations were driving big changes in film business models, particularly toward greater collaborations with tech industries. For example, IMAX announced in 2016 its new partnership with Google to develop a state-of-the-art VR camera for 2018, a US$50 million fund for financing VR content, and its plans to start building high-end VR arcades. As CEO Rich Gelfond explained, "I just think IMAX has the right brand. . . . There aren't many companies that have expertise in technology, real estate, and relationships with filmmakers and studios." From an interview with Gelfond, one *Wired Magazine* journalist described VR as "poised to be the biggest shift in the history of filmmaking . . . and just as MGM and Warner Bros. made a killing at the dawn of the movie industry, there's a gold rush happening around the future of frame-free cinema" (Walzer 2017). While VR viewing spaces opened sporadically across the globe, Paramount Pictures took up a different strategy and launched a virtual movie theater viewing platform. Rather than going to a physical theater, Paramount consumers would be able to log in to a website and enter a virtual one through their personal VR headsets at home. Paramount's senior vice president of new media explained, "Paramount wants to be where the consumers are and the media landscape is changing and we want to be as vanguard as possible. . . . There is quite a cultural difference between high-tech and Hollywood. Here we are testing something that is a page turner in the history of media" (quoted in Busch 2017a).

This industry vision of VR as potentially the biggest cultural bridge yet to link cinema to Silicon Valley also demonstrates Hollywood's indoctrination into an increasingly hegemonic temporal orientation associated with twenty-first century technoscience. Scholarship on biomedical practice and climate change, for example, has explored how contemporary scientific knowledge, increasingly presented as speculative forecasts, produces "regimes of anticipation" that structure affective states of anxiety, dread, and hope (Adams, Murphy, and Clarke 2009). Encouraged by neoliberal logics, anticipation has become for many a predominant mode of being in time, one in which the future exists as a palpable influence that orientates subjectivities and lifeworlds in the present (Adams, Murphy, and Clarke 2009, 247–248). Put another way, "one inhabits time out of place as the future" (247). Moreover, as Lana Swartz (2017, 89) describes in her piece "Blockchain Dreams," in Silicon Valley "technology is always one step behind its promises," while its presumed socioeconomic consequences are treated as though having already happened.

Notably, source material for imagining film futures often comes from a romanticized view of an industrial past that positions VR film as the inevitable next phase of cinema's evolution. An example of this was the commonly shared opinion at the time of this research that "we are now in the Lumière phase of VR." For Samuel Collins (2008, 121), such future-focused yet teleological modes of time reckoning are examples of the continuation of nineteenth-century evolutionary ideology. Logics that point to phenomena in the present as belonging to stages in a linear path already traveled by some other present-object are precisely the temporal models that deny the copresence of observer and observed (Fabian 1983), or, as described above, that relegate certain contemporaneous practices to either the past or the present, foreclosing all but certain futures.

Futures have long been colonized in the name of the present (Giddens 1991; Swartz 2017, 89), but as Vincanne Adams, Michelle Murphy, and Adele Clarke claim, "anticipation now names a particular self-evident 'futurism' in which our 'presents' are necessarily understood as contingent upon an ever-changing astral future that may or may not be known for certain, but still must be acted upon nonetheless" (2009, 247). And as Eshun (2003, 291) observes, noting the rise of "New Economy" theories and the role of "the scenario" in serving corporate interests, "powerful descriptions of the future have an increasing ability to draw us towards them, to command us to make them flesh." Futurism in this case, he adds, seeks to "model variation over time by oscillating between anticipation and determinism" (291). Imaginaries of the future therefore do a tremendous amount of work in the present. In addition to justifying radical interventions in its name, operating as if the future, however uncertain, is merely a matter of time also becomes a way of taming disruption—now a popular and perhaps overused term in technocultural and economic parlance—as merely a timely call for capitalization.

Industry attitudes toward VR film therefore present a discursive field where the structures, values, and habits of visual culture production become uniquely visible, as do perceptions of film's influence on broader social relations and even philosophical meditations. Even if these strategic moves by major film companies ultimately fail, or if VR is again sidelined as it was in the mid-1990s as a gimmick rather than a game changer, VR still exists for film industries in the present as, following Swartz, an "inventory for desire" (2017, 83). Experimental beginnings also have the potential to open new doors and permit different perspectives, which is especially valuable to those historically excluded from established industry structures and processes. Stakeholders and creatives in the Global South, as African Futures showed, are likely to relate to these desired industry futures differently from those in either Southern or Northern California. In a time and place where calls for decolonization have reemerged in popular discourse and as public protest, the promise of decentering Western conventions and inventing new ones makes for a powerfully charged field of possibility. The tricky position in which industry stakeholders in South Africa seemed to find themselves was to promote the potential for African VR film as somehow distinct from its imaginings in the Global North, but without precluding the chance to participate in its markets.

One of the most striking differences between discourses around VR voiced in popular U.S. and U.K. industry news, and the industry talks I attended in South Africa, was about funding. Big companies like IMAX, Paramount, Facebook, and Google have their own capital to invest in developing VR content for distribution, often on their own platforms. Contrastingly, VR film production in Africa tends to rely on foreign investment, often from departments of arts and culture in former colonial metropoles, which fund projects as a form of cultural exchange and a means to maintain diplomatic ties. As Mich Nyawalo (2016, 215) and others have pointed out, reliance on European agencies for funding has created resentment among many African filmmakers who may face patronizing demands from less experienced foreign producers dubbed "mentors" by funders, or even struggle to maintain creative control over their own projects. Additional opportunities exist through international film festivals, many of which have launched new media programs with funds for incubation and development. But in addition to a lack of local funding, international grants amount to relatively few opportunities for artists in Africa. According to Kopp (2017), in her article titled "Who Is VR For?," these small and not very diverse pots for financing risk dissuading artists and organizations from collaborating. Speaking at a film industry mart in Durban, she emphasized the harsh realities of VR filmmaking as an independent artist: "Most people I know are not getting funded to make VR, and that's just the reality you should know. . . . Right now VR is a very unstable space to be in, and you need to go into it with eyes wide open."[25] Far from the production resources of IMAX or Paramount, these

VR projects were relatively small yet complicated undertakings, with limited equipment and crew.

Second, access for consumers was also a critical question for both creatives and funders looking into VR film. While companies like Facebook and Sony are updating their hardware to enable greater interactivity at increased computing power, it is developments in mobile phones that many VR film enthusiasts working in Africa see as enabling their future audience. For instance, Yetunde Dada is a first-time VR filmmaker with support from France's Digital Lab Africa initiative and Atlas V (a VR studio) to produce a project promoting empathy for LGBTQ communities in Kenya. She wanted to be certain that the piece could be viewed in Kenya, despite the likelihood that the current regime would ban the film. In their project pitch, Dada and her production partner, Shariffa Ali, addressed this head on, stating, "Once core communities and sites have been identified, our aim is to send a traveling platform called the VR Mobile Unit, a custom-made VR station equipped with solar panels, as well as creating a cardboard headset dispersal initiative called Share-Board."[26] Given the often-cited boom in information and communication technologies across Africa (GMSA 2017), and the availability of the Google Cardboard headset as an open-source design, VR seemed to some almost specially suited for imagined African audiences. However, VR-capable smartphones remain expensive, and data costs are disproportionately high while bandwidth is still relatively low in many areas. Still, as one nonprofit funder optimistically stated, "equipment and access matter when it comes to immersive experiences . . . yet this phone can be the great equalizer" (Barret 2017). In line with twenty-first-century technoculture time reckoning, the general feeling was that the tools and platforms will get better and cheaper eventually anyway (or else fade away entirely).

This brings me to a particularly thought-provoking set of industry events I attended about VR's filmic future in 2017, including a VR master class that explored recent popular literature on "exponential technology, born of the Fourth Industrial Revolution," through the lens of Afrofuturism.[27] With an emphasis on critical practice, the presenter proposed that an Afrofuturist perspective, when combined with the emergence of new visual technologies like VR, could offer film students in Africa "new narratives" for envisioning futures beyond a white Eurocentric modernism. Citing seminal Afrofuturist scholars and recent works (such as Anderson and Jones 2016; Dery 1994; Eshun 2003; Phillips 2015), as well as psychiatrist and critical theorist Frantz Fanon (1967) and economist Moeletsi Mbeki (2009), the presenter contextualized "narrative" in this instance as the historical, structural, and psychological positioning of Africa and Africans within a global order organized under European imperialism.

"Historically, progress in Africa has always come at a price.... You can see already from the sixteenth century onwards how Africa was set up in terms of the global narrative to be the reserve of cheap labor.... I think VR is a way for us to resist those narratives." "Afrofuturism," the speaker explained with enthusiasm, "is liberating in the context of VR [because] it enables the construction of radical new languages." The presenter then met this broader theoretical imperative with a socioeconomic one relating more directly to young filmmakers and students, for whom many educators felt a duty to help "future-proof" for a soon-to-be dramatically changed industrial landscape. "It's very seldom now that filmmakers, and certainly those coming out of the born-free generation, are only writers, or only directors, or only actors, or only sound designers. Everybody has to have a multiplicity of skill sets. So as much as the technology we use is becoming exponential, we also need to become exponential in our skill sets."[28]

This was one of two presentations at this particular industry meeting to discuss "exponential technologies"—such as robotics, 3D printing, VR, and artificial intelligence—and to specifically reference the works of best-selling author Peter Diamandis, of *Abundance: The Future Is Better Than You Think* (Diamandis and Kotler 2012), and Yuval Noah Harari's (2017) *Homo Deus: A Brief History of Tomorrow.*[29] These authors presume an evolutionary model of technology with inevitable social consequences, both good and bad. More than one presenter at this film industry event also cited Moore's law, the eponymous observation made in 1965 by the cofounder of the Intel Corporation, which posits that the processing power of new microchips doubles every two years. This is a favorite framework for Diamandis, who uses Africa as a kind of archetype when making his case for exponential technologies as evolutionary mechanisms. "From the mitochondria-enabled eukaryote to the mobile-phone-enabled Masai [*sic*] warrior, improved technology enables increasing specialization that leads to more opportunities for cooperation. It's a self-amplifying mechanism. In the same way that Moore's law is the result of faster computers being used to design the next generation of faster computers" (Diamandis and Kotler 2012, 79–80). But instead of challenging the Euro-modern narrative of progress that the industry presenter quoted above calls on filmmakers to resist, Diamandis, Harari, and other thought leaders of what the World Economic Forum has extolled as "the Fourth Industrial Revolution" (Schwab 2016) seem to rather double down on existing industrial-capitalist imaginations of technosocial evolution. Moreover, contrary to its common characterization, Moore's law is not a scientific rule but rather a mid-twentieth-century observation that became a schedule for technology industries to follow (Waldrop 2016). Consumers are told to expect a new generation of electronics every couple of years, and engineers and factory workers are tasked to deliver.[30]

Harari, on the other hand, misinterprets the material connection between mineral and knowledge economies when he claims that humanity has finally "broken the Law of the Jungle"—a Rudyard Kipling reference (the British Empire's narrator par excellence) used to describe a propensity toward warfare. Harari writes:

> In 1998 it made sense for Rwanda to seize and loot the rich coltan mines of neighboring Congo, because this ore was in high demand for the manufacture of mobile phones and laptops. . . . In contrast, it would have made no sense for China to invade California and seize Silicon Valley, for even if the Chinese could somehow prevail on the battlefield, there were no silicon mines to loot in Silicon Valley. Instead, the Chinese have earned billions of dollars from cooperating with hi-tech giants such as Apple and Microsoft, buying their software and manufacturing their products. What Rwanda earned from an entire year of looting Congolese coltan, the Chinese earn in a single day of peaceful commerce. (2017, 15–16)

In addition to overlooking the fact that contemporary knowledge economies run on mobile devices, Harari misses the link between "peaceful commerce" and violent extraction in transnational circuits of production (see Parikka 2015). He also describes these two economies as if belonging to different times when he states that "wars became increasingly restricted to those parts of the world—such as the Middle East and Central Africa—where the economies are still old-fashioned material-based economies" (Harari 2017, 15). Never mind that the technological centers of the Global North have been reliant on the violent exploitation of mineral wealth from the Global South since the dawn of the first Industrial Revolution, as the speaker above points out in their comment about "progress" historically coming at a high price for Africa.

The invocation of these best-sellers—and what Eshun (2003), Sherryl Vint (2016), and others have termed the futures industry—at film industry dialogues about VR's future in Africa helped to elucidate tensions between Afrofuturist (and Africanfuturist) discourses and the temporal orientations of capitalist-driven techno-optimism.[31] Namely, that Euro-modern frameworks and imaginaries remain hegemonic in the reproduction of neoliberal logics, transnational economic policies, and the global circuits of materials, minerals, and labor that technology industries both rely on and render invisible.[32] Under the weight of industrial capitalism, whether digital or analogue, even Afrofuturist projects can be co-opted by Euro-modern outlooks, especially when powerful affective states of urgency can be found in both. Such urgencies are also distinguishable, however. While Afrofuturism is not a homogenous movement or monolithic worldview, a common theme in works emanating from North America—where the aesthetic genre first gained curatorial recognition (Dery 1994; Nelson 2002)—is an urgency to imagine any future beyond the dystopian present. At a time when merely proclaiming that Black lives matter becomes a radical rallying cry, to imagine a future at all becomes an act of political resistance (see Brown and Imarisha 2015; Dahya 2018). Imagining African futures from contexts within the African continent can pose different though deeply interrelated imperatives.[33]

For industry stakeholders in the Global South, there is a palpable desire not to be left behind, or, more optimistically, to "catch up." As one South African film student explained after coproducing one of the first commercially focused VR films in the country, "This is a brand new thing. Overseas it's been in play for a little while . . . so we wanted to kind of hightail South Africa into the international market. . . . We believe that virtual reality being so interactive and such an awesome experience . . . that's going to definitely fast-forward our film industry [to] an international level" (Expresso Show 2017, 00:00:47). Importantly, leapfrog or "fast-forward" narratives galvanized by emerging technologies are motivating passionate creatives and funders to take on very real infrastructural limitations in imaginative ways, and often to pursue more sustainable and equitable innovations. They can also hold in place a view of historical and technological progress that still presumes that the West leads the world. As the speaker quoted earlier who promotes VR to film students also rightly pointed out about Harari's dystopian prediction of a majority "useless" class, however: "you can argue with him and you can critique his point of view," but in a context like South Africa where unemployment is at nearly 30 percent, "you can't really dismiss him."

I will return to some of the imaginative strategies used by the VR filmmakers I followed to create immersive narratives that, each in their own way, challenged a Euro-modern framing of time as linear and inevitable to produce unframed experiences of African virtual worlds. The intention here is not to delineate boundaries between mutually exclusive temporal orientations, or to suggest some radical alterity to be found in modes of time reckoning. Rather I have tried to describe how novel technologies relate to existing frameworks for conceiving time and wield powerful affective influence over ways of being in the world. A critical temporality can also offer a politics for revealing particular frameworks as hegemonic, and for forming counternarratives to its structuring logic.[34] With the preceding examples, I have tried to more specifically show how contemporary discourse around technofutures tends to frame conversations concerning film's global futures. By privileging a view from the Global South, however, Euro-modern perspectives of technological progress now ensconced in visions of an arriving dematerialized industrial future can be critically questioned.

* * *

You are in a forest. A voice reads a lyrical poem about dreams and memories. A person dressed in black, another in red, and a third in yellow dance around you. Holographic forms hover above them. You are transported to a campfire; the steps of a dilapidated building; the bottom of a swimming pool. Butterfly-like creatures flutter around you and the dancers underwater. The dreamy, surreal scene continues until the poem's end. I feel like I've been swaying back and forth in my chair, in concert with the dancers. (Author's viewing notes)

> *VR Film Title:* Nairobi Berries *(Kenya)*
> *Creator: Ng'endo Mukii*
> *"Two women and a man wrangle. Each must hollow out the other's core for fruits promised but only ever borne in dreams. A poetic symphony on Nairobi"*
> *(Encounters 2017).*
> *Watch it here: https://youtu.be/dfsJ1CQRYqs*

Making VR Film

While filmmakers and industry leaders alike emphasized an imperative to proliferate African stories, it was the form these stories might take that posed the greatest questions for artists endeavoring to make VR film. The accustomed filmic narrative, which moves through a progression of images in front of the viewer, is exploded without the formative restrictions of the frame. With 360 degrees of image, a filmmaker can never guarantee that the viewer will look in one intended direction. Nor can viewers ever see the immersive image in its totality from any perspective, provoking them to turn their bodies to make sense of a plot. Yet each glance offers a new array of possibilities for experiencing the VR story world. The reorientation required for the time-space of 360-degree visual storytelling might then best be described by Hendricks's reflection on "madness": "It's avant-garde, almost surrealism. You, being a person through my [the director's] eyes, but you've got your own agenda.... I'm looking in my direction, but maybe you want to look at other things ... so I've completely thrown out this notion of a film language—it's more of an experience. I'm trying to create narrative through madness. That's what I call it for now."[35] Making VR film therefore meant remaking a filmic sensibility. It also meant unmaking a hegemonic mode of visual representation with roots in a Euro-imperialist worldview.

As visual anthropologist Christopher Pinney argues in his 1992 article on VR and the "future history" of travel, the sixteenth century saw the rise of a Cartesian perspectivalism in Renaissance painting coalesce with technologies of travel to frame the world as an image. "The world as picture," according to Heidegger, was to be appreciated and apprehended at a distance. Through a worldview predicated on particular subject-object relations, the white European male consumer subject had the privilege to travel across landscapes where he could see curiosities and decipher the similarities and differences between the world and himself.[36] As travel became a pastime of the elite, the world increasingly came to be conceptualized as "a pictorial surface" (Pinney 1992, 41). The Western subject was purported to stand apart from or above the world as though it were an object, in order to survey it, to grasp its totality, and finally to know it (41–44, 47).

The immersive image, however, undoes this sense of mastery by subjecting the viewer to a visual field that overwhelms any single point of view, or any authoritative way of knowing it (Pinney 1992). This duration of visual space opens up the story world to a multiplicity of potential viewings and experiences. As Collins (2008) avers, following Elizabeth Grosz (2004), in a conception of time (and space) that is open to multiple "virtualities," time is no longer "a negative force whereby the future is winnowed away through a series of possibles" (Collins 2008, 120), leaving us with only the inevitable. "The future" can rather be understood "less as the dismal consequences of the present than as the excess production of fecund contingencies" (121). The space-time of VR storytelling, unbounded by the frame, opens up a visual field of possibility to tell stories in new ways, where one viewpoint need not foreclose another, and where surprise as much as directorial planning moves a narrative forward. That said, there were key pragmatic challenges that gave shape to what the VR filmmakers I followed eventually produced. In the paragraphs that remain, I describe how directing without a frame, the compounded degree of contingency in 360-degree images, and the technological imperfections of image stitching became akin to what Mary Ann Doane (2007, 38) has called "enabling impediments" from which these early VR film languages were made.

First, the directorial question was viewed as a problem to be solved by some creatives more than others. The inability to guarantee the direction of a viewer's attention, combined with the potential of cuts between scenes to disorient the viewer, and the need to remove oneself from the VR camera rig so as not to be included in the 360-degree scene, all dramatically compounded the tension found in traditional filmmaking between control and contingency. As with framed cinema, some VR filmmakers embraced contingency as part of the artistic form. For others, the key to unlocking VR's filmic potential was to figure out how to control, or at least effectively guide, the viewer's experience.[37]

At the time of this research, Jessica Brillhart—Google's former principal VR developer and adviser at the "New Dimensions" workshop—had created the closest thing to a manual for directing and editing VR film. Through a series published on her blog, Brillhart (2016) developed a way of mapping what might be called concentric circles of attention. In place of a storyboard, she presents a series of circular diagrams of color-coded rings expanding outward like a cross-section of a tree's trunk. Dots in each ring represent characters or features in the landscape likely to draw viewers' attention. By matching these points of interest between shots, the VR filmmaker had a better chance of holding viewers' attention in a particular direction, and of keeping them oriented in virtual space. Ng'endo Mukii, creator of *Nairobi Berries*, developed her own method, however, by making sure to always include simultaneous action both "north" and "south" of the viewer's assumed perspective (re:publica 2017, 00:07:45). Less concerned with directing the viewer's gaze, Mukii's strategy encouraged exploration of the virtual, surreal world she choreographed. Like the lyricism of her poem, Mukii's piece is less a narrative to follow than an experience to be moved by.

Another challenge brought up by VR filmmakers and viewers alike was the occasional visibility of "stitch lines," the result of stitching together images from multiple cameras on a rig to create the coherent 360-degree image in postproduction. The consensus was that stitch lines were merely an imperfection of the medium to contend with in the short term; they would disappear as the tech improved over time. One VR film stood out for its creative mitigation of this problem, however. The viewer of *Let This Be a Warning* (*LTBW*)—made by Jim Chuchu and the Nairobi-based Nest Collective of artists—is positioned in the story as a character trapped inside a broken space suit. Near the end, a woman walks a slow circle around the viewer while delivering a speech about their fate and twice passes through visible stitch lines. The filmmakers ingeniously made this part of the narrative by adding an AR effect that draws attention to the split image as though it is a malfunction in the visual interface of the viewer's damaged suit. Turning a filmic imperfection into a diegetic element, the makers of *LTBW* thereby also turned a technological flaw, already treated as a problem of the soon-to-be past, into a visual index for a high-tech future. Moreover, the parenthetical insertion into the closing text, "If black worlds exist(ed) . . . ," effectively interrupts while also calling out presumptions of a

Eurocentric linear imaginary. The text emphasizes the story's allegorical warning for the present about the cosmic consequences of white supremacy while simultaneously disrupting the (Western) science fictional notion that such a story—with ray guns, spacesuits, and world of Black sovereignty—could only make sense in a distant future.

Moments when "something untimely disrupts our expectations," contends Grosz (2004, 5), allow us to be "jarred out of our immersion" in time's continuity and to assume a stance from which to think critically about time as both an ontological and political element. Jacques Rancière (2010, 139) posits that it is art's ability to create "dissensus"—"a conflict between a sensory presentation and a way of making sense of it, or between several sensory regimes"—that enable it to affectively disrupt uncritical consensus. For an Africanist perspective, we might turn to artist and theorist Pamela Phatsimo Sunstrum, who specializes in speculative panoramas, film, performance art, and immersive installations, and who also presented at the African Futures festival in Johannesburg. Sunstrum has sought to locate an "African sensibility with regards to futurism" (2013, 113), and is interested in "the de-defining, de-writing, and transcendence of these historical, geographic, national, political, cultural, economic, and temporal specifiers" (114). With this aim, Sunstrum practices an artistic methodology that she describes as "a 're-seeing' of Afro-mythologies through the lens that SF provides" (2013, 113), and cites literary criticism that claims an affinity between SF's own interest in mythology, time travel, and alternative dimensions, and the "mythical mode" of African oral histories and storytelling that draw on Indigenous beliefs to resist teleological arrangement (Carstens and Roberts 2009, 79–80; Quayson 1997, 149; Sunstrum 2013, 113–114).

While *LTBW* might inspire temporal estrangement through familiar SF-themed signifiers and its closing text, other VR films mentioned here utilize mythology and surrealism to explore how vision "unframed" from Western aesthetic conventions might articulate a new film language. Dada's VR film, *Round Round*, for instance, follows a gender-nonconforming protagonist as they enact a Gĩkũyũ myth by walking seven circles around a Mũgumo tree in order to change their sex/gender.[38] Notably, this particular myth also features in an earlier, nonimmersive film by the makers of *LTBW*, which they also imbue with SF aesthetics.[39] Dotse's *Pandora*, on the other hand, inserts Greek mythology into a contemporary Ghanaian context, while Selly Raby Kane's *The Other Dakar* is described as "an homage to Senegalese mythology" (Tribeca Film Festival 2017). Sunstrum is careful to avoid cataloguing her notion of Afro-mythology "on geographical, historical, or any sort of imagined ethnic or cultural categorization," and rather advocates a "thoroughly subjective descriptor of

Africa-originating modes of narrative practice and orality" (2013, 115). Mythic subject matter is thereby drawn from eclectically, similarly to the ways authors like Wole Soyinka, Ben Okri, and Amos Tutuola draw on Indigenous resources for signs and symbols to elaborate on a "mythopoesis rather than a straight forward realism" (Quayson 1997, 18, 67–68). For "realism," argues literary scholar Ato Quayson, "promotes a view of reality which is inadequate to engaging with the problematic fusion of the real with the other-worldly" (1997, 149).

To this end, many of the filmmakers I followed employed a surrealist aesthetic, for which, as Hendricks points out, VR film seems particularly suited. Stitch lines, for instance, seem to lend themselves to worlds that intentionally disrupt realism, as do elements of the unexpected or the seemingly undirected. For example, Kane's *The Other Dakar* follows a young girl given privileged access to an invisible world. Kane, an SF-inspired fashion designer by trade, fills *The Other Dakar* with neon lights, eccentrically dressed spirits, and regal artists, and the viewer's perspective oscillates from just above the ground to several feet in the air. Undoing or playing with camera-height conventions was something Mukii also described in the making of *Nairobi Berries*, which shares a surreal or dreamlike sensibility.[40]

These gestures, which disrupted viewers' ability to orientate themselves conventionally in cinematic time-space, became VR-filmic tools for "otherworlding" in an Afro-mythic mode that could challenge Euro-modern worldviews historically associated with framed Cartesian perspectivalism and realism. Sunstrum reminds us, however, that the Afro-mythic mode she advocates in contemporary artistic practice is not related to "an essentialist or nostalgic distant past" (2013, 116). This is not, in other words, a case for supplanting Western artistic perspectives with precolonial ones, which might reinforce Western claims to the present while relegating African perspectives to the past. Nor is it to strictly delineate between European, African, or Afro aesthetic and temporal sensibilities. Rather, to return to a visual politics of untimeliness, the suggestion here is that an African futurism, variously being made visible in VR-filmic practice on the continent, is more about refusing a temporal order of things than about making claims on a future that still sees itself as emerging from only particular centers of technological and cultural production. As Mbembe also explains, commenting on Africa's futurity, "that Africa is gradually perceived as the place where our planetary future is at stake—or is being played out—is due to the fact that, all around the world and especially in Africa itself, older senses of time and space based on linear notions of development and progress are being replaced by newer senses of time and of futures founded on open narrative models. . . . [W]ithin the continent itself, Africa's future is more and more thought of as full of un-actualized possibilities, of would-be-worlds, of potentiality" (2016a, 96).

* * *

"The Other Dakar is a manifesto in a sense, it is for me a way to reconnect the urban space with its mythology and to use design and creativity as a platform for the invisible Dakar to express her uniqueness. In a time where materialism occupies the mainstream, there is a need to re-invest imaginary spaces and use them as a fertile soil for the necessary adjustments we need to implement as a country facing several cultural and political changes." (Filmmaker's note, Kane 2017)

VR Film Title: The Other Dakar (Senegal)
Creator: Selly Raby Kane
"A little girl is chosen to discover the invisible Dakar" (Encounters 2017).
"An homage to Senegalese mythology . . . this magical 360-degree film transports viewers to a place where past and future meet and where artists are the beating heart of the city" (Tribeca Film Festival 2017).
Watch it here: https://youtu.be/2OhCMhYMazA

FIGURE 7.4. *The Other Dakar.* Photo: Electric South/Selly Raby Kane.

To Be Continued . . .

This chapter has sought to explore how contested yet entangled modes of temporality have informed—and have been made visible through—creative practices and discursive endeavors to make VR film in Africa. By relating critical discourses around themes of African futurity to industry conversations about the future of film in light of VR technology, I show how a sense of urgency to disrupt Eurocentric narratives can become co-opted by industry narratives of urgency; how new technologies and their economies become seen as the movers of time, their disruptions something to be actively anticipated, prepared for, and capitalized on. The temporal orientations of creativity, its industries, and the varying worldviews of those involved are not mutually exclusive, but pragmatically entangled and made flexible to accommodate the necessities of economic livelihoods in what, for many, are increasingly precarious lifeworlds.[41] For these reasons, untimely interventions that need not cohere in some distinct other-timely claim, but can rather dwell in the disorientation of the seemingly surreal, may be preferable to notions of technological disruption now so easily converted into business as new, but made usual.[42] The VR films discussed here, I have argued, each in their own way resulted from practices in critical and experimental worlding that resisted teleological or Euro-modern narratives.

But to return briefly to Riaan Hendricks's claim at our meeting in 2017: can we still call this film? In the spirit of resisting foreclosures, the case for VR as film (in addition to many other things) remains an open question. The creators discussed here did, however, use technological and structural processes closely associated with filmmaking in their bids to create visual stories told through moving images. And unlike the filmmakers of Sherry Ortner's (2013) ethnographic study of the U.S. Indie-film scene "at the twilight of the American Dream," who deployed a harsh realism in ideological opposition to the "unreality" of early twenty-first-century Hollywood, these VR storytellers from Ghana, Kenya, Senegal, and South Africa made their virtual worlds untimely experiences by diversely deploying other aesthetic tactics borrowed from framed cinema. Science fiction–themed estrangement, avant-gardism, and surrealism were used to effectively resist a realist worldview associated with white Euro-modernism, a worldview in which, even according to Heidegger, "the accepted principles of metaphysical truth work to set 'experience on a definite path' without allowing themselves—or their very frame as worldview—to be called into question" (Robiadek 2016, 388).[43] Moreover, instead of being specially enabled by a new technology, making VR into film may have more importantly presented opportunities to explore different narrative modes, and to draw from marginalized forms of storytelling, made possible by a willingness to experiment despite the risk-averse character of most film industries.

This openness by industry stakeholders is not a given, however. And although VR is an emerging medium for which conventions have yet to be established, it is also an iconic pop-culture object—what VR will (or ought to) be able to do has, for many, seemingly already been worked out in decades of popular, predominantly Euro-American, science fiction. To approach the question of VR as film another way then, one could also ask: is film not always a virtual reality? Ingrid Kopp often emphasized at film industry events, in her usual cautiously optimistic tone, that while it is unclear whether 360-degree video VR—or game-engine VR, or AR, or something in between—is actually poised to be the next big thing, it is definitely becoming something. "So it's really important that Africans are involved in this prototyping phase." She once added, while closing her talk with a famous press image of Facebook founder Mark Zuckerberg presiding over an auditorium filled with what appears to be exclusively white men in VR headsets, "if Silicon Valley and Hollywood get to decide what VR is, then we are in a lot of trouble, because this episode of *Black Mirror* sucks."[44]

Notes

In addition to the editors and reviewers of this volume, I am indebted to my colleagues, friends, and mentors who offered invaluable feedback at various stages of this chapter's creation, including Jean Comaroff, Warrick Moses, and Ahmed Ragab, as well as the members of my 2020 virtual writing clinic—Gbemisola Abiola, Zabeen Khamisa, Ping-hsiu Alice Lin, and Anna Neumann—who provided much more than just scholarly support throughout a difficult year. And also to Luke Hollis for kindly reviewing my use of still-emerging VR terminologies.

1 Markovitz's recent producer credits include the award-winning *aKasha* (Kuka 2018) and *Rafiki* (Kahiu 2018).

2 Riaan Hendricks, personal communication with author, November 1, 2017.

3 I am especially grateful to Ingrid Kopp and Steven Markovitz for their time and generosity, and for connecting me with VR filmmakers working in various African cities.

4 The problem of a persistent triangle of concentration concerning gear, information, and access to limited funding in South Africa, Nigeria, and Kenya was often brought up at VR-related industry meetings, as was the need to better include filmmakers in Francophone countries in these networks.

5 The political boundaries of which are the result of regional, imperial, and colonial histories, and are cross-cut by speakers of an estimated two thousand different languages that also extend beyond the continent (Mugane 2015; Ndhlovu 2018).

6 For examples of studies of African futures, see, for instance, Comaroff and Comaroff (2011), Goldstone and Obarrio (2016), Guyer (2007), Honwana (2012), Mbembe (2016b), Roitman (2013), Stasik, Hänsch, and Mains (2020), and Sunstrum (2013).

7 Including Brown (2005), Eshun (2004), Goldstone and Obarrio (2016), Grosz (2004), Pandian (2012), Rabinow (2008), and Wilder (2009).

8 The rights for which were later acquired by Facebook for a highly publicized US$2 billion.

9 Examples of AR in popular culture at the time of this writing are Niantic's mobile game *Pokemon Go* and Google's wearable AR glasses, Google Glass.

10 Both AR and VR, as well as less-common designations like mixed reality (MR) and extended reality (XR), are still contested terminologies that have as much to do with marketing strategies as distinctions of design and technological capacity. "Virtual reality" is often used colloquially as shorthand to refer to the umbrella category of immersive media.

11 The format preferred would seem to depend on the industry looking to incorporate the new visual technology—such industries include everything from film to video games, porn, communication, advertising, medicine, architecture, archaeology, planetology, mining, and real estate—as well as the perceived desires of its consumers and the resources of producers.

12 When reviewing my notes about my own impressions of these VR films, which I jotted down immediately after viewing them, I noticed that I tended to describe their plot structure in the second person. Questions over how VR film might utilize first-, second-, or third-person narration inform screenwriting scholarship (see Larsen 2018), as well as demonstrate how limitations of the technology in fact provoke a broad range of possibilities.

13 Jonathan Dotse, Skype interview with author, November 3, 2017.

14 Agbogbloshie, a dumping site in Accra, has garnered particular global attention in recent years as various news outlets published images of young men extracting hazardous materials from the site, highlighting the transnational circulation of e-waste from the Global North to the Global South and its impact on global health inequality (Hirsch 2013; Ottaviani 2015; Schiller 2015). See Onuoha (2016), however, for an important rethinking of this region's representation.

15 Quotes from the edited volume produced postfestival (Heidenreich-Seleme and O'Toole 2016).

16 See, for instance, Gilroy (1994) and Hanchard (1999).

17 See Comaroff and Comaroff (2011), Mbembe (2016a), and Standing (2011).

18 For example, Adejunmobi (2016), Bould (2013, 2015), Carstens and Roberts (2009), Hugo (2017), and Nyawalo (2016).

19 See also Eshun, however, on B. Kojo Laing's 1992 novel *Major Gentl and the Achimota Wars*, in which Eshun argues, "Instead of integrating the Laingian text into the canon of African science fiction or belatedly admitting it into the canon of Afrofuturism, perhaps a more generative procedure would be to think with the ways in which a Laingian grammar reorganizes the predicates that compose the 'futures' and 'futurities' of science fiction. In doing so, it might indicate ways of reconfiguring the ground, the stakes and the object of the 'future'" (2019, 86).

20 African Futures, panel discussion, October 30, 2015.

21 A second workshop has since been held, and VR films are being developed with support from Electric South by artists in Nigeria, Malawi, the Democratic Republic of Congo, Zimbabwe, South Africa, and Uganda (Electric South 2017).

22 Eshun's use of "untimely" is particularly apposite here. Following the enthusiastic reception of *Handsworth Songs* (Akomfrah 1986) by the Black Audio Film Collective (BAFC) at the *Documenta11* contemporary art exhibition in 2002, Eshun employs his own "untimely meditation" (a reference to Nietzsche) as a critical intervention to the supposed linear progression of the arts industry, and provides a review of the BAFC's body of work stretching back to the early 1980s. Moreover, Eshun describes their artistic practice, which involved reediting, redubbing, and recontextualizing archival and broadcast video footage as "a radical interruption of the smooth teleology of twentieth century European film culture" (2004, 40). Eshun concludes his review by stating, "in refashioning the documentary into an untimely meditation, the Black Audio Film Collective created a politics of the image that simultaneously functioned as a new image of politics" (45). The launch of the #FeesMustFall movement also sparked intergenerational reflections at the African Futures festival, leading one presenter to comment that "students have discovered their parents' struggle." This chapter looks to capture a sense that these were times that pushed against the very notion of "the times," and that, like the Black British visual artists of interest to Eshun's 2004 review, the VR filmmakers I followed from 2015 to 2017 also sought to deploy a critical filmic practice of untimeliness, while nonetheless working within an industry-oriented field preoccupied with timely capitalization for Africa.

23 As mentioned previously, and also highlighted in the introduction to Brian Goldstone and Juan Obarrio's (2016, 16–17) edited volume *African Futures*, several anthropologists have taken up "the untimely" as a critical perspective and intellectual strategy in recent years. See, for instance, Pandian (2012), Rabinow (2008), and Wilder (2009).

24 Ortner has referred to this kind of "cultural ethnography through discourse" (2013, 31)—that draws on formal industry forums like film festivals, screenings with Q&As, panel discussions, published interviews with entertainment journalists, and so on—in which members of a creative or industrial community explicitly "interface with the public" as "interface ethnography" (26).

25 Ingrid Kopp, Durban, South Africa, July 17, 2017.

26 Yetunde Dada, personal communication with author, November 1, 2017.

27 All quotes from industry master class held in South Africa in 2017. The presenter did not wish to be identified.

28 South Africa's "born free" generation refers to those people born after South Africa's first democratic election in 1994.

29 Harari's work in particular had garnered a popular readership in South Africa by this time. On my return flight from Durban to Cape Town, I purchased a copy of *Homo Deus*—a stack of which was prominently displayed at the airport bookshop. Before my flight departed, I was approached by two different people who saw me reading it and wanted to speak with me about it.

30 The sustainability of Moore's law beyond the present decade has increasingly been called into question (Khan, Hounshell, and Fuchs 2018; Simonite 2016).

31 Eshun defines "the futures industry" as "the intersecting industries of technoscience, fictional media, technological projection, and market prediction" (2003, 290). And the critical essays of Vint's edited volume for *Paradoxa* on the same subject concern "the need to reclaim the power to imagine the future outside of industry-produced

advertising images" as well as "our imaginative capacity to think about estranged and new worlds rather than to capitulate to the future as envisioned by global capital" (2016, 8, 9).

32　For more on the invisible labor of the internet and computing service industries, see Lemov (2015) on "clickwork" and the data-driven body, and Gray and Suri (2019) on "ghost work."

33　Debates regarding aesthetic and thematic distinctions between works of Black SF produced within Africa and those produced in the diaspora continue to inform Afrofuturist and Africanfuturist scholarship. South African author Mohale Mashigo explains her own desire to avoid the label of Afrofuturism in terms that echo the skepticism of an emphasis on the future voiced by many of the participants at the African Futures festival quoted earlier. In an essay titled "Afrofuturism Is Not for Africans Living in Africa," which serves as the preface of her 2018 collection of short stories, Mashigo states, "May this _____ (insert the name you've all agreed on) also focus on Now and not just The Future. Let us use our folktales if need be—use them to imagine us being fantastical in the Africa we occupy right now." Mich Nyawalo, however—in his comparison of "the aesthetics of hope" in Jean-Pierre Bekolo's vision of a future Cameroon in the film *Les Saignantes* (2005) and Wanuri Kahiu's portrait of a postapocalyptic Kenya in her film *Pumzi* (2009)—considers Afrofuturism a poetics deployed by both films to "destabilize eurocentric depictions of the continent" (2016, 219). For Nyawalo, Afrofuturism is an aesthetic and narrative tool that is contextual and relevant to Africans living in Africa because, as he explains, "afro-futurists do not simply place black bodies into previously whitewashed futuristic and technology-enhanced spaces, they also deconstruct the very idea of progress, including the evolutionary continuum associated with such locations. In this way, it is not just 'western' notions of modernity and progress that are redefined, essentialized ideas about African tradition are also taken to task" (212). More recently, Nnedi Okorafor (2019) has put forward a definition of Africanfuturism as similar and sometimes overlapping with Afrofuturism. "The difference," she explains "is that Africanfuturism is specifically and more directly rooted in African culture, history, mythology and point-of-view as it then branches into the Black Diaspora, and it does not privilege or center the West." The nuances of these debates are not adequately summarized here, but as Grace Gipson points out, many conversations between key Afrofuturism scholars, authors, artists, and activists have taken place on social media, bridging geographical distances and national borders. For Gipson, who advocates for an inclusive and additive view of Afrofuturism's meaning and creative utility, any tweet using #Afrofuturism meaningfully should be understood as adding to Afrofuturist scholarship (2019, 85).

34　See also Muñoz (2009).

35　Riaan Hendricks, personal communication with author, November 1, 2017.

36　See Mudimbe (1988, 11–12) on the empire of sameness and otherness. See also Urry (1990).

37　See Doane (2002) for more on cinematic time and contingency.

38　This description borrows language used in the production pitch for the film, provided by the filmmaker.

39 See *Stories of Our Lives* (Chuchu 2014) as well as Henriette Gunkel's analysis of this film and its use of cinematic time in her chapter "Alienation and Queer Discontent" in *We Travel the Space Ways* (Gunkel and Lynch 2019).

40 Ng'endo Mukii, personal communication with author, July 14, 2017.

41 See Curtin and Sanson (2016) and Standing (2011).

42 For more on productive disorientation, see Ahmed (2006).

43 For more on Heidegger's distinction between "worlding" and "worldview," see Robiadek (2016).

44 Ingrid Kopp, industry talk, July 17, 2017. *Black Mirror* is an SF anthology television series, often referred to as *The Twilight Zone* for the digital age.

8. THE MOROCCAN FILM INDUSTRY *À CONTRE-JOUR*
The Unpredictable Odyssey of a Small National Cinema

KEVIN DWYER

Prologue/Πρόλογος

In my first writing on Moroccan cinema, in 1999, I compared Moroccan films'
newfound success in the nation's theaters with the Mediterranean epic *The Odyssey*: like Odysseus, the Moroccan filmmaker was "returning in rags from a
long voyage, finally reconciled with his wife Penelope, his privileged [home]
audience, after vanquish[ing] other suitors"—in this case "satellite television,
video clubs, and big-budget films from the West." Uncertainty remained, however, and it was quite possible that the Moroccan filmmaker, in the face of these
and other threats, might, "after reuniting with his audience for a time, ... set
off on a new long voyage" (Dwyer 2002, 358–359).[1]

Introduction

In the global film world, countries such as Brazil, South Korea, and Nigeria
have successfully expanded what were relatively small national industries, using
a variety of measures, such as instituting quotas in the theaters, allowing the development of video distribution circuits, and promoting an encouraging legal
environment.[2]

Morocco's film industry, also very successful over the past few decades, has
been, both within Morocco and outside, something of a model for how a small
national industry might thrive. We see this with regard to other industries in
Africa where, as some have argued, "many on the [African] continent look
with envy at the way films are financed in Morocco ... [where] government
funding has made the country the envy of the continent" (Ahram Online 2013;

see also Rogez 2019). Even in Tunisia—a country that for several decades saw itself as playing the leading role among Maghrebian film industries—this argument is made, as in a headline in the main French-language newspaper that posed the question "Le cinéma marocain, un modèle à suivre?" and answered it largely in the affirmative, although with some qualifications (Gharbi 2013).

Now, as we look at Morocco's film industry's arduous voyage over the past several decades, we find that even given its significant successes—which include a relatively high number of films produced and a very creative cohort of filmmakers—it has not beaten back several disturbing trends, trends that are cited in most writings on small national film industries and that cast a dark shadow over the sector: rapid falls in the number of theaters, in overall cinema attendance, and in box office receipts. Since the early 1980s, Morocco has lost about three-quarters of its film screens, and attendance has fallen to about one-thirtieth of what it was then. In the five-year period from 2014 to 2018, attendance fell by 15 percent, although box office receipts fell by only 2 percent (*Bilan* 2018, 52).[3] These overall declines are even more striking given that the Moroccan population has more than doubled in size since the early 1980s.

The glare, or backlighting (*contre-jour*), cast by these various trends of decline makes it difficult to see the fuller face of the Moroccan film industry—its successes, its failures, and its potential. As we look over the past few decades and into the present, we find that although the sector has continued to be very dynamic, it now finds itself at a critical juncture. Among the new problems arising are sharpened criticisms of the way the sector is organized—it is governed by the Centre Cinématographique Marocain (CCM, Moroccan Film Center), a state organization founded in 1944 while Morocco was still under French rule and which exerts a commanding influence over the entire sector—and a general atmosphere of conflict and controversy. All these aspects put the Moroccan film industry in a situation where, even while creators continue to show considerable resourcefulness and inspiration, its past achievements are threatened with becoming historical curiosities and its future is very much in doubt.

Morocco's Film Industry: National and International Aspects

Two Decades and More: A Brief Overview

For a broader appreciation of Morocco's film industry we need, at the very least, to look historically at a number of dimensions—for a start, at the production and attendance figures for Moroccan films. In the sixteen years from 1988 to

2003, Morocco produced an average of roughly six feature films per year, which increased to thirteen over the period from 2004 to 2012, and to an average of more than twenty-seven feature films per year entering into production over the period 2014 through 2018.[4]

These Moroccan films have performed rather well in the nation's theaters, a trend that began in the late 1990s. In 1999, Moroccan films ranked first, second, and ninth in receipts and occupied three of the top five places in admissions. This trend has continued: in 2017, five of the top six films in audience were Moroccan, as were the top three and four of the top ten in 2018.[5]

When compared to films from abroad in terms of box office receipts, Moroccan films have shown great resilience, as table 8.1 shows: after falling to only an 18 percent share of receipts (with 22 percent of films shown, 68 of 303) in 2016, Moroccan films in 2018 reached approximately one-third of total receipts for approximately one-third of films shown (81 of 246 films; *Bilan* 2018, 60).

TABLE 8.1. The Top Five Countries by Percentage of Box Office Receipts (2014 to 2018)

2014	2015	2016	2017	2018
US	US	US	US	US
47	50	64	51.50	43.26
Morocco	Morocco	Morocco	Morocco	Morocco
24	23	18	28	32.05
France	France	India	France	France
8	5	4	4	6.93
India	Egypt	France	Egypt	India
6	3	1	3	2.12
Egypt	India	Egypt	India	Great Britain
4	3	1	0.50	1.14
Other	Other	Other	Other	Other
11	13	12	13	14.50

On the whole then, while the Moroccan film industry has maintained its increased production over the past decade or so, trends along other dimensions, among them the closing of theaters and decreasing attendance, have increased concerns about maintaining higher production numbers and the position of Moroccan cinema in the public sphere. In addition, in the midst of this growing sense of crisis we are now seeing increasing discontent among film sector professionals, to which its organizations have given voice.

These developments have pushed Morocco's film industry toward what seems like a precipice. How did this small national industry, in the face of what appear to be overwhelming global trends pushing such industries into ever more precarious situations, manage to struggle rather successfully over the past few decades, only to face existential issues at the end of the second decade of the twenty-first century?

The National Level

The CCM—the state institution that governs the film sector—has, among its many functions, the tasks of providing state funding, deciding which films are suitable to be shown, granting permission to film, and overseeing foreign productions in Morocco.

On the national level, financing is a central issue, but to evaluate the film sector's performance it is also important to consider diversity among filmmakers and in their films, and how public interest in cinema is being encouraged.

INDUSTRY FINANCING: THE AID FUND, THE STATE, TV

Private financing for Moroccan films is difficult to obtain, given the country's scarce investment capital and its relatively small national market; also, the many foreign films shot in Morocco distort the demand for actors and technicians and encourage higher fees than local producers can pay. In addition, international distributors are unwilling to take on such local films because they are hard to market abroad. This forces Moroccan film producers to target only national distributors, from whom they must seek relatively high payments to offset their costs, leading national distributors to turn away from Moroccan films since payments to Moroccan film producers would tend to be higher than those for films from abroad, which have earned money elsewhere and are usually available on the national market at rock-bottom prices. This leads to a vicious circle, where locally produced films are often not screened and have little or no chance of recouping costs, and distributors and theater owners end up showing mostly foreign imports.

In such a situation, Moroccan filmmakers are forced to depend on other sources of financing, here mainly from the state, but also from television and from abroad (in the form of coproductions and/or foreign aid).

The main state financial support for Moroccan film production companies comes via the Aid Fund, administered by the CCM. Since 2004, this aid has resembled the French system of advances on a film's receipts, where the film is supposed to repay the state's financing based on a certain percentage of its

Moroccan box office receipts. This system, together with a greater willingness on the part of the state to support Moroccan cinema, has led to significant increases in funding, going from roughly 20 million dirhams awarded in 2003 to 74 million in 2018 (*Bilan* 2018, 39). However, the Aid Fund can provide no more than two-thirds of a film's budget, so the producers must seek the remainder of the funding elsewhere.[6]

Significant financial support for Moroccan films also comes from the two Moroccan television channels (TVM and 2M), which was made more solid in 2005 with the announcement that each would increase their commitment to films so that a total of some thirty films per year—television films and feature films—would be produced or coproduced with the stations' financial aid. This enabled television not only to support feature films and add to the corpus of Moroccan films but also to become a main workplace for film professionals. Morocco's major filmmakers have been involved (including Farida Belyazid, Hakim Noury, Daoud Oulad-Syad, Saad Chraibi, Jilali Ferhati, Narjess Nejjar, Hakim Belabbes, Noureddine Lekhmari, and Muhammad Abderrahman Tazi, among many others), enabling them to survive financially in a situation where they cannot count on making more than one feature film every few years. And, as some filmmakers have argued, in the current situation it may be more satisfying and challenging to make a television series with an audience of 5 million, rather than a feature film one is not even sure will be released in the theaters.

As far as theaters are concerned, theater owners themselves are partly to blame for their problems. Following the process of Moroccanization in the early 1970s (where foreign ownership was transferred to Moroccans), many theater owners treated the theaters simply as a source of rent and did not invest in improvements that might continue to attract customers. In their defense, it was not made easy for them to make such investments then, nor is it now, since a large share of the ticket price goes to the distributor and to the state in the form of taxes, so that the theater owner may receive less than half of the ticket price. In this economic context, many of the older theaters do not meet basic standards.

The theater crisis has led, in the last few years, to measures designed to provide aid to theater owners, including subsidies for theater improvement, renovation, and digitalization. In 2018, six theaters (four in Rabat and two in Tangier) received such aid, totaling 6 million dirhams. In addition, 2.5 million dirhams were provided to open a theater with three screens in El-Jadida (*Bilan* 2018, 62). The opening of Megarama's eight screens in Tangier in 2016 has also been a positive development.

Much of the credit for the success of the Moroccan film sector must go to the filmmakers themselves and the films they have made. The most important trends with regard to the filmmakers involve ongoing renewal of the younger generation (many of whom are from the Moroccan diaspora), a growing number of women filmmakers (although it is still quite limited), and the sustained contribution of Morocco's first and second generations of filmmakers (roughly, those born from the 1930s through the 1950s), some of whom now have a considerable oeuvre to their credit.[7] There have also been important shifts in the themes and genres of the films produced and a significant presence of Amazigh films.[8]

Since the late 1990s, young Moroccan filmmakers, including many who spent a substantial portion of their lives outside Morocco, have been getting consistent support, through the Aid Fund as well as from several programs abroad supporting fledgling filmmakers. As a result, twenty filmmakers produced their first features between 2001 and 2005.[9] This trend continues and has even increased: over the years 2014–2016, 25 percent of the films awarded support by the Aid Fund were first films (*Bilan* 2016, 43–44), and this number increased to almost 50 percent in 2017–2018 (*Bilan* 2018, 42).

The first film directed by a Moroccan woman was Farida Bourquia's *La Braise* (*Embers*, 1984), followed soon thereafter by Farida Belyazid's *Une porte ouverte sur le ciel* (*A Door to the Sky*, 1988). These two were the only women filmmakers until almost the turn of the century. In the first decade of the twenty-first century, women began to appear behind the camera in greater numbers, with a number of first features directed by women in the early 2000s, among them some very highly acclaimed films.[10] The numbers, however, are still relatively low, with women directing only 25 percent of first films over the period 2014–2018 (*Bilan* 2018, 41–42), and receiving only 13.3 percent of authorizations (four of thirty) to film full-length feature films in 2018 (*Bilan* 2018, 3–4).

Starting in the early 2000s, both the continuation of old themes (with some new twists) and the emergence of new ones provide good evidence of creative vitality in Moroccan cinema. Some of the new themes that began to appear before 2010 brought to light previously unexplored aspects of historical memory, with a number focusing on *les années de plomb* (the leaden years—a period from the late 1960s through the mid-1980s when King Hassan II's rule was marked by harsh repression, disappearances, arrests, imprisonment, and torture), and others on the period in the early 1960s that saw the large-scale emigration of Morocco's Jewish community. Even farther back historically, several films have portrayed the evils under colonialism.

Social injustice and social questions in general have long been a dominant theme in Moroccan filmmaking, which continues to be expressed frequently. Also, subjects related to women have continued to constitute a strong theme, as was the case even during the 1990s when Farida Belyazid was the only active woman filmmaker and many men made films focusing on women's lives and problems. Emigration has been another strong theme over the past decades, and in recent years a "metafilmic" theme has appeared—films that present various aspects of filmmaking as well as some that are studded with film references.

As with themes, Moroccan filmmakers have been producing films in a wide variety of genres. New trends here include a growing number of comedies, along with crime films, road movies, dramas, and melodramas. The trend toward comedy has been marked, in recent years, by the great success of *Road to Kabul* (Brahim Chkiri, 2012), which almost succeeded in dethroning Muhammad Abderrahman Tazi's earlier comedy, *Looking for My Wife's Husband* (1992), as the Moroccan film with the largest audience.[11]

The making of short films, always an important step toward making feature films, has been particularly important in Morocco since the 1990s, when then-CCM director Souheil Ben Barka issued a directive that required filmmakers to produce three shorts in order to obtain a professional card. Recent years have seen in the neighborhood of one hundred short films produced per year, with a total of 207 produced in 2017–2018 (*Bilan* 2017, 10; 2018, 11).[12]

There is continuing controversy and activism concerning the role of Amazigh culture and language(s) in Moroccan national life. With the creation of the Institut Royal pour la culture amazighe (IRCAM) following a speech by King Muhammad VI in 2001 that called for integrating Amazigh language and culture into the national media, and the new constitution of 2011 making Amazigh a national language alongside Arabic, important steps were taken to give official recognition to Amazigh culture, and hopes were raised among the Amazigh community and others that Amazigh cultural expression and activities would be allowed more space in the Moroccan public sphere. One vibrant area in Amazigh cultural production is straight-to-video/DVD, and Amazigh feature films, while still constituting a minority genre, are increasing in number.[13] In 2018, three of Morocco's sixty-seven CCM-supported film festivals were devoted to Amazigh films (*Bilan* 2018, 66–70), as was the case for one of the eighteen festivals that did not receive CCM support (*Bilan* 2018, 71); in addition, a number of Amazigh films were shown at other Moroccan film festivals.

In addition, there has been a very important expansion in the area of documentary, including both nonfiction and fiction films in a documentary style, involving patrimonial as well as politically relevant films. While many of these documentaries have been made without CCM authorization (this is discussed further below, in the section "Filmmaking outside the Purview of the CCM"), the CCM began to provide significant support for documentaries in a program called Documentaries on Hassani Sahraoui Culture, History, and Space (Documentaires sur la Culture, l'Histoire et l'Espace Sahraoui Hassani), which was announced by the minister of communication in October 2014, stating that "funds from the CCM amounting to 15 million dirhams will be allocated specifically to support documentary production on Hassani and Sahraoui culture."[14] For the years 2017 and 2018, the amounts awarded to films in this program were approximately 20 percent of all production aid (*Bilan* 2017, 34; 2018, 39), amounts which, as we will see below, have been challenged. Outside of this program, CCM financial support had been limited to fiction films, but starting in 2018, the CCM began to provide financial support for documentaries, beginning very modestly with funding for two documentaries, which amounted to 2.6 percent of all film funding.[15]

STIMULATING PUBLIC INTEREST: FESTIVALS, FILM CLUBS, FILM CRITICISM, TRAINING

One of the main tasks in keeping the film sector vibrant is to stimulate public interest in cinema. In Morocco, some of the ways in which this occurs are discussed below.

Numerous film festivals are held throughout the country.[16] The National Film Festival, first established in 1982 as an itinerant festival and held irregularly, became an annual festival in 2007, with a permanent home in Tangier. Each festival shows all, or almost all, national films produced in the intervening period, and leads to wide discussion in the press, on radio and television, in everyday conversation, and on the internet.

Besides the National Film Festival, between fifty and one hundred film festivals are now being held each year.[17] Among the most important are those focusing on African films (Khouribga), Mediterranean cinema (Tetouan), short films (Tangier), women's films (Salé), Amazigh films (Agadir and Ouarzazate), trans-Saharan films (Zagora), immigration films (Agadir), and international documentary films (Agadir). To bring cinema to areas that do not have theaters—particularly important in a situation where very few theaters are located outside a handful of major urban areas—for years the CCM used a practice that went back to the early years of the film industry in Morocco, when mobile film structures, known as film caravans, were sent into the countryside to show films. However, this practice is no longer systematic but does occur occasionally, as in the context of the annual international documentary film festival in Agadir (FIDADOC).[18]

Film clubs in Morocco have a long and distinguished history in the country. Carrying on a tradition dating from the period of French colonialism, a federation of film clubs was formed in the early 1970s, and it became, like many cultural organizations during that period of heavy political repression, a site where expression was relatively free. There were at that time roughly a hundred film clubs with over forty thousand members, and this very successful period was marked by the presidency in 1973 of film critic and activist Noureddine Sail, who held the position until 1982 (and who from 2003 to 2014 headed the CCM). However, by 2012 and very much in line with general filmgoing trends, fewer than a dozen film clubs attended the annual meeting of Morocco's Fédération des Ciné-Clubs. An effort is now afoot to revive this institution, and in early 2013 new management was elected to the federation, with eleven members, two of whom were women (*Le Matin* 2013).

A number of film critics work in Morocco, either in the press, as members of the various university structures, or independently. This has led to a vast corpus of articles as well as a large number of books in Arabic and French. However, much still remains to be done, as a statement in 2011 by the Association Marocaine des Critiques de Cinéma indicates, referring to "the constraints faced by those writing about cinema which hinders the development of effective criticism, given the almost total absence of specialized written and audiovisual supports that would help propagate film culture."[19]

For decades, many in Morocco lamented the lack of training institutions for film specialties, but 2007 saw the birth of the School of Visual Arts (Ecole supérieure des arts visuels) in Marrakesh and a second school, in Ouarzazate, that welcomed some 120 trainees (Wilson-Goldie 2007). Then, in fall 2013, an ambitious institution opened in Rabat—the Higher Institute of Audiovisual and Cinema Occupations (L'Institut supérieur des métiers de l'audiovisuel et du cinéma), which was to be a major public institution with some two hundred teaching positions that would provide professional qualifications in any of six technical fields (screenwriting, cinematography, sound, production, directing, editing), and later master's degrees in some of these fields (EuroMed Audiovisuel 2013, 144). All in all there are now more than twenty institutions, public and private, that provide training in audiovisual arts and techniques.[20]

The International Level

In recent years, Morocco has worked hard to promote its cinema internationally. This has involved efforts to enter into coproduction agreements and expand regional cooperation, to attract foreign productions, to raise Moroccan cinema's international profile via commercial and festival screenings abroad, and to establish a major international festival (the Marrakesh International Film Festival).

COPRODUCTIONS AND REGIONAL COOPERATION

Coproduction may involve relationships with other countries on a number of different levels—gaining financing from abroad that may contribute significantly to a Moroccan film's budget (in this case financing will usually be European), or sharing in some way in the production or postproduction of a foreign film, usually with Morocco's Maghreb neighbors and with countries in sub-Saharan Africa. Over the period 2006–2011, 38 percent of Moroccan feature films were coproduced with either one or several countries, mainly European countries, with France participating in approximately 40 percent of these coproduced Moroccan films (EuroMed Audiovisuel 2013, 106).

And Morocco has made a major effort to coproduce with other countries of the South, particularly in Africa. As of 2018, Morocco had coproduction agreements with six other African countries (Benin, Ivory Coast, Egypt, Mali, Niger, Senegal), a joint accord among countries of the Arab Maghreb Union, and accords with nine other nations.[21] This has led to a total of twenty-six coproductions over the period 2009–2018, twenty-one of these being with African countries (including five with other countries of the Maghreb; CCM 2017).

Efforts to enhance cooperation at the Maghreb regional level have not been very successful. Maghreb Cinemas was formed in 2005, joining many Moroccan filmmakers with their Algerian and Tunisian colleagues, with the aim of promoting Maghreb cinemas and strengthening relations with the European Union community. This went together with the establishment of an annual festival of Maghreb films to be held in Oujda, but only one session, in 2005, appears to have been held. From 2009 to 2018, only five of the twenty-six films coproduced by Morocco involved other Maghreb countries (three from Tunisia, two from Algeria), and the most recent of these was in 2014 (CCM 2017).

Morocco also participates actively in the EU's Euromed Audiovisuel programs, which support data gathering, analysis, and cross-border distribution of Mediterranean and European films in member countries.

Morocco has a long history of providing locations for foreign productions, among them films by Orson Welles, Alfred Hitchcock, David Lean, John Huston, and, more recently, Martin Scorsese, Ridley Scott, and Oliver Stone. While Morocco has benefited from Western filmmakers' desire for Middle Eastern locations, it is facing increasing competition from other countries, such as Jordan and the Gulf Emirates of Dubai and Abu Dhabi. Among Morocco's advantages in attracting foreign productions are its willingness to allow films on controversial political subjects—for example, two films set in Egypt (Shirin Neshat's *Looking for Oum Kulthum*, 2017, and Tarek Saleh's *The Nile Hilton Incident*, 2017) were in fact filmed in Morocco because of restrictions they would have faced in Egypt—and its economies of production, with expenses very low and competitive.[22] And Morocco gains a number of benefits from foreign productions. In addition to the employment opportunities for individuals (actors, technicians, and extras), some 30 percent of the foreign production's local budget accrues to the local economy in the form of tourism, hotel, and restaurant expenditures. However, because of competition from other countries, Morocco is unable to impose the kinds of restrictions and taxes that might benefit it to a considerably greater extent, and it has moved to refund some 20 percent of any major foreign production's expenditures in the country.

The amount of money invested in Morocco for these films varies greatly year by year—for example, 2008 saw what was then a record investment of 913 million dirhams, almost double the figures for 2007, but then investment fell by more than 50 percent in 2009, to 415 million dirhams (*Bilan* 2009, 13). By 2016 this had fallen further to 280 million dirhams (*Bilan* 2016, 32).[23] However, budget plans produced by the Ministry of Culture and Communication for the period 2017–2021 sought a tripling of investments for foreign productions in Morocco, and by 2018, with a foreign investment of 732 million dirhams for the year, this aim had almost been achieved (Maghress 2017).

INTERNATIONAL PROFILE: COMMERCIAL AND FESTIVAL SCREENINGS ABROAD AND THE MARRAKESH INTERNATIONAL FILM FESTIVAL

By far the most important market for distributing Moroccan films abroad lies in Europe, most particularly in France, but the figures here are not very encouraging. Between 1996 and 2012, seventy-four Morocco-produced films appeared on European screens, but of these, only twenty-five were fully Moroccan, and in fourteen Morocco had a majority share.[24] These thirty-nine films averaged just over seven thousand tickets per film, with France overwhelmingly their main market, with 67.1 percent of the tickets sold, followed by Spain (23.8 percent) and the Netherlands (8 percent). The conclusion is unavoidable, given the fact that non-European and non-U.S. films represent, cumulatively, only 1–2 percent of European tickets, that "for Moroccan films and Arab films in general, the European market remains extremely closed."[25]

While very few Moroccan films gain commercial screenings abroad, many have appeared and won prizes in international festivals. Morocco's success in international festivals was first noticed at Cannes in 2003, when two of its feature films were presented outside the main competition—the first time in more than thirty years that the country's films were selected for the world's most prestigious film festival—and Faouzi Bensaidi's *A Thousand Months* won the prize for best first feature in the section called Un Certain Regard. Since then many Moroccan films have won prizes at international festivals. Over the years 2014–2018 the number of prizes has varied considerably, but there has been some improvement most recently.[26] At the 2018 Cannes festival, Maryam Touzani's first film, *Adam*, won high praise, also in the section Un Certain Regard.

Another sign of Morocco's growing presence internationally is the recent naming of Moroccan film figures to the U.S. Academy of Motion Picture Arts and Sciences, whose members vote for the Academy Awards: film directors Houda Benyamina and Maryam Touzani were named in 2019, following actor Saïd Taghmaoui, director and producer Nabil Ayouch, and producer Khadija Alami, all named in recent years.

But perhaps the most striking symbol of Morocco's enhanced international film profile was the establishment in 2001 of the annual Marrakesh International Film Festival (Festival International du Film de Marrakech, FIFM). Attracting celebrities from all over, this festival has enabled Morocco to gain greater visibility in the international film world and to strengthen its attraction as a location for foreign films. In a separate section, the FIFM also usually offers a panorama of Moroccan films, enabling the international audience at the festival to gain some knowledge of the national cinema. Over the years it has had leading figures in the film world on its jury, among them Martin Scorsese, Béla Tarr, Isabelle Huppert, and Francis Ford Coppola as heads of the jury and, as jury members, Marion Cotillard, Fatih Akin, Paolo Sorrentino, and film figures from Mexico, Iran, India, and South Korea, as well as Morocco; and master classes have been led by James Gray, Abbas Kiarostami, Nicolas Winding Refn, and Régis Debray, among others. Its truly international lineup is a clear sign of both the success of the festival and Morocco's relative success in carving for itself a place, albeit limited, in global cinema.

Another sign of growing recognition of Morocco's contribution to world cinema is that two of Ahmed Maanouni's films—*Alyam, Alyam* (The days, the days, 1978) and *Transes* (*Trances*, 1981)—were among the thirty-one films from twenty-one nations chosen to be fully restored by the Film Foundation's World Cinema Project, founded by Martin Scorsese at Cannes in May 2007 and dedicated to the preservation of films from around the world.[27]

Areas of Controversy, Areas of Construction

Over the past two decades or so, we have seen the Moroccan film industry's significant achievements in a number of crucial areas—funding and production, success with local audiences, outreach, training, filmmaker demographics, cinematic themes and genres, and in enhancing its international profile. Very recently, however, downward trends have started to predominate and become more critical, threatening, perhaps, to eventually become lethal. It is not surprising, given this context, that controversy, tensions, and discontent in the film sector have increased.

This has manifested itself in criticism of several CCM programs, such as how the FIFM has been handled and the funding given to the program Documentaries on Hassani Sahraoui Culture, History, and Space. This criticism is but one aspect of broader objections coming from Moroccan filmmakers, both informally and through their organizations, to the way the film sector is being managed by the CCM and the CCM's overall role in the film sector. The CCM has also been challenged by filmmakers operating outside the CCM's control. And all this is taking place in a context where issues relating to freedom of expression are never far from the surface and where general government policy with regard to the film sector is being questioned, especially since the coming to power in 2011 of the Parti de Justice et Démocratie (PJD), which presents itself as a moderate Islamist party. Let us look at each of these aspects in turn.

The FIFM and the Hassani Sahraoui Documentary Project

Over its first decade and a half, the FIFM was very successful. However, the 2016 edition occasioned great controversy, in part because no Moroccan films were in the competition, nor was there a specific section devoted to Moroccan films (this had been standard practice), and only one Moroccan film was shown under the rubric "outside competition." This, among other problems, led to a cancellation of the 2017 edition. However, the 2018 edition went ahead as planned and included a "panorama" devoted to Moroccan films.

The controversy over the 2016 edition provides some insight into ongoing tensions within the Moroccan film industry. The defense offered by the CCM and the selection committee for the absence of any Moroccan films in the competition was that none were sufficiently worthy. Of course, this was disputed by many critics, filmmakers, and members of the public. For example, Muhammad Abderrahman Tazi, president of the National Chamber of Film Producers (Chambre Nationale des Producteurs de Films, CNPF), argued in a newspaper interview at the time of the festival, "When you're in France or Spain, the national cinema's presence is obligatory. You can't say that of the four or five [Moroccan] projects presented, not one was acceptable. . . . And the Panorama of Moroccan films was also absent [from this festival]. If it continues in this manner, next year it will be useless to invite Moroccans. It will be an international festival in Morocco and financed to a major degree by Morocco."[28]

In addition to problems related to this festival, there have been other disputes over festival funding, including the criticism that the FIFM has received the lion's share of festival funding (it gained almost 40 percent of all festival funding in 2016, although this went down to 32 percent in 2018), and that smaller festivals do not receive enough funding.[29] And there have also been arguments over the large amounts given to the program Documentaries on Hassani Sahraoui Culture, History, and Space, which, for the years 2017 and 2018, as mentioned earlier, was awarded approximately 20 percent of all production aid (*Bilan* 2017, 34; 2018, 39). Among those critical of this funding was the prominent film director and producer Nabil Ayouch, who, alluding to the conflict over the Western Sahara, said, "Is this a matter of funds to support the war effort? Creative artists are free and must be so."[30] Some informal comments from filmmakers suggest that the significant amounts awarded to this program, as well as the CCM's acceptance of applications for documentary films and the television station 2M's heightened interest in documentaries in recent years, is related to the coming to power of the PJD in 2011, and its desire to use documentaries to promote its political agenda, which, while disavowing violence and adhering to democratic processes, includes support for the monarchy, for Morocco's territorial integrity (as in the case of the Western Sahara), for Morocco's Islamic nature, and also, as we shall see below, for the notion of clean art.

Filmmakers' Critiques

CRITICISM FROM FILMMAKER ORGANIZATIONS

The criticisms related to the FIFM and other festival funding are part of a broader critique that has been building over the past few years, coming from filmmakers and filmmaker organizations toward film sector practices and policies put forward by the CCM.

In a communiqué released in October 2016 for the annual National Film Day, the Moroccan Chamber of Film Producers (Chambre Marocaine des Producteurs de Films, CMPF), headed by Ahmed Maanouni, called for a "Rescue plan" for Moroccan cinema, which it characterized as in "a state of crisis at all levels of the film chain: theaters, distribution, film quality, the precariousness of film professions, the burden of administrative procedures and authorizations, the dysfunctions with the Aid Fund and with the promotion and visibility of film production on the national and international level."[31]

A short time later, in a press release on December 15, 2016, immediately after the end of the FIFM, the executive committee of a separate organization, the National Chamber of Film Producers (Chambre Nationale des Producteurs de Films, CNPF), criticized "unilateral decisions taken by the director of the Moroccan Film Center that strike deeply and painfully at the national cinema's development and tend to throttle its impetus."[32] It also strongly criticized "the exclusion, unjustified and very prejudicial to the national cinema, of Moroccan films from the last FIFM," as well as the "exclusion of the CNPF from all film festivals and professional commissions."[33]

Furthermore, in a joint press release on March 5, 2017, a unified group bringing together the CNPF, the CMPF, and the Union des Auteurs Réalisateurs Marocains (URAM), headed respectively by some of the best-known names in Moroccan cinema—Muhammad Abderrahman Tazi, Ahmed Maanouni, and Hassan Benjelloun—indicated their intention to join together in one united organization and proposed a number of steps to improve the Moroccan film sector. These proposed measures included "maintaining national film production at more than twenty films per year; defending the freedom of expression and creation; finding the necessary means to distribute national films...; [seeking] better organization for the film industry sector, the audiovisual, and live performances; ... creating an appropriate structure to distribute our films internationally."[34]

And, in preparing for the October 26, 2017, Journée Nationale du Cinéma (National Cinema Day), the CNPF prepared a "memorandum for structuring the national cinema [industry] in conformity with the kingdom's aspirations and the expectations of its populations," which laid out in detail its concerns for freedom of expression, improving financial support from TV and other sources, for raising the amounts awarded per film—necessary given increasing expenses—increasing support for theaters, and forming a specialized organization to promote Moroccan films internationally.[35] It also accused the supervising institutions (mainly the CCM, under the tutelage of the Ministry of Culture and Communication) of "lacking a coherent vision able to contribute to the development and defense of the national culture. Rather than listening to the professionals in the sector, they [the supervising institutions] to the contrary assume the right to regulate and legislate without real consultation with them [the professionals]."[36]

This discontent led to a sit-in by film professionals in front of the Parliament in Rabat in January 2018, protesting against the "mediocrity" of public television and film production, which was followed several weeks later by an audit of the CCM's finances and procedures, carried out by the Court of Auditors (Cour des Comptes; see H24 Info 2018).

The CCM's head has also been directly challenged. From 2003 to 2014— what some would argue was the Moroccan film industry's most fertile and productive period—the CCM director was Noureddine Sail, an individual with a long history in the film and audiovisual sector as cinephile, film club federation leader, television contributor and executive in both France and Morocco, and, finally, CCM head. As the filmmaker Muhammad Abderrahman Tazi described him, "Noureddine Sail is a man of the cinema. He created the Film Club Federation; he personified the radio and television programs that constituted the high points of film criticism. He is also the initiator of television films. He encouraged a cinema of value, thinking of both quantity and quality."[37] (Sail died in December 2020 at the age of seventy-three, and his death led to a flow of testimonies and tributes from across Morocco's creative sphere.)[38]

Any successor to Sail would probably suffer by comparison, and that man— Sarim Fassi Fihri, by profession a film producer and provider of film services— has clearly not escaped this fate. While the situation of the Moroccan film industry, as we have seen, is certainly not any one individual's responsibility, one of the most common criticisms of the current CCM leadership is that it has responded too passively and has not stood up sufficiently for the sector's interests in the face of political and other pressures (Savage 2016). For example, in a 2018 statement, the CNPF challenged Fassi Fihri frontally, arguing, "We believe, in all reason and honesty, that responsibility for the regression in the national cinema and the deterioration in working conditions in the sector falls entirely on the CCM director, the sole manager and organizer of the center and of the funds and budgets that come from it. . . . It is the director's policies that have led the national cinema into the advanced state of crisis that is suffocating it today." Foremost among its specific criticisms was the following: "Since his nomination more than four years ago, the director has completely neglected the national cinema's interests, focusing on two essential concerns: to travel the world and strut around at film festivals, and to use the shooting of foreign films in Morocco to benefit his own companies that service them."[39]

FILMMAKING OUTSIDE THE PURVIEW OF THE CCM

Another challenge to the CCM's control over the film sector lies in the growing number of films being financed, filmed, and shown outside the centralized system—initiatives made possible in part by lighter filming equipment, digitalization, internet viewing, and so on. Many of these films are documentaries, and some directly confront the film establishment. Among the first such films were several by Nadir Bouhmouch, cofounder of a group called Guerrilla Cinema Movement. His first film (*My Makhzen & Me*, 2011) follows the Moroccan protest group known as the 20th February movement, which came into being in February 2011 in the early popular enthusiasm of the "Arab Spring"; his second (*475: When Marriage Becomes Punishment*, 2013) focuses on the case of Amina Filali, a sixteen-year-old rape victim who was forced to marry her rapist and then committed suicide a year after her marriage, and challenges media and public representations of this case, both within and outside Morocco. A third film (*Basta*, Younes Belghazi and Hamza Mahfoudi, 2013) was made by a team that accompanied Bouhmouch when he was filming *475* and recounts its efforts to secure film authorization from the CCM, directly confronting the role of the CCM as the centralized source of money and permission to film in Morocco. These films have been funded from private sources—personal contributions and crowdfunding—and are often filmed with hidden cameras without CCM authorization.[40] Bouhmouch does not shy away from confrontation, and the opening credits of his film *475* include the statement, "this is not a commercial film," and, at greater length, "This film was made illegally, as a form of civil disobedience to call for freedom of expression of the arts in Morocco and as a stand against the state regulation of filmmaking through the Centre Cinématographique Marocain." Bouhmouch's most recent film, *Amussu* (2019), a documentary dealing with a protest in an Amazigh village against a mining company's effects on the village water supply, was also filmed without CCM authorization, and it won first prize at the 2019 FIDADOC festival.[41]

Censorship and Freedom of Expression

In the film sector, the institution charged with enforcing limits to the freedom of expression is the Supervisory Film Commission (Commission de contrôle des films cinématographiques), housed in the CCM. After viewing a film, the commission either issues the so-called *visa d'exploitation* that allows the film to be screened as is, imposes cuts, or judges the film unsuitable and denies it a visa.

In Morocco it is commonly understood that while censorship is limited and expression relatively free, one should not cross the "red lines" by challenging the monarchy, the nation's territorial integrity (with specific reference to the area known as the Western Sahara, but also referring to the contentious Spanish-controlled enclaves of Sebta and Melilla and some islands off Morocco's Mediterranean coast), or religion. While the public freedoms to discuss, criticize, and mobilize in defense of objectives that might challenge authority are sometimes curtailed, the freedom that Moroccans have come to enjoy in the public sphere, and in Moroccan cinema as one of its most important sectors, has expanded significantly over the past two decades, compared to the control that existed under King Hassan II. This greater freedom in the field of cinema can be seen, for example, in the strength of the theme of political repression and political criticism that has been strongly in evidence in a number of Moroccan films over the past decade and more, referring primarily to the period of King Hassan II's rule, which ended with his death in 1999.[42]

Over the past decade, several particularly controversial Moroccan films have encountered opposition from the Supervisory Film Commission. Abdellah Taïa's *The Salvation Army* (*L'Armée du Salut*, 2013), based on his novel of the same name, deals directly with homosexuality among Moroccans in Europe. Taïa is based in Paris, and this, his first film, was a French production and thus did not go through the Moroccan financing process. But it was still subject to CCM authorization for filming and, as Taïa says, "Before shooting, I submitted the screenplay in its original form to the authorities at the National Centre for Moroccan Cinema. I didn't cut anything. I didn't want to sugarcoat things in order to get the green light to shoot. They approved the screenplay, and I hope they end up following through by allowing the film to be released" (Frosch 2013). In fact, the film was never released in Morocco despite winning several prizes at international festivals. More recently, in the case of Nabil Ayouch's widely publicized film *Much Loved* (2015), the Ministry of Culture and Communication ruled, before the film was even sent to the Supervisory Film Commission, that it could not be shown in Morocco because "the film undermines the moral values, and dignity of Moroccan women, as well as all the image of Morocco."[43]

While the films by Ayouch and Taïa remain among the rare cases of censorship of Moroccan films, cuts in foreign films, where neither the producer nor distributor has much recourse, are much more frequent. Important also is the indirect role of the commission in influencing filmmakers' assessments of what they believe is permissible—leading to the phenomenon of self-censorship.

There has been some recent, if limited, progress on the legal level with regard to freedom of expression in the press, with implications for the film sector. A new press code adopted in 2016 eliminated prison terms as a punishment for offenses, with penalties now restricted to fines and the suspension of publications. However, as a Human Rights Watch report argues, this progress is circumscribed in two ways: (1) "many of the offenses that the new press code punishes with fines and suspensions of publications should be decriminalized entirely in order to conform with Morocco's obligations to protect international norms with respect to freedom of expression"; (2) the new press code must be seen in conjunction with the penal code, "which continues to punish with prison a range of nonviolent speech offenses, whether committed by journalists or non-journalists. In fact, Parliament adopted, in tandem with the new press code, additions to the penal code that criminalized 'causing harm' to Islam and the monarchy, giving offense to the king or members of the royal family, and inciting against territorial integrity, to be punished by prison and/or a fine" (Human Rights Watch 2017, 2).

The ongoing tension between freedom of expression and censorship is not likely to go away, although it may abate or stiffen with changing circumstances, as we will see below.

Government Policy and Clean Art

Into this complicated overall situation a new element was introduced shortly after the 2011 parliamentary elections that brought the PJD into power. The attitudes of this party toward art had already drawn attention before these elections when Abdelilah Benkirane, the party's leader, had condemned, among other forms of cultural expression, Noureddine Lekhmari's critically praised film *Casanegra* (2008). Laïla Marrakchi's *Marock* (2005) had also drawn criticism from party officials, as had several other films and a number of public performances. When the party came to power in 2011 and Benkirane became prime minister, creative artists were on guard against attacks on cultural activity, which were not long in coming. For example, in November 2011, PJD member and Minister of Economic and General Affairs Muhammad Najib Boulif began to discuss the importance of "clean art" (French, *l'art propre*; Arabic, *fenn nadhif*) as art that is "morally acceptable" (Akdim 2012). A short time later, in May 2012, Minister of Communication Mustapha El Khalfi, whose ministry supervises the CCM and who is a PJD member, also used the term "clean art" and argued in the Advisory Chamber of the Moroccan Parliament that "Moroccans cannot finance media that will provoke disruption and deviations among their children."[44] Two years later, in June 2014, he criticized Moroccan television before Parliament, posing the question, "Do you want to transform Morocco into a Mexican whorehouse?" (Tourabi 2014).

Artists reacted strongly to these attacks, and filmmakers were among those who felt and continue to feel targeted. Some filmmakers argued that the Aid Commission was taking the notion of clean art into account when making funding decisions, applying restrictions on certain subjects that had not previously faced such scrutiny, and was asking questions like, "Why do Fatima and Mohamed go out together if they're not married? Why is there a bar in your scenario? Why is there dancing? That's not part of Moroccan culture. Don't touch marriage—leave Moroccan traditions alone."[45]

Weaponizing the term "clean art" in attempts to stifle freedom of expression is perhaps better seen as a repressive tactic employed by those in authority, rather than as a program tied to one political party or religious orientation. Evidence for this lies in the fact that after elections in October 2016 led to a broad coalition government that was still led by the PJD but where the minister of culture and communication was a member of another political party, disputes over clean art continued.[46]

In one such incident beyond the film sector, in early 2018 the artist Khadija Tnana saw her installation, *Kamasutra*, which includes 246 hands as the background for couples in amorous poses, withdrawn from the Modern Art Center in Tetouan. The work had already been exhibited in ceramic form in 2014 at the Second Art Biennial in Casablanca, where, although the municipal authorities sought to have it withdrawn, the organizers refused, and it remained in the exhibition. After her work was removed from the Tetouan exhibition, Tnana directly accused the minister of culture, a member of the Popular Movement political party, of being behind the removal, and commented sarcastically, "The theory of clean art still has some beautiful days ahead of it."[47]

Conclusion

When the conclusions of a study commissioned by the CCM—the Diagnostic and Strategic Study for the Development of the Film Sector in Morocco—were adopted in 2007 as a national strategy, these conclusions were nothing if not optimistic: over the following ten years, annual feature film production would increase from eight to forty; state financing would double; incentives would pro-mote theater construction and renovation, with a target of some 250 theaters; support would be provided for distributing and screening Moroccan films; and educational programs would develop the public's taste for films. To promote the internationalization of Moroccan cinema, the number of Moroccan films shown on foreign screens would grow, and foreign productions would dou-ble: some thirty feature films, twelve television films, and fifty advertising spots were to be shot annually.[48]

Some of these projections have been met—funding has indeed more than doubled; Morocco has met the official middle-term target of producing be-tween fifteen and twenty features per year, and it has also continued to attract foreign productions. Yet distribution and screening—keys to the health of the film sector—continue to constitute weak points, and we have seen declines in a number of other areas as well.

One of the characteristics of the Moroccan film sector, governed as it is by the CCM, is its strongly centralized structure. In this critical situation, it is not surprising that the central role of the CCM is being challenged more frequently, more broadly, and more sharply than in the past where, while there were always some who were discontented with the way the system functioned, these were largely isolated cases.

Add to this the ever-growing group of filmmakers of Moroccan origin with grounding in two countries or more who form the very rich Moroccan film-making diaspora and who are not tied, in the same degree or sometimes in any degree at all, to the Moroccan state and its institutions and who, therefore, may show more independence in their filmmaking. Add further the growing ease of digital filming and the diversification of ways for films to reach the Moroccan public at home or abroad. Taken all together, we have many of the conditions set for a serious challenge to the institutions and practices in place and perhaps for a new burst of creativity in the sector, from somewhat unexpected places.[49]

In addition, the overall political context in Morocco needs to be taken into account. Following the self-immolation of Muhammad Bouazizi on Decem-ber 17, 2010, in the southern Tunisian city of Sidi Bouzid—the spark that set off uprisings throughout the Arab world—Morocco was the scene of serious protests and demonstrations, although never strong enough to threaten the stability of the monarchy. King Muhammad VI coordinated the adoption by referendum of a new Moroccan constitution in July 2011, and in the first elec-tions following this adoption the Islamically oriented PJD emerged victorious, forming a government in a coalition with other parties. Since the coming to power of the PJD, we have seen that the film sector, and artistic creativity more broadly, has faced pressure to conform to notions of clean art. It is far from clear, at this point, what long-term effect this heightened censorious attitude by governmental figures will have on creative activity.

In any event, as we consider the future prospects for Moroccan cinema, among the most important questions to keep in mind are the following:

1 What will be the role of the state and the CCM, as the state institution that controls the film sector, in promoting filmmaking? Already today we see the CCM's role and functioning being challenged on several fronts—not only by independent filmmakers who choose to raise money independently, to film without official authorization, or to distribute outside official circuits—but also by professional organizations such as both the CMPF and the CNPF, which see the CCM as not providing the leadership necessary to reverse negative trends in filmgoing and the state of theaters, not sufficiently promoting national film production and the construction of national film culture via festivals and other film presentations, and not working to update outdated legal and administrative procedures.

These issues became critically important with the advent of the COVID-19 pandemic beginning in early 2020, which, as elsewhere, had severe negative effects on all aspects of the Moroccan film industry: film and television productions were interrupted, film distribution and exhibition plummeted, foreign productions in Morocco were suspended or canceled, film festivals were annulled, and so on. There were calls from across the sector for government aid to help the industry survive, but this was slow in coming and only involved small amounts. In at least one area, however, the CCM responded with a positive and very successful program, putting online a large corpus of Moroccan films, watchable from across the globe.[50]

2 How will television and other home viewing systems and internet access affect Moroccan cinema? To what extent will we begin to see in Morocco, as we are seeing in some other countries, a splintering and growing division within national populations fostered by social media and individualized viewing, rather than the family or group practices that are characteristic of television and theatergoing?

3 Related to both of these issues are questions having to do with the role of the state in promoting cultural practices and behavior that promote free expression, social cohesion, artistic creativity, and progressive attitudes.

Epilogue/επίλογος

As I look back on my roughly two decades of research on Moroccan cinema and the Moroccan film industry, I return to the parallel I drew with the *Odyssey* in my first article on the subject, where my final words suggested that the Moroccan filmmaker might, "after reuniting with his audience for a time, ... set off on a new long voyage" (Dwyer 2002, 359).

Now, as we attempt to take stock of Moroccan cinema's development over these past two decades—and it took Odysseus about that much time to return home to Ithaca after leaving for the war in Troy—we should recall that Odysseus was, like many Moroccan filmmakers, persistent, dedicated, and sharp-witted. How else could he (and they) have endured such an extended and hazardous voyage, survived its many ordeals and challenges, and succeeded, finally, in reuniting with Penelope, the privileged domestic audience, and in assuming an eminent place at home?

Homer's *Odyssey* ends with the successful return home. Yet continuing success is never assured, and what happens to Odysseus afterward is a subject for speculation. Some stories have Odysseus leaving Ithaca, marrying again, and finding new audiences away from home; others have him leading a full life in Ithaca and dying only of old age, as prophesied by the seer Tiresias; and still others find him unhappy back in Ithaca or even not returning to Ithaca at all.[51]

Yet another story sees Odysseus unintentionally slain by Telegonus, the son he fathered with the magician goddess Circe. In a playful spirit, yet with no small amount of foreboding, we might imagine this slaying of Odysseus (the father and master copy) as the act of a son so much in his father's image (like a pirated copy or a smaller home-screen version) that he is able to push his progenitor aside and replace him.

(And let me propose one final act for Odysseus's journey, as we finish writing this text in the midst of the COVID-19 pandemic: how useful Odysseus might be today if he remodeled for our world the feat he performed in the *Iliad* when, before embarking on his long odyssey, he succeeded in having Apollo end the plague that the god had visited upon the Greeks.)

Which of these scripts—or others yet to be written—Moroccan filmmakers will bring to the screen, whether that screen will be a public or private one, and how creative activity will be culturally and societally embedded and expressed are impossible to know at this stage. In addition, today's Moroccan film industry and its filmmakers (mostly men but with a growing number of women) have been so nurtured by images from all over the world and have spent so much time in so many different places that distinctions between home and abroad, between Morocco and elsewhere, have become unsettled. In this sense, and in many others as well, Moroccan filmmakers have much in common with their global counterparts, embarked as they all are on an always uncertain and risky journey, on an odyssey that inevitably links the Moroccan industry's fate to that of the world film industry as a whole.

Notes

1 That first writing on Moroccan cinema was a paper presented at the 1999 conference of the Middle East Studies Association, Washington, DC, which led to the 2002 publication cited here.

2 See, for example, Jin (2020); Larkin (2008); Nagib (2003). See Mette Hjort's (2005) study of New Danish Cinema for a thought-provoking discussion of the challenges of "small nation" cinemas in a global context. Hjort argues, "What is needed, then, is not only a more general understanding of the place of small filmmaking nations in a global film culture but also a series of detailed case studies focusing on the way in which state policies, the workings of particular civil societies, and the contributions of key individuals combine at a given moment to reconfigure the networks and dynamics of cultural circulation" (33).

3 The Moroccan Film Center (CCM) publishes an annual summary of developments in the film sector, *Bilan cinématographique*. Citations will simply be in the form (*Bilan* year, page number). In the early 1980s, Morocco's 251 theaters were attended by 45 million spectators—the highest totals ever reached—yet by 2009, attendance was under 3 million and the number of theaters had fallen to fifty, with seventy-four screens. By 2018 attendance was below 1.5 million and the number of theaters down to sixty-five, increasingly concentrated in the three cities of Casablanca, Marrakesh, and Tangier and of which sixty were digitally equipped (*Bilan* 2018, 61). The growing concentration of cinemas in these three cities followed investment in these areas by the French company Megarama, starting in 2002 in Casablanca—the company's first investment on the African continent. As of 2018, of the sixty-five screens in Morocco, forty-seven are in the three cities (*Bilan* 2018, 61), with eight new screens opened by Megarama in Tangier in 2016. More than ten Moroccan cities with a population greater than 300,000 have no cinemas at all. Although varying somewhat, total receipts have remained relatively steady over the past decade through 2018, rising from 68 million dirhams in 2009 (*Bilan* 2011, 20) to 74 million in 2015 (*Bilan* 2016, 59), and then decreasing to just over 71 million in 2018 (*Bilan* 2018, 61).

4 For 2004–2012, see EuroMed Audiovisuel (2013, 92). There were twenty-four in 2014 (*Bilan* 2014, 3–4), twenty-eight in 2015 (*Bilan* 2015, 4–5), twenty-four in 2016 (*Bilan* 2016, 5), thirty-one in 2017 (*Bilan* 2017, 13–14), and thirty in 2018 (*Bilan* 2018, 3–4).

5 For 2017 figures, see *Bilan* (2017, 48); for 2018, see *Bilan* (2018, 54).

6 "Conformément à l'article 4 du cahier des charges du CCM ... (Cahier des charges du Centre Cinématographique Marocain accessible au http://www.ccm.ma)" (EuroMed Audiovisuel 2013, 95).

7 Among them Farida Belyazid, Mustapha Derkaoui, Jilali Ferhati, Abdelkader Lagtaa, Nabyl Lahlou, Hakim Noury, and Muhammad Abderrahman Tazi—all of whom have now made at least five films. Several have made in the neighborhood of ten films each.

8 Following current usage in Morocco, the term "Amazigh" is used in this chapter, rather than "Berber."

9 The 2001–2005 figure comes from the Moroccan film critic Muhammad Bakrim, cited in Zyad (2007).

10 For example, Narjiss Nejjar's *Les Yeux Secs* (2002), Yasmine Kassari's *L'Enfant endormi* (2004, which won the Best Film award at the 2005 National Film Festival), and Laïla Marrakchi's top-grossing and very controversial *Marock* (2005).

11 For a discussion of two Moroccan film comedies, and the role of comedy in Moroccan cinema to that time, see Dwyer (2004b); for a study of Moroccan crime films, see Smolin (2013).

12 There has been controversy over these increasing numbers, with some arguing that this is a sign of the sector's vitality, others saying that the administrative requirement has led to churning out mediocre films just to fulfill the requirement.

13 For an optimistic prognosis for Amazigh filmmaking, see Idtnaine (2008).

14 "Un fonds du CCM de 15 millions de dirhams va être alloué spécifiquement pour soutenir la production de documentaires de la culture hassanie et sahraouis" (Pauline 2015).

15 For more detailed information on filmmaker demographics, themes, and genres, with reference to specific films in the various categories, see Dwyer (2011); for an exploration of the work of women filmmakers from Morocco and other Maghreb countries, see Martin (2011); for a fuller discussion of Moroccan documentary, see Dwyer (2020); and for a look at Moroccan and Maghrebian documentary from a feminist perspective, see Van de Peer (2012). For the figures on documentary film funding outside the Hassani project, see *Bilan* (2018, 37).

16 Film festivals are important in the film industry as venues in which films can gain national and transnational recognition, which in turn enhances their marketability and profitability. Films are often rushed to be completed in order to meet festival deadlines. At the same time, such films may or may not be part of promoting a national or transnational cinema project.

17 In 2017 there were sixty-seven festivals, of which forty-eight received financial support from the Aid Commission; in 2018, sixty-seven of eighty-five festivals received such support, to the amount of 37 million dirhams (*Bilan* 2017, 61; 2018, 70–71).

18 See Bouhmouch and Terrass (2017). For the FIDADOC use of film caravans, see *Hespress* (2019).

19 "Les contraintes auxquelles fait face la pratique de l'écriture cinématographique au vu des limites qui empêchent le développement d'une critique efficiente à la suite de l'absence presque totale des supports écrits et audiovisuels spécialisés qui permettent de propager la culture cinématographique" (see Association des critik 2011).

20 A list can be found at EuroMed Audiovisuel (2013, 143–144).

21 The other nations are Argentina, Belgium, Canada, Spain, France, the United Kingdom, Italy, Portugal, and Syria (CCM n.d.).

22 As one line producer for Nabil Ayouch's *Whatever Lola Wants* stated, "nine weeks of shooting in Casablanca cost only slightly more than nine days filming in New York" (see Hopewell 2006).

23 With regard to numbers of films, in 2018, for example, Morocco welcomed the filming of seventeen features, eight shorts, and sixteen television series, as well as many advertising clips, télévision reports, and so on (*Bilan* 2018, 22–29).

24 EuroMed Audiovisuel (2013, 126–129), Moroccan films abroad.

25 "Pour les films marocains et arabes en général, le marché européen reste extrêmement fermé" (EuroMed Audiovisuel 2013, 129).

26 Moroccan feature films won twenty-seven prizes in fifty-five foreign festivals in 2014 (*Bilan* 2014, 22–24), twelve prizes in thirty-three festivals in 2015 (*Bilan* 2015, 58, 62–63), sixteen prizes in forty-five festivals in 2016 (*Bilan* 2016, 72), twenty-five prizes in eighty-nine festivals in 2017 (*Bilan* 2017, 67, 74–75), and thirty prizes in eighty festivals in 2018 (*Bilan* 2018, 75, 80–91).

27 Another symptom of international attention devoted to Moroccan cinema is a three-year project, Transnational Moroccan Cinema, funded by the Arts and Humanities Research Council (UK) and led by Profs. Will Higbee of the University of Exeter (UK) and Florence Martin, Goucher College, Baltimore, Maryland. The project, which began in 2016, "analyses the rise of Moroccan cinema over the last two decades from relative obscurity to a position where it is arguably now amongst the most important national cinemas within Africa and the Arab world" (see the project website at http://moroccancinema.exeter.ac.uk/en/). The project also provides some fellowships for Moroccans working in the film sector.

28 "Quand vous êtes en France ou en Espagne, la présence du cinéma national est obligatoire. On ne peut pas dire que sur les quatre ou cinq projets présentés, il n'y a pas un seul qui soit valable. . . . Le panorama du film marocain fait aussi défaut. . . . Si on continue à ce rythme, l'année prochaine ce n'est pas la peine d'inviter des Marocains. Ce sera un festival international fait au Maroc et financé en grande partie par le Maroc" (*Le Matin* 2016).

29 In 2018, 12 million dirhams of a total festival support of 33 million dirhams was awarded to the FIFM, exactly twice as much as its nearest competitor, the Festival National du Film (*Bilan* 2018, 66).

30 "Est-ce qu'il s'agit d'un fond pour soutenir l'effort de guerre? Les créateurs sont libres et doivent l'être" (Pauline 2015).

31 "L'état de crise à tous les niveaux de la chaîne cinématographique: dans les salles, dans la distribution, dans la qualité des films, dans la précarité des métiers, dans la lourdeur des démarches administratives et des autorisations, dans le dysfonctionnement du Fonds de Soutien, dans la promotion et la visibilité de la production cinématographique aussi bien au niveau national qu'à l'international" (*Menara* 2016).

32 "Décisions unilatérales de la Direction du Centre Cinématographique Marocain qui portent des coups graves et douloureux au développement du cinéma national et tendent à stopper son élan."

33 "L'exclusion, injustifiée et très préjudiciable au cinéma national, des films marocains du dernier FIFM"; "l'exclusion de la CNPF de toutes les manifestations cinématographiques et commissions professionnelles."

34 "Maintenir la production cinématographique nationale à plus de 20 films par an. Défendre la liberté d'expression et de création. . . . Trouver les moyens nécessaires pour une diffusion nationale de nos films. . . . Œuvrer . . . en vue d'une meilleure organisation du secteur de l'industrie du cinéma, de l'audiovisuel et du spectacle vivant. . . . Création d'un organisme adéquat pour la diffusion de nos films sur le plan international" (CNPF 2017).

35 "Memorandum pour une structuration de la cinematographie nationale conforme aux aspirations du royaume et aux attentes de ses populations"

36 "Manquer de vision cohérente susceptible de contribuer au développement et à la défense de la culture nationale. Au lieu d'être à l'écoute des professionnels du secteur, elles s'arrogent au contraire le droit de réglementer et de légiférer sans concertation réelle avec eux" (3).

37 "Noureddine Saïl est un monsieur du cinéma. C'est le créateur de la Fédération des ciné-clubs, c'est lui les émissions de radio et de télé qui ont fait les belles heures de la critique de cinéma. Il est aussi l'initiateur des films à la télévision. Il a encouragé un cinéma de valeur, en pensant à la fois à la quantité et à la qualité" (Savage 2016).

38 A broad sample of these tributes can be found in a special issue (a "dossier hommage") devoted to Sail of the Moroccan magazine *Telquel*, December 18, 2020.

39 "Nous estimons, en toute rationalité et honnêteté . . . que la responsabilité de la régression du cinéma national et la détérioration des conditions du travail dans le secteur incombent entièrement au directeur CCM, unique gestionnaire et ordonnateur du centre et des fonds et budgets qui en dépendent. . . . C'est bien la politique du directeur . . . qui a conduit le cinéma national à l'état de crise avancée qui l'asphyxie aujourd'hui." "Depuis sa nomination, il y a plus de quatre ans, le directeur a totalement négligé les intérêts du cinéma national, se concentrant sur deux préoccupations essentielles: parcourir le monde pour se pavaner dans les festivals de cinéma, et le tournage de films étrangers au Maroc pour faire travailler ses propres sociétés de prestation de services" (Quid 2018).

40 Bouhmouch, who was born in Casablanca, grew up in Rabat, and was a student at San Diego State University, is not afraid to court controversy, as he did in crossing one of the clear red lines by attending the Western Sahara International Film Festival, which took place in the refugee camp of Dakhla in October 2013 and where he presented *My Makhzen & Me*. Aware that he would be attacked by many Moroccans for this act, he has put on his blog a statement titled "Why I'm a Moroccan Standing with the Sahrawi People," where he says, "My presence in the festival is a show of solidarity with the Sahrawi *people*, not with the Polisario. I can never agree with any entity that has used or uses violence as a mean of resistance" (Bouhmouch 2013, emphasis in original).

41 Bouhmouch describes filming *Amussu* without CCM authorization: "The *muqaddim* [village head who acts as government representative] reacts quite quickly to our presence in the village. This basically just means that we have to plan better to avoid him. The muqaddim doesn't have the right to arrest us, but if the muqaddim spots us, he could call the gendarmes who have the power to stop us and confiscate our equipment. Knowing that there are gendarmes 15 minutes away from the village where we're shooting, we avoid as much as we can him spotting us. If he does spot us,

we know we have 15 minutes to hide in a house somewhere, which isn't very difficult to do when the entire community is supporting the movement and the movement is producing the film" (Jiang 2019).

42 For a broad examination of films with this theme, see Bahmad (2019).

43 Morocco World News 2015. The film led to physical threats against both the filmmaker and members of the cast, particularly against Loubna Abidar, who played the role of a prostitute and who, for her own safety, moved from Morocco to France. Ayouch had already faced a similar problem with his earlier film *One Minute Less in the Sun* (2003), when it was ruled unsuitable for screening unless several scenes were shortened or cut. The filmmaker refused, and the film was not allowed in the theaters. The case of Ayouch's films is particularly striking given that his earlier film, *Ali Zaoua* (2000), had been a great popular and critical success, gained some international commercial distribution and many festival awards, and was also awarded the prize for best film at the Sixth National Film Festival in Marrakesh in 2001.

44 "Les Marocains ne peuvent pas financer des médias qui vont provoquer leur démembrement et des déviations de leurs enfants" (Savage 2016).

45 "Pourquoi Fatima et Mohamed sortent ensemble s'ils ne sont pas mariés," "Pourquoi y a-t-il un bar dans votre scénario," "Pourquoi la danse? Ça ne fait pourtant pas partie de la culture marocaine," "Ne touchez pas au mariage, laissez la tradition marocaine tranquille" (Savage 2016).

46 After five months of stalemate following elections in October 2016, agreement was reached in March 2017 on the formation of a new coalition government where the prime minister would remain in the hands of the PJD (with PJD member Saad Eddin El Othmani replacing Abdallah Benkirane), but five other political parties would share in governmental positions (Le Rassemblement national des indépendants, RNI; Le Mouvement populaire, MP; L'Union constitutionnelle, UC; L'Union socialiste des forces populaires, USFP; and Le Parti pour le progrès et du socialisme, PPS). In this situation, the new minister of culture and communication, from 2017–2019, was Muhammad Laaraj, a member of the Popular Movement party, which was founded in 1958 and had its historical roots in rural Amazigh communities.

47 "La théorie de l'art propre a encore de beaux jours devant elle!" (Ouamer-Ali 2018). On this incident, see also Lévy (2018). For a discussion of clean art with regard to a theatrical production—a 2013 Moroccan adaptation of Eve Ensler's *Vagina Monologues*—see Reihaye (2013). For a broad assessment of the role of the PJD and the impact of its notion of clean art on Moroccan cultural production, see Graiouid and Belghazi (2013).

48 The study was carried out by the international firm Valyans Consulting and is available at the CCM's website.

49 Hicham Lasri is perhaps the best known of the many Moroccan filmmakers who make films without CCM approval—he made four films independently before his fifth, *Headbang Lullaby*, was awarded Aid Fund support, and several of his films have won international awards. He distributes much of his film work via social media.

50 Starting at the end of March 2020 and lasting into early 2021, the CCM put several series of films online, and by mid-June 2020 these films had been seen by almost half

a million viewers in 101 countries (APA 2020). By the end of 2020, the CCM had put online some one hundred full-length fiction films and documentaries that were seen by more than a million viewers, ending with a series of four films in homage to the actor and former minister of culture Touria Jabrane and then six short films made by well-known filmmakers (Hakim Belabbes, Faouzi Bensaidi, Tala Hadid, Muhammad Mouftakir, and others), filmed with cell phones and directly addressing matters related to the COVID-19 pandemic (press release, CCM, https://www.ccm.ma/actualite-1799).

51 These last two scenarios are seen, respectively, in Alfred Lord Tennyson's poem "Ulysses" and in Constantine Cavafy's poem "Ithaca," both of which are discussed in Mendelsohn (2017, 190–195).

References

Abu-Lughod, Lila. 2005. *Dramas of Nationhood: The Politics of Television in Egypt*. Chicago: University of Chicago Press.

Achebe, Chinua. 1977. "An Image of Africa." *Massachusetts Review* 18 (4): 782–794.

Acland, Charles R. 2003. *Screen Traffic: Movies, Multiplexes, and Global Culture*. Durham, NC: Duke University Press.

Adams, Vincanne, Michelle Murphy, and Adele E. Clarke. 2009. "Anticipation: Technoscience, Life, Affect, Temporality." *Subjectivity* 28 (1): 246–265.

Adejunmobi, Moradewun. 2016. "Introduction: African Science Fiction." *Cambridge Journal of Postcolonial Literary Inquiry* 3 (3): 265–272.

Adichie, Chimamanda Ngozi. 2009. "The Danger of a Single Story." TED, July. https://www.ted.com/talks/chimamanda_ngozi_adichie_the_danger_of_a_single_story?

Adorno, Theodor. 1975. "Culture Industry Reconsidered." *New German Critique* 6: 12–19.

African Futures: Four Interdisciplinary Festivals. 2015. Johannesburg Programme Poster. Goethe-Institut. https://issuu.com/goethejoburg/docs/africanfutures_a2poster_r1_cmyk_lor.

Ahmad, Ali Nobil. 2010. "Is There a Muslim World?" *Third Text* 24 (1): 1–9.

Ahmed, Asad Ali. 2009. "Spectres of Macaulay: Blasphemy, the Indian Penal Code and Pakistan's Postcolonial Predicament." In *Censorship in South Asia: Cultural Regulation from Sedition to Seduction*, edited by Raminder Kaur and William Mazzarella, 172–205. Bloomington: Indiana University Press.

Ahmed, Nazneen. 2014. "The Poetics of Nationalism: Cultural Resistance and Poetry in East Pakistan/Bangladesh, 1952–71." *Journal of Postcolonial Writing* 50 (3): 256–268.

Ahmed, Sara. 2006. *Queer Phenomenology: Orientations, Objects, Others*. Durham, NC: Duke University Press.

Ahram Online. 2013. "African Film Enjoys Rare Cannes Outing." May 20. http://english.ahram.org.eg/NewsContent/5/32/71872/Arts—Culture/Film/African-film-enjoys-rare-Cannes-outing.aspx.

Akdim, Youssef. 2012. "Maroc: L'art et la manière forte." Jeune Afrique, June 25. https://www.jeuneafrique.com/140890/culture/maroc-l-art-et-la-mani-re-forte/.

Akomfrah, John, dir. 1986. *Handsworth Songs* [film]. London: Black Audio Film Collective.

Allen, Robert, and Douglas Gomery. 1985. *Film History: Theory and Practice*. New York: Knopf.

Al-Maswari, Hizaa'. 2004. Friday sermon at Al-Hadda Mosque, early February. Tape transcript and translation by Steven C. Caton. Sana'a, Yemen.

Anderson, Reynaldo, and Charles E. Jones, eds. 2016. *Afrofuturism 2.0: The Rise of Astro-Blackness*. Lanham, MD: Lexington.

Annamalai, E. 2004. "Nativization of English in India and Its Effect on Multilingualism." *Journal of Language and Politics* 3 (1): 151–162.

Anonymous. n.d. Felix Films [printed brochure]. London: Sana'a.

APA. 2020. "Maroc: Plus de 485.000 visionnages complets provenant de 101 pays enregistrés sur les serveurs du ccm." June 12. http://apanews.net/mobile/uneInterieure.php?id=4941044.

Appadurai, Arjun. 1986. "Introduction: Commodities and the Politics of Value." In *The Social Life of Things: Commodities in Cultural Perspective*, edited by Arjun Appadurai, 3–63. Cambridge: Cambridge University Press.

Appel, Hannah. 2012. "Offshore Work: Oil, Modularity, and the How of Capitalism in Equatorial Guinea." *American Ethnologist* 39 (4): 692–709.

Armbrust, Walter. 1996. *Mass Culture and Modernism in Egypt*. Cambridge: Cambridge University Press.

Ascheid, Antje. 1997. "Speaking Tongues: Cinema as Cultural Ventriloquism." *Velvet Light Trap* 40 (fall): 32–41.

Askew, Kelly, and Richard R. Wilk, eds. 2002. *The Anthropology of Media: A Reader*. Malden, MA: Blackwell.

Association des critik. 2011. "Communiqué." Cinemaroc, November 26. http://cinemaroc.wordpress.com/graphiques-expos/6780-2/.

Atwood, Blake. 2016. *Reform Cinema in Iran: Film and Political Change in the Islamic Republic*. New York: Columbia University Press.

Badger, Clarence C., dir. 1917. *Teddy at the Throttle*. Hollywood, CA: Keystone Studios.

Bahmad, Jamal. 2019. "Art of Peacebuilding Transitional Justice and Unfinished Reconciliation in Moroccan Cinema." In *Dialogic Configurations in Post-colonial Morocco: Rhetorical Conjectures in Arts, Culture and Politics*, edited by Najib Mokhtari, 167–180. Rabat, Morocco: International University of Rabat.

Bajoghli, Narges. 2019. *Iran Reframed: Anxieties of Power in the Islamic Republic*. Stanford, CA: Stanford University Press.

Balio, Tino, ed. 1985. *The American Film Industry*. Rev. ed. Madison: University of Wisconsin Press.

Balio, Tino. 1993. *Grand Design: Hollywood as a Modern Business Enterprise, 1930–1939*. Berkeley: University of California Press.

Bamzai, Kaveree. 2005. "Shakti Kapoor Caught in Sting Operation Offering Work in Bollywood for Sex." *India Today*, March 28. http://indiatoday.intoday.in/story/shakti-kapoor-caught-in-sting-operation-offering-work-in-bollywood-for-sex/1/194058.html.

Bamzai, Sandeep. 2009. "K Soap Queen Seeks a Fresh Lease of Life." Exchange4media, October 21. https://www.exchange4media.com/media-tv-news/guest-column-retrofitk-soap-queen-seeks-a-fresh-lease-of-life-36214.html.

Banks, Miranda J., Bridget Conor, and Vicki Mayer, eds. 2016. *Production Studies, the Sequel! Cultural Studies of Global Media Industries*. New York: Routledge.

Barrett, Diana. 2017. "Virtual Reality: A Funder's Perspective." *Immerse*, May 30. https://immerse.news/virtual-reality-a-funders-perspective-8ab369a1e063.

Batabyal, Somnath. 2012. *Making News in India: Star News and Star Ananda*. New Delhi: Routledge.

Bekolo, Jean-Pierre, dir. 2005. *Les Saignantes* [film]. Cameroon: Quartier Mozart Films.

Benjamin, Walter. 1969. *Illuminations: Essays and Reflections*. Translated by Harry Zohn. Edited by Hannah Arendt. New York: Schocken Books.

Benjamin, Walter. 1979. "A Small History of Photography." In *One-Way Street and Other Writings*, translated by Edmund Jephcott and Kingsley Shorter, 240–257. London: Verso.

Benveniste, Emile. 1971. "The Nature of Pronouns." In *Problems in General Linguistics*, translated by Mary Elizabeth Meek, 217–222. Coral Gables, FL: University of Miami Press.

Bernabo, Laurena Elizabeth Nelson. 2017. "Translating Identity: Norms and Industrial Constraints in Adapting *Glee* for Latin America." PhD diss., University of Iowa.

Berry, Chris. 2010. "What Is Transnational Cinema? Thinking from the Chinese Situation." *Transnational Cinemas* 1 (2): 111–127.

Berry, Chris, and Mary Farquhar. 2005. "Shadow Opera: Towards a New Archaeology of the Chinese Cinema." In *Chinese Language Film: Historiography, Poetics, Politics*, edited by Sheldon H. Lu and Emilie Yueh-yu Yeh, 27–51. Honolulu: University of Hawai'i Press.

Bielskyte, Monika. 2017. "Virtual Reality as Possibility Space." *Medium*, March 4. https://medium.com/@monikabielskyte/virtual-reality-as-possibility-space-24a8600a59ff.

Bilton, Nick. 2017. "Why Hollywood as We Know It Is Already Over." *Vanity Fair*, January 29. https://www.vanityfair.com/news/2017/01/why-hollywood-as-we-know-it-is-already-over.

Black, Shirley Temple. 1988. *Child Star: An Autobiography*. New York: Warner.

Bolter, Jay David, and Richard Grusin. 2000. *Remediation: Understanding New Media*. Cambridge, MA: MIT Press.

Bordwell, David. 2001. "Aesthetics in Action: *Kungfu*, Gunplay, and Cinematic Expressivity." In *At Full Speed: Hong Kong Cinema in a Borderless World*, edited by Esther C. M. Yau, 73–94. Minneapolis: University of Minnesota Press.

Bordwell, David. 2006. *The Way Hollywood Tells It: Story and Style in Modern Movies*. Berkeley: University of California Press.

Bordwell, David, Janet Staiger, and Kristin Thompson. 2003. *The Classical Hollywood Cinema: Film Style and Mode of Production to 1960*. London: Routledge.

Bordwell, David, and Kristin Thompson. 2008. *Film Art: An Introduction*. 8th ed. Boston: McGraw Hill.

Bosseaux, Charlotte. 2015. *Dubbing, Film and Performance: Uncanny Encounters*. Oxford: Peter Lang.

Bouhmouch, Nadir. 2013. "Why I'm a Moroccan Standing with the Sahrawi People." *Ciranda*, October 4. http://www.ciranda.net/?Why-I-m-a-Moroccan-Standing-with&lang=pt_br.

Bouhmouch, Nadir, and Elias Terrass. 2017. "The Rise and Fall of Moroccan Cinema." *Al Jazeera*, November 17. http://www.aljazeera.com/news/2017/10/rise-fall-moroccan-cinema-171015133631178.html.

Bould, Mark, ed. 2013. "Africa SF." Special issue, *Paradoxa* 25.

Bould, Mark. 2015. "African Science Fiction 101." *SFRA Review* 311: 11–18.

Bourdieu, Pierre. 1984. *Distinction: A Social Critique of the Judgment of Taste*. Translated by Richard Nice. Cambridge, MA: Harvard University Press.

Braudy, Leo. 2004. "Genre: The Conventions of Connection." In *Film Theory and Criticism: Introductory Readings*, 6th ed., edited by Leo Braudy and Marshall Cohen, 663–679. New York: Oxford University Press.

Bright, Jake. 2015. "Meet 'Nollywood': The Second Largest Movie Industry in the World." *Fortune*, June 24. http://fortune.com/2015/06/24/nollywood-movie-industry.

Brillhart, Jessica. 2016. "In the Blink of a Mind—Prologue." *Medium*, January 12. https://medium.com/the-language-of-vr/in-the-blink-of-a-mind-prologue-7864c0474a29.

Brooker, Will, and Deborah Jermyn, eds. 2003. *The Audience Studies Reader*. London: Routledge.

Brown, Adrienne Maree, and Walidah Imarisha, eds. 2015. *Octavia's Brood: Science Fiction Stories from Social Justice Movements*. Oakland, CA: AK Press.

Brown, Wendy. 2005. *Edgework: Critical Essays on Knowledge and Politics*. Princeton, NJ: Princeton University Press.

Burt, Richard. 1994. *The Administration of Aesthetics: Censorship, Political Criticism, and the Public Sphere*. Minneapolis: University of Minnesota Press.

Busch, Anita. 2015. "'Midnight Rider' Director Randall Miller Issues Statement from Jail—Updated." *Deadline*, March 20. https://deadline.com/2015/03/randall-miller -midnight-rider-accepts-responsibility-accident-1201396236/.

Busch, Anita. 2017a. "Paramount Pictures Launching First Virtual Reality Movie The-ater." *Deadline*, December 20. http://deadline.com/2017/12/paramount-pictures-first -ever-virtual-reality-movie-theater-with-top-gun-3d-1202209276/.

Busch, Anita. 2017b. "Sarah Jones Family v. CSX: Local Manager Charley Baxter's Big Reveal." *Deadline*, July 15. https://deadline.com/2017/07/midnight-rider-sarah-jones -csx-trial-location-manager-testimony-charley-baxter-1202129595/.

Butcher, Melissa. 2003. *Transnational Television, Cultural Identity and Change: When STAR Came to India*. New Delhi: Sage.

Caldwell, John Thornton. 2008. *Production Culture: Industrial Reflexivity and Critical Practice in Film and Television*. Durham, NC: Duke University Press.

Carroll, Noël. 2016. "Art Appreciation." *Journal of Aesthetic Education* 50 (4): 1–14.

Carstens, Delphi, and Mer Roberts. 2009. "Protocols for Experiments in African Science Fiction." *Scrutiny2: Issues in English Studies in Southern Africa* 14 (1): 79–94.

Casetti, Francesco. 2015. *The Lumière Galaxy: 7 Key Words for the Cinema to Come*. New York: New York University Press.

Caton, Steven C. 1999. *Lawrence of Arabia: A Film's Anthropology*. Berkeley: University of California Press.

Caton, Steven C. 2000. "The Sheik: Instabilities of Race and Gender in Transatlantic Popular Culture of the Early 1920s." In *Noble Dreams, Wicked Pleasures: Orientalism in America, 1870–1930*, edited by Holly Edwards, 99–117. Princeton, NJ: Princeton University Press.

CCM. n.d. "Traités de Coproduction." Accessed July 5, 2019. http://www.ccm.ma/traites -coproduction.

CCM. 2017. "Liste de coproductions." http://www.ccm.ma/docs/liste-cooperations -internationales.pdf.

Chakrabarty, Dipesh. 1999. "Nation and Imagination: The Training of the Eye in Bengali Modernity." *Topoi* 18, no. 1: 29–47.

Chakravartty, Paula, and Srirupa Roy. 2015. "Mr. Modi Goes to Delhi: Mediated Populism and the 2014 Indian Elections." *Television and New Media* 16 (4): 311–322.

Chan, Melanie. 2014. *Virtual Reality: Representations in Contemporary Media*. New York: Bloomsbury.

Chimurenga Chronic. 2016. "The Corpse Exhibition and Older Graphic Stories." August 14. http://www.chimurenga.co.za/archives/5123.

Chin, Zela. 2018. "Celluloid Ceiling" [video]. *Money Magazine*, March 30. http://news .tvb.com/programmes/moneymagazine/5abe9051e60383141ae5c928.

Chion, Michel. 1999. *The Voice in Cinema*. Edited and translated by Claudia Gorbman. New York: Columbia University Press.

Chowdhry, Angad. 2011. "MMS Scandals and Challenges to the Authority of News Mediation." In *Indian Mass Media and the Politics of Change*, ed. Somnath Batabyal, Angad Chowdhury, Meenu Gaur, and Matti Pohjonen, 122–139. New Delhi: Routledge.

Chuchu, Jim, dir. 2014. *Stories of Our Lives* [film]. Kenya: Nest Collective and Big World Cinema.

Chung, Hye Jean. 2011. "Spectral Bodies and Uncanny Effect: Cosmopolitan Anxieties in *Shutter*." *Spectator* 30 (1): 10–16.

Chung, Hye Jean. 2018. *Media Heterotopias: Digital Effects and Material Labor in Global Film Production*. Durham, NC: Duke University Press.

Clarke, David B., ed. 1997. *The Cinematic City*. New York: Routledge.

CNPF. 2017. "Communique de Presse Commun." March 15. https://www.cnpf.ma /communique-de-presse-commun/.

"The Code for Censorship of Films in Bangladesh." 1985. Government of the People's Republic of Bangladesh Ministry of Information Notification, Dhaka, November 16. http://bfcb.portal.gov.bd/sites/default/files/files/bfcb.portal.gov.bd/policies /7ed53658_63e5_4doc_afee_3dcd60e3a396/The%20Code%20for%20Censorship%20 of%20Films%20in%20Bangladesh%201985.pdf.

Coleman, E. Gabriella. 2010. "Ethnographic Approaches to Digital Media." *Annual Review of Anthropology* 39 (1): 487–505.

Collins, Samuel Gerald. 2008. *All Tomorrow's Cultures: Anthropological Engagements with the Future*. New York: Berghahn Books.

Comaroff, Jean, and John L. Comaroff. 1991. *Of Revelation and Revolution*, vol. 1: *Christianity, Colonialism, and Consciousness in South Africa*. Chicago: University of Chicago Press.

Comaroff, Jean, and John L. Comaroff. 2011. *Theory from the South: Or, How Euro-America Is Evolving toward Africa*. New York: Paradigm.

Copjec, Joan. 1994. *Read My Desire: Lacan against the Historicists*. Cambridge, MA: MIT Press.

Crittenden, Roger. 2006. *Fine Cuts: The Art of European Film Editing*. Boston: Focal.

Curtin, Michael. 2007. *Playing to the World's Biggest Audience: The Globalization of Chinese Film and TV*. Berkeley: University of California Press.

Curtin, Michael, and Kevin Sanson, eds. 2016. *Precarious Creativity: Global Media, Local Labor*. Oakland: University of California Press.

Dabashi, Hamid. 2001. *Close-Up: Iranian Cinema, Past, Present and Future*. London: Verso.

Dahya, Reza. 2018. "Afrofuturism, Sci-Fi and Why 'It Is a Radical Act for Black People to Imagine Having a Future.'" CBC Arts, January 30. http://www.cbc.ca/arts /exhibitionists/afrofuturism-sci-fi-and-why-it-is-a-radical-act-for-black-people-to -imagine-having-a-future-1.4510844.

Dancyger, Ken. 2007. *The Technique of Film and Video Editing: History, Theory, and Practice*. 4th ed. Oxford: Focal.

Dass, Manishita. 2015. *Outside the Lettered City: Cinema, Modernity, and the Public Sphere in Late Colonial India*. Delhi: Oxford University Press.

Davier, Lucile. 2014. "The Paradoxical Invisibility of Translation in the Highly Multilingual Context of News Agencies." *Global Media and Communication* 10 (1): 53–72.

Davila, Arlene. 2001. *Latinos, Inc.* Berkeley: University of California Press.

Decherney, Peter, and Blake Atwood, eds. 2015. *Iranian Cinema in a Global Context: Policy, Politics, and Form*. London: Routledge.

de Klee, Katie. 2016. "Jonathan Dotse Makes Virtual Reality Experiences in Accra." *Design Indaba*, July 18. http://www.designindaba.com/videos/interviews/jonathan-dotse -virtual-reality-accra.

Derné, Steve. 2000. *Movies, Masculinity, and Modernity: An Ethnography of Men's Movie-Going in India*. Westport, CT: Greenwood.

Dery, Mark. 1994. "Black to the Future: Interviews with Samuel R. Delany, Greg Tate, and Tricia Rose." In *Flame Wars: The Discourse of Cyberculture*, 179–222. Durham, NC: Duke University Press.

Diamandis, Peter, and Steven Kotler. 2012. *Abundance: The Future Is Better Than You Think*. New York: Free Press.

Dickey, Sara. 1993. *Cinema and the Urban Poor in South India*. Cambridge: Cambridge University Press.

Dickey, Sara. 1997. "Anthropology and Its Contributions to Studies of Mass Media." *International Social Science Journal* 153: 413–427.

Directors Guild of America. n.d. "The Founding of the Women's Steering Committee." Accessed May 23, 2018. https://www.dga.org/The-Guild/Committees/Diversity /Women/WSC-Founding-Video.aspx.

Doane, Mary Ann. 1980. "The Voice in the Cinema: The Articulation of Body and Space." *Yale French Studies* 60: 33–50.

Doane, Mary Ann. 2002. *The Emergence of Cinematic Time: Modernity, Contingency, the Archive*. Cambridge, MA: Harvard University Press.

Doane, Mary Ann. 2007. "The Indexical and the Concept of Medium Specificity." *Differences* 18 (1): 128–152.

Dodson, Michael S. 2005. "Translating Science, Translating Empire: The Power of Language in Colonial North India." *Comparative Studies in Society and History* 47 (4): 809–835.

Donoghue, Courtney Brannon. 2014. "Sony and Local-Language Productions: Conglomerate Hollywood's Strategy of Flexible Localization for the Global Film Market." *Cinema Journal* 53 (4): 3–27.

Doostdar, Alireza. 2019. "Hollywood Cosmopolitanisms and the Occult Resonance of Cinema." *Comparative Islamic Studies* 13 (1–2): 121–149.

Dorian, Marc, Lauren Putrino, and Alexa Valiente. 2014. "*Midnight Rider* Hairstylist Describes When Train Hit Her, Killed Fellow Crew Member." ABC News, October 31.

Dornfeld, Barry. 1998. *Producing Public Television, Producing Public Culture.* Princeton, NJ: Princeton University Press.

Drew, Bernard A. 2013. *Motion Pictures Series and Sequels: A Reference Guide.* Oxford: Routledge.

Ďurovičová, Nataša, and Kathleen Newman, eds. 2010. *World Cinemas, Transnational Perspectives.* New York: Routledge.

Dwoskin, Elizabeth, and Annie Gowen. 2018. "On WhatsApp, Fake News Is Fast, and Can Be Fatal." *Washington Post,* July 23. https://www.washingtonpost.com/business /economy/on-whatsapp-fake-news-is-fast-and-can-be-fatal/2018/07/23/a2dd7112-8ebf -11e8-bcd5-9d911c784c38_story.html.

Dwyer, Kevin. 1982. *Moroccan Dialogues: Anthropology in Question.* Baltimore: Johns Hopkins University Press.

Dwyer, Kevin. 2002. "Moroccan Filmmaking: A Long Voyage through the Straits of Paradox." In *Everyday Life in the Muslim Middle East,* edited by Donna Lee Bowen and E. A. Early, 349–359. Bloomington: Indiana University Press.

Dwyer, Kevin. 2004a. *Beyond Casablanca: M.A. Tazi and the Adventure of Moroccan Cinema.* Bloomington: Indiana University Press.

Dwyer, Kevin. 2004b. "Un pays, une décennie, deux comédies." In *Cinémas du Maghreb,* edited by Michel Serceau, 86–91. Cinemaction no. 111. Paris: Corlet.

Dwyer, Kevin. 2007. "Moroccan Cinema and the Promotion of Culture." *Journal of North African Studies* 12 (3): 277–286.

Dwyer, Kevin. 2011. "Morocco: A National Cinema with Large Ambitions." In *Film in the Middle East and North Africa: Creative Dissidence,* edited by J. Gugler, 325–338. Austin: University of Texas Press.

Dwyer, Kevin. 2020. "Family Resemblance: An Anthropologist Looks at Moroccan Documentary." In *Cinema of the Arab World: Contemporary Directions in Theory and Practice,* edited by T. Ginsberg and C. Lippard, 231–278. London: Palgrave Macmillan.

Dwyer, Rachel, and Christopher Pinney. 2001. *Pleasure and the Nation: The History, Politics, and Consumption of Public Culture in India.* New Delhi: Oxford University Press.

Dwyer, Rachel, and Jerry Pinto. 2011. *Beyond the Boundaries of Bollywood: The Many Forms of Hindi Cinema.* New Delhi: Oxford University Press.

Economist. 2011. "Africa Rising." December 3.

Eisenstein, Sergei. 1949. *Film Form: Essays in Film Theory.* New York: Harcourt, Brace and World.

Electric South. 2017. "Electric South Announces Participants for New Dimensions VR Lab." *Medium,* July 20. https://medium.com/@electric_south/electric-south -announces-participants-for-new-dimensions-vr-lab-a3b6bede76a8.

Elsaesser, Thomas. 2013. "Digital Cinema: Convergence or Contradiction?" In *The Oxford Handbook of Sound and Image in Digital Media,* edited by Carol Vernallis, Amy Herzog, and John Richardson. Oxford Handbooks. New York: Oxford University Press. doi:10.1093/oxfordhb/9780199757640.013.014.

Elsaesser, Thomas. 2019. "National, Transnational, and Intermedial Perspectives in Post-2008 European Cinema." In *Contemporary European Cinema: Crisis Narratives and Narratives in Crisis*, edited by Betty Kaklamanidou and Ana M. Corbalán, 20–36. London: Routledge.

Encounters. 2017. "Virtual Encounters: Programme." Twentieth Encounters South African International Documentary Festival. https://encounters.co.za/archived -programmes/.

Ernst & Young. 2018. *Re-imagining India's M&E Sector*. New Delhi: Federation of Indian Chambers of Commerce and Industry.

Eshun, Kodwo. 2003. "Further Considerations of Afrofuturism." *CR: The New Centennial Review* 3 (2): 287–302.

Eshun, Kodwo. 2004. "Untimely Meditations: Reflections on the Black Audio Film Collective." *Nka: Journal of Contemporary African Art* 19 (summer): 38–45.

Eshun, Kodwo. 2019. "To Win the War, You Fought It Sideways: Kojo Laing's *Major Gentl and the Achimota Wars*." In *We Travel the Space Ways: Black Imagination, Fragments, and Diffractions*, edited by Henriette Gunkel and Kara Lynch. Bielefeld: Transcript Verlag.

EuroMed Audiovisuel. 2013. "Projet de collecte de données statistiques sur les marchés cinématographiques et audiovisuels dans 9 pays méditerranéens. Monographies nationales: 2. Maroc." https://www.ebu.ch/files/live/sites/ebu/files/Publications/euromed _MA_report.pdf.

Expresso Show. 2017. "AFDA Students Produce South Africa's First VR Film" [video]. YouTube, November 23. https://www.youtube.com/watch?v=uTds-Q9cxC4.

Fabian, Johannes. 1983. *Time and the Other: How Anthropology Makes Its Object*. New York: Columbia University Press.

Fairservice, Don. 2001. *Film Editing: History, Theory and Practice—Looking at the Invisible*. Manchester: Manchester University Press.

Fanon, Frantz. 1967. *Black Skin, White Masks*. New York: Grove.

Fernandes, Leela. 2006. *India's New Middle Class: Democratic Politics in an Era of Economic Reform*. Minneapolis: University of Minnesota Press.

Ferrari, Chiara Francesca. 2011. *Since When Is Fran Drescher Jewish? Dubbing Stereotypes in The Nanny, The Simpsons, and The Sopranos*. Austin: University of Texas Press.

Ferrell, Jeff. 1993. *Crimes of Style: Urban Graffiti and the Politics of Criminality*. New York: Garland.

Fischer, Lucy. 1999. "Film Editing." In *A Companion to Film Theory*, edited by Toby Miller and Robert Stam, 64–83. Malden, MA: Blackwell.

Fischer, Michael M. J. 2004. *Mute Dreams, Blind Owls, and Dispersed Knowledges: Persian Poesis in the Transnational Circuitry*. Durham, NC: Duke University Press.

Flaherty, Robert J. 1922. "How I Filmed Nanook of the North." *World's Work*, October, 632–640.

Freud, Sigmund. (1919) 1955. "The 'Uncanny.'" In *An Infantile Neurosis and Other Works (1917–1919)*, vol. 17 of *The Standard Edition of the Complete Psychological Works of Sigmund Freud*, 219–252. London: Hogarth.

Friedkin, William, dir. 1971. *The French Connection*. New York: Twentieth Century Fox.

Friedkin, William. 2014. *The Friedkin Connection: A Memoir*. New York: HarperCollins.

Fritz, Ben. 2017. "The End of the Feature Film." *Wall Street Journal*, July 11. https://www
.wsj.com/articles/movie-whats-a-movie-1499787223.

Frosch, Jon. 2013. "Exclusive Interview: 'There Is a Place for Gays in Islam.'" France24,
September 5. https://www.france24.com/en/20130905-venice-film-festival-abdallah
-taia-gay-muslim-islam-homosexuality-morocco-arab-salvation-army.

Furstenau, Marc. 2018. "Film Editing, Digital Montage, and the 'Ontology' of Cinema."
Cinémas 28 (2–3): 29–49. doi: 10.7202/1067492ar.

Gal, Susan. 2015. "Politics of Translation." *Annual Review of Anthropology* 44: 225–240.

Ganti, Tejaswini. 1998. "Centenary Commemorations or Centenary Contestations?—
Celebrating a Hundred Years of Cinema in Bombay." *Visual Anthropology* 11 (4): 399–419.

Ganti, Tejaswini. 2012a. *Producing Bollywood: Inside the Contemporary Hindi Film Industry*. Durham, NC: Duke University Press.

Ganti, Tejaswini. 2012b. "Sentiments of Disdain and Practices of Distinction: Boundary-
Work, Subjectivity, and Value in the Hindi Film Industry." *Anthropological Quarterly*
85 (1): 5–43.

Ganti, Tejaswini. 2014. "The Value of Ethnography." *Media Industries Studies Journal* 1
(1): 16–20. doi:10.3998/mij.15031809.0001.104.

Ganti, Tejaswini. 2021. "Blurring the Boundaries between Hollywood and Bollywood:
The Production of Dubbed Films in Mumbai." In *Industrial Networks of Indian
Cinema: Shooting Stars, Shifting Geographies and Multiplying Media*, edited by Monika
Mehta and Madhuja Mukherjee, 208–221. London: Routledge.

Gaonkar, Dilip P., and Elizabeth Povinelli. 2003. "Technologies of Public Forms: Circulation, Transfiguration, Recognition." *Public Culture* 15 (3): 385–397.

Geertz, Clifford. 1973. *The Interpretation of Cultures: Selected Essays*. New York: Basic Books.

Gharbi, Neila. 2013. "Le cinéma marocain, un modèle à suivre?" *La Presse Magazine*,
February 17, 6–8.

Ghose, Bhaskar. 2005. *Doordarshan Days*. New Delhi: Penguin.

Giddens, Anthony. 1991. *Modernity and Self-Identity: Self and Society in the Late Modern
Age*. Stanford, CA: Stanford University Press.

Gilroy, Paul. 1994. *The Black Atlantic: Modernity and Double Consciousness*. Cambridge,
MA: Harvard University Press.

Ginsburg, Faye D. 1991. "Indigenous Media: Faustian Contract or Global Village?" *Cultural Anthropology* 6 (1): 92–112.

Ginsburg, Faye D., Lila Abu-Lughod, and Brian Larkin. 2002. *Media Worlds: Anthropology on New Terrain*. Berkeley: California University Press.

Gipson, Grace. 2019. "Creating and Imagining Black Futures through Afrofuturism."
In *#Identity: Hashtagging Race, Gender, Sexuality, and Nation*, edited by Abigail de
Kosnik and Keith P. Feldmann. Ann Arbor: University of Michigan Press.

Gitlin, Todd. 1994. *Inside Prime Time*. Rev. ed. London: Routledge.

Gleich, Joshua. 2019. "'Good Oriental Setting': Negotiating San Francisco Locations."
Velvet Trap 83 (spring): 18–31.

Gleich, Joshua, and Lawrence Webb, eds. 2019. *Hollywood on Location: An Industry History*. New Brunswick, NJ: Rutgers University Press.

Goethe-Institut South Africa. 2015. "New Dimensions: A Virtual Reality Exhibition." Issuu, October 19. https://issuu.com/goethejoburg/docs/virtualreality_dl_digital.

Goldstone, Brian, and Juan Obarrio, eds. 2016. *African Futures: Essays on Crisis Emergence, and Possibility*. Chicago: University of Chicago Press.

Gomery, Doug. 2005. *The Hollywood Studio System: A History*. London: British Film Institute.

Gopalan, Lalitha. 2001. "Indian Cinema." In *An Introduction to Film Studies*, 3rd ed., edited by Jill Nelmes, 359–388. London: Routledge.

Gopalan, Lalitha. 2003. *Cinema of Interruptions: Action Genres in Contemporary India*. Delhi: Oxford University Press.

Govil, Nitin. 2013. "Recognizing 'Industry.'" *Cinema Journal* 52, no. 3 (spring): 172–176.

Govil, Nitin. 2015a. "On Comparison." *Media Industries Studies Journal* 1 (3): 1–6. doi:10.3998/mij.15031809.0001.301.

Govil, Nitin. 2015b. *Orienting Hollywood: A Century of Film Culture between Los Angeles and Bollywood*. New York: New York University Press.

Graiouid, Said, and Taieb Belghazi. 2013. "Cultural Production and Cultural Patronage in Morocco: The State, the Islamists, and the Field of Culture." *Journal of African Cultural Studies* 25 (3): 261–274.

Gray, Mary L., and Siddharth Suri. 2019. *Ghost Work: How to Stop Silicon Valley from Building a New Global Underclass*. New York: Eamon Dolan Books.

Grosz, Elizabeth. 2004. *The Nick of Time: Politics, Evolution, and the Untimely*. Crows Nest, NSW: Allen and Unwin.

GSMA. 2017. "The Mobile Economy—Sub-Saharan Africa 2017." Global Systems for Mobile Communications Association. https://www.gsma.com/subsaharanafrica/resources/mobile-economy-2017-sub-saharan-africa-2017.

Guback, Thomas H. 1969. *The International Film Industry: Western Europe and America since 1945*. Bloomington: Indiana University Press.

Gunkel, Henriette, and Kara Lynch, eds. 2019. *We Travel the Space Ways: Black Imagination, Fragments, and Diffractions*. Bielefeld: Transcript Verlag.

Gunning, Tom. 2006. "The Cinema of Attraction[s]: Early Film, Its Spectator, and the Avant-Garde." In *The Cinema of Attractions: Reloaded*, edited by Wanda Strauven, 381–388. Amsterdam: Amsterdam University Press.

Guyer, Jane. 2007. "Prophecy and the Near Future: Thoughts on Macroeconomic, Evangelical, and Punctuated Time." *American Ethnologist* 34 (3): 409–421.

H24 Info. 2018. "Après le ras-le-bol des professionnels du cinéma, le CCM audité par Jettou." February 3. https://www.h24info.ma/culture/apres-ras-bol-professionnels-cinema-ccm-audite-jettou/.

Habermas, Jürgen. (1962) 1989. *The Structural Transformation of the Public Sphere: An Inquiry into a Category of Bourgeois Society*. Cambridge, MA: MIT Press.

Hanchard, Michael. 1999. "Afro-Modernity: Temporality, Politics, and the African Diaspora." *Public Culture* 11 (1): 245–268.

Hansen, Miriam. 1991. *Babel and Babylon: Spectatorship in American Silent Film*. Cambridge, MA: Harvard University Press.

Harari, Yuval Noah. 2017. *Homo Deus: A Brief History of Tomorrow*. New York: HarperCollins.

Hardt, Michael. 2007. Foreword to *The Affective Turn: Theorizing the Social*, edited by Patricia Ticineto Clough and Jean Halley, ix–xiii. Durham, NC: Duke University Press.

Harper, Graeme, and Jonathan Rayner, eds. 2010. *Cinema and Landscape: Film, Nation and Cultural Geography*. Bristol: Intellect.

Heidegger, Martin. (1927) 1962. *Being and Time*. Translated by John Macquarrie and Edward Robinson. New York: Harper.

Heidenreich-Seleme, Lien, and Sean O'Toole, eds. 2016. *African Futures: Thinking about the Future through Word and Image*. Bielefeld: Kerber.

Herbert, Daniel, Amanda D. Lotz, and Aswin Punathambekar. 2020. *Media Industry Studies*. Cambridge, UK: Polity.

Hespress. 2019. "FIDADOC d'Agadir: Des projections ambulantes de films dans plusieurs communes." May 31. https://fr.hespress.com/75038-fidadoc-dagadir-des-projections-ambulantes-de-films-dans-plusieurs-communes.html.

Higbee, Will, and Song Hwee Lim. 2010. "Concepts of Transnational Cinema: Towards a Critical Transnationalism in Film Studies." *Transnational Cinemas* 1 (1): 7–21.

Hirsch, Afua. 2013. "'This Is Not a Good Place to Live': Inside Ghana's Dump for Electronic Waste." *Guardian*, December 14. https://www.theguardian.com/world/2013/dec/14/ghana-dump-electronic-waste-not-good-place-live.

Hirsi, Bader Ben, dir. 2000. *The British Sheikh and the Yemeni Gentleman*. London: Felix Films.

Hirsi, Bader Ben. 2004. *A New Day in Old Sana'a* [script]. London: Felix Films.

Hirsi, Bader Ben, dir. 2005. *A New Day in Old Sana'a*. London: Felix Films.

Hjort, Mette. 2005. *Small Nation, Global Cinema: The New Danish Cinema*. Minneapolis: University of Minnesota Press.

Hjort, Mette, and Scott MacKenzie, eds. 2000. *Cinema and Nation*. London: Routledge.

Hoek, Lotte. 2010. "Unstable Celluloid: Film Projection and the Cinema Audience in Bangladesh." *BioScope: South Asian Screen Studies* 1 (1): 49–66.

Hoek, Lotte. 2014. *Cut-Pieces: Celluloid Obscenity and Popular Cinema in Bangladesh*. New York: Columbia University Press.

Hoek, Lotte. 2019. "Pictures on Paper: Censoring Cinematic Culture through the Bangladesh Film Club Act." *Terrain* 72. https://doi.org/10.4000/terrain.19361.

Holt, Jennifer, and Alisa Perren, eds. 2009. *Media Industries: History, Theory, and Method*. Malden, MA: Wiley-Blackwell.

Holt, Jennifer, and Alisa Perren. 2019. "Media Industries: A Decade in Review." In *Making Media: Production, Practices, and Professions*, edited by Mark Deuze and Mirjam Prenger, 31–43. Amsterdam: Amsterdam University Press.

Honwana, Alcinda. 2012. *The Time of Youth: Work, Social Change, and Politics in Africa*. Sterling, VA: Kumarian.

Hopewell, John. 2006. "'Morrywood' Lures More O'seas Prod'n." *Variety*, November 26.

Horkheimer, Max, and Theodor Adorno. (1944) 1989. "The Culture Industry: Enlightenment as Mass Deception." In *Dialectic of Enlightenment*, translated by John Cumming, 120–167. New York: Continuum.

Horst, Heather A., and Daniel Miller. 2012. *Digital Anthropology*. London: Berg.

Hughes, Stephen P. 2000. "Policing Silent Film Exhibition in Colonial South India." In *Making Meaning in Indian Cinema*, edited by Ravi S. Vasudevan, 39–64. New Delhi: Oxford University Press.

Hugo, Esthie. 2017. "Looking Forward, Looking Back: Animating Magic, Modernity and the African City-Future in Nnedi Okorafor's Lagoon." *Social Dynamics* 43 (1): 46–58.

Hull, Mathew. 2012. *Government of Paper: The Materiality of Bureaucracy in Urban Pakistan*. Berkeley: University of California Press.

Human Rights Watch. 2017. *The Red Lines Stay Red: Morocco's Reforms of Its Speech Laws*. https://www.hrw.org/report/2017/05/04/red-lines-stay-red/moroccos-reforms-its-speech-laws.

Hyde, Lewis. 2010. *Trickster Makes This World: Mischief, Myth and Art*. New York: Farrar, Straus and Giroux.

Idtnaine, Omar. 2008. "Le cinéma amazigh au Maroc: Éléments d'une naissance artistique." *Africultures*, October 19. http://africultures.com/le-cinema-amazigh-au-maroc-8117/.

Irvine, Judith. 1988. "When Talk Isn't Cheap: Language and Political Economy." *American Ethnologist* 16 (2): 248–267.

Jacobson, Brian R. 2015. *Studios before the System: Architecture, Technology, and the Emergence of Cinematic Space*. New York: Columbia University Press.

Jaikumar, Priya. 2006. *Cinema at the End of Empire: A Politics of Transition in Britain and India*. Durham, NC: Duke University Press.

Jayadeva, Sazana. 2018. "'Below English Line': An Ethnographic Exploration of Class and the English Language in Post-liberalization India." *Modern Asian Studies* 52 (2): 576–608.

Jedlowski, Alessandro. 2016. "Avenues of Participation and Strategies of Control: Video Film Production and Social Mobility in Ethiopia and Southern Nigeria." In *Production Studies, the Sequel! Cultural Studies of Global Media Industries*, edited by Miranda J. Banks, Bridget Conor, and Vicki Mayer, 175–186. New York: Routledge.

Jedlowski, Alessandro, and Giovanna Santanera, eds. 2015. *Lagos Calling: Nollywood e la reinvenzione del cinema in Africa*. Rome: Ariccia.

Jeffrey, Robin. 2000. *India's Newspaper Revolution: Capitalism, Politics, and the Indian-Language Press, 1977–99*. Delhi: Oxford University Press.

Jenkins, Henry. 2006. *Convergence Culture: Where Old and New Media Collide*. New York: New York University Press.

Jiang, Irene. 2019. "Silver and Water in Morocco: Q&A with Nadir Bouhmouch." *Roads and Kingdoms*, March 29. https://roadsandkingdoms.com/2019/silver-water-morocco-qa-nadir-bouhmouch/.

Jin, Dal Yong. 2020. *Transnational Korean Cinema: Cultural Politics, Film Genres, and Digital Technologies*. New Brunswick, NJ: Rutgers University Press.

Johnson, Scott. 2014a. "Exclusive Interview with Parents of 'Midnight Rider' Victim Sarah Jones." *Hollywood Reporter*, March 4. https://www.hollywoodreporter.com/news/midnight-rider-victim-sarah-jones-685846.

Johnson, Scott. 2014b. "A Train, a Narrow Trestle, and 60 Seconds to Escape: How Midnight Rider Victim Sarah Jones Lost Her Life." *Hollywood Reporter*, March 4. https://

www.hollywoodreporter.com/news/midnight-rider-accident-sarah-jones-death-gregg
-allman-685976.

Kaes, Anton, Nicholas Baer, and Michael Cowan. 2016. *The Promise of Cinema: German Film Theory, 1907–1933*. Oakland: University of California Press.

Kahiu, Wanuri, dir. 2009. *Pumzi* [film]. Kenya: Inspired Minority Pictures.

Kahiu, Wanuri, dir. 2018. *Rafiki* [film]. Kenya: Big World Cinema.

Kane, Selly Raby. 2017. *The Other Dakar*. MIT Open Documentary Lab _docubase. https://docubase.mit.edu/project/the-other-dakar/.

Kaplan, Robert D. 1994. "The Coming Anarchy: How Scarcity, Crime, Overpopulation, Tribalism, and Disease Are Rapidly Destroying the Social Fabric of Our Planet." *Atlantic Monthly*, February, 44.

Kar, Law. 2000. "The American Connection in Early Hong Kong Cinema." In *The Cinema of Hong Kong: History, Arts, Identity*, edited by Poshek Fu and David Desser, 44–70. Cambridge: Cambridge University Press.

Kaur, Raminder, and William Mazzarella, eds. 2009. *Censorship in South Asia: Cultural Regulation from Sedition to Seduction*. Bloomington: Indiana University Press.

Keil, Charlie, and Kristen Whissel. 2016. *Editing and Special/Visual Effects*. New Brunswick, NJ: Rutgers University Press.

Khan, Hassan N., David A. Hounshell, and Erica R. H. Fuchs. 2018. "Science and Research Policy at the End of Moore's Law." *Nature Electronics* 1 (January): 14–21. doi:10.1038/s41928-017-0005-9.

Kohli-Khandekar, Vanita. 2010. *The Indian Media Business*. New Delhi: Sage.

Kong, Travis. 2015. "Buying Sex as Edgework: Hong Kong Male Clients in Commercial Sex." *British Journal of Criminology* 56 (1): 105–122. doi:10.1093/bjc/azv040.

Kopp, Ingrid. 2017. "Who Is VR For?" *Immerse*, August 30. https://immerse.news/who-is
-vr-for-20b3f077a912.

Kottak, Conrad. 1990. *Prime-Time Society: An Anthropological Analysis of Television and Culture*. Belmont, CA: Wadsworth.

KPMG. 2017. *Media and Entertainment Industry Report: Media for the Masses: The Promise Unfolds*. New Delhi: Federation of Indian Chambers of Commerce and Industry.

Kracauer, Siegfried. (1947) 2004. *From Caligari to Hitler: A Psychological History of the German Film*. Rev. and expanded ed. Edited by Leonardo Quaresima. Princeton, NJ: Princeton University Press.

Kracauer, Siegfried. (1960) 1997. *Theory of Film: The Redemption of Physical Reality*. Princeton, NJ: Princeton University Press.

Kracauer, Siegfried. (1963) 1995. *The Mass Ornament: Weimar Essays*. Translated and edited by Thomas Y. Levin. Cambridge, MA: Harvard University Press.

Krauss, Rosalind. 1986. *The Originality of the Avant-Garde and Other Modernist Myths*. Cambridge, MA: MIT Press.

Kuhn, Annette. 1988. *Cinema, Censorship and Sexuality, 1909–1925*. London: Routledge.

Kuka, Hajooj, dir. 2018. *aKasha* [film]. Sudan: Big World Cinema.

LaDousa, Chaise. 2014. *Hindi Is Our Ground, English Is Our Sky: Education, Language, and Social Class in Contemporary India*. New York: Berghahn.

Lamont, Charles, dir. 1933. *Kid in Africa* [film]. Hollywood, CA: Educational Films.

Lamprakos, Michele. 2015. *Building a World Heritage City*. Surrey, UK: Ashgate.

Langford, Michelle. 2008. "Negotiating the Sacred Body in Iranian Cinema(s): National, Physical and Cinematic Embodiment in Majid Majidi's *Baran* (2002)." In *Negotiating the Sacred 2: Blasphemy and Sacrilege in the Arts*, edited by Elizabeth Burns Coleman and Maria Suzette Fernandes-Dias, 161–171. Canberra: ANU E Press.

Larkin, Brian. 2008. *Signal and Noise: Media, Infrastructure, and Urban Culture in Nigeria*. Durham, NC: Duke University Press.

Larsen, Mads. 2018. "Virtual Sidekick: Second-Person POV in Narrative VR." *Journal of Screenwriting* 9 (1): 73–83.

Lauzen, Martha M. 2018. "The Celluloid Ceiling: Behind-the-Scenes Employment of Women on the Top 100, 250, and 500 Films of 2017." San Diego, CA: Center for the Study of Women in Television and Film, San Diego State University. https:// womenintvfilm.sdsu.edu/wp-content/uploads/2018/01/2017_Celluloid_Ceiling _Report.pdf.

Lee, Benjamin, and Edward LiPuma. 2002. "Cultures of Circulation: The Imaginations of Modernity." *Public Culture* 14 (1): 191–213.

Lefebvre, Martin, and Marc Furstenau. 2002. "Digital Editing and Montage: The Vanishing Celluloid and Beyond." *Cinémas/Revue d'études cinématographiques* 13 (1–2): 69–107.

Le Matin. 2013. "Le nouveau souffle des ciné-clubs." October 21. https://lematin.ma /journal/2013/7e-art_le-nouveau-souffle-des-cine-clubs/189804.html.

Le Matin. 2016. "16e Festival international du film de Marrakech." December 6. https://lematin.ma/journal/2016/shinya-tsukamoto-le-plus-innovant-des-cineastes -independants-japonais/259364.html.

Lemov, Rebecca. 2015. "On Not Being There: The Data-Driven Body at Work and at Play." *Hedgehog Review* 17, no. 2 (summer). https://hedgehogreview.com/issues/the-body-in -question/articles/on-not-being-there-the-data-driven-body-at-work-and-at-play.

Lévi-Strauss, Claude. 1966. *The Savage Mind*. Chicago: University of Chicago Press.

Lévy, Noémie. 2018. "Une œuvre figurant le Kamasutra dans une main de Fatma censurée au Maroc." March 5. https://www.lefigaro.fr/arts-expositions/2018/03/05/03015 -20180305ARTFIG00263-une-oeuvre-figurant-le-kamasutra-dans-une-main-de-fatma -censuree-au-maroc.php.

Liang, Lawrence. 2011. "Media's Law: From Representation to Affect." *BioScope: South Asian Screen Studies* 2 (1). 23–40.

Lindsay, Jennifer. 2005. *Speaking the Truth: Speech on Television in New Order Indonesia*. ARI Working Paper Series, no. 34. Singapore: Asia Research Institute.

Lo, Dennis. 2016. "From Experiencing Life to Life Experiences: Location Shooting Practices in Chinese and Taiwanese New Wave Cinemas." In *Production Studies, the Sequel! Cultural Studies of Global Media Industries*, edited by Miranda J. Banks, Bridget Conor, and Vicki Mayer, 187–195. New York: Routledge.

Lois, Jennifer. 2001. "Peaks and Valleys: The Gendered Emotional Culture of Edgework." *Gender and Society* 15 (3): 381–406. doi:10.1177/089124301015003004.

Lukács, Gabriella. 2010. *Scripted Affects, Branded Selves: Television, Subjectivity, and Capitalism in 1990s Japan*. Durham, NC: Duke University Press.

Lyng, Stephen. 1990. "Edgework: A Social Psychological Analysis of Voluntary Risk Taking." *American Journal of Sociology* 95 (4): 851–886.

Lyng, Stephen, ed. 2004. *Edgework: The Sociology of Risk-Taking*. New York: Routledge.

Maghress. 2017. "Plan d'action 2017–2021 du Ministère de la Culture." August 7. https://www.maghress.com/fr/lopinion/56648.

Mahon, Maureen. 2000. "The Visible Evidence of Cultural Producers." *Annual Review of Anthropology* 29 (1): 467–492.

Majumdar, Rochona. 2012. "Debating Radical Cinema: A History of the Film Society Movement in India." *Modern Asian Studies* 46 (3): 731–767.

Makhulu, Anne-Maria, Beth A. Buggenhagen, and Stephen Jackson, eds. 2010. *Hard Work, Hard Times: Global Volatility and African Subjectivities*. Berkeley: University of California Press.

Mankekar, Purnima. 1999. *Screening Culture, Viewing Politics: An Ethnography of Television, Womanhood, and Nation in Postcolonial India*. Durham, NC: Duke University Press.

Manovich, Lev. 2001. *The Language of New Media*. Cambridge, MA: MIT Press.

Martin, Florence. 2011. *Screens and Veils: Maghrebi Women's Cinema*. Bloomington: Indiana University Press.

Martin, Sylvia J. 2012a. "Of Ghosts and Gangsters: Capitalist Cultural Production and the Hong Kong Film Industry." *Visual Anthropology Review* 28 (1): 32–49.

Martin, Sylvia J. 2012b. "Stunt Workers and Spectacle: Ethnography of Physical Risk in Hollywood and Hong Kong." In *Film and Risk*, edited by Mette Hjort, 97–114. Detroit: Wayne State University Press.

Martin, Sylvia J. 2017. *Haunted: An Ethnography of the Hollywood and Hong Kong Media Industries*. New York: Oxford University Press.

Mashigo, Mohale. 2018. "Afrofuturism Is Not for Africans Living in Africa." *Johannesburg Review of Books*, October 1. https://johannesburgreviewofbooks.com/2018/10/01/afrofuturism-is-not-for-africans-living-in-africa-an-essay-by-mohale-mashigo-excerpted-from-her-new-collection-of-short-stories-intruders.

Mavhunga, Clapperton Chakanesta, ed. 2017. *What Do Science, Technology, and Innovation Mean from Africa?* Cambridge, MA: MIT Press.

Mayer, Vicki. 2011. *Below the Line: Producers and Production Studies in the New Television Economy*. Durham, NC: Duke University Press.

Mayer, Vicki, Miranda J. Banks, and John T. Caldwell. 2009. *Production Studies: Cultural Studies of Media Industries*. London: Routledge.

Mazumdar, Ranjani. 2007. *Bombay Cinema: An Archive of the City*. Minneapolis: University of Minnesota Press.

Mazumdar, Ranjani. 2009. "That Elusive Object of Cinema." *Television and New Media* 10 (1): 105–107.

Mazzarella, William. 2004. "Culture, Globalization, Mediation." *Annual Review of Anthropology* 33 (1): 345–367.

Mazzarella, William. 2013. *Censorium: Cinema and the Open Edge of Mass Publicity*. Durham, NC: Duke University Press.

Mbeki, Moeletsi. 2009. *Architects of Poverty: Why African Capitalism Needs Changing*. Johannesburg: Picador Africa.

Mbeki, Thabo. 1998. "The African Renaissance: South Africa and the World." Address at United Nations University, Tokyo, Japan, April 9.

Mbembe, Achille. 2016a. "Africa in the New Century." *Massachusetts Review* 57 (1): 91–104.

Mbembe, Achille. 2016b. "Africa in Theory." In *African Futures: Essays on Crisis Emergence, and Possibility*, edited by Brian Goldstone and Juan Obarrio, 212–230. Chicago: University of Chicago Press.

McKernan, Brian. 2005. *Digital Cinema: The Revolution in Cinematography, Postproduction, and Distribution*. New York: McGraw Hill.

Mehta, Monika. 2011. *Censorship and Sexuality in Bombay Cinema*. Austin: University of Texas Press.

Mehta, Nalin. 2008. *India on Television: How Satellite News Channels Have Changed the Way We Think and Act*. New Delhi: HarperCollins.

Menara. 2016. "Cinéma: Les producteurs marocains appellent à un 'plan de sauvetage.'" October 27. https://www.menara.ma/fr/article/cinema-les-producteurs-marocains -appellent-a-un-plan-de-sauvetage.

Mendelsohn, Daniel. 2017. *An Odyssey*. New York: Knopf.

Metz, Christian. 1982. *The Imaginary Signifier: Psychoanalysis and the Cinema*. Bloomington: Indiana University Press.

Meyer, Birgit. 2015. *Sensational Movies: Video, Vision, and Christianity in Ghana*. Berkeley: University of California Press.

Millar, Kathleen. 2014. "The Precarious Present: Wageless Labor and Disrupted Life in Rio de Janeiro, Brazil." *Cultural Anthropology* 29 (1): 32–53. doi:10.14506/ca29.1.04.

Miller, Jade L. 2016. *Nollywood Central*. London: Palgrave.

Miller, Randall, dir. 2014. *Midnight Rider*. Savannah, GA: Film Allman LLC, Unclaimed Freight Productions.

Miller, Toby, Nitin Govil, John McMurria, Richard Maxwell, and Ting Wang. 2005. *Global Hollywood 2*. London: British Film Institute.

Mitter, Partha. 2007. *The Triumph of Modernism: India's Artists and the Avant-Garde, 1922–47*. London: Reaktion.

Miyao, Daisuke. 2013. *The Aesthetics of Shadow: Lighting and Japanese Cinema*. Durham, NC: Duke University Press.

Mokammel, Tanvir. 2013. "The Short-Film Movement." In *The Bangladesh Reader: History, Culture, Politics*, edited by Meghna Guhathakurta and Willem van Schendel, 390–393. Durham, NC: Duke University Press.

Monteiro, Anjali, and K. P. Jayasankar. 1994. "The Spectator-Indian: An Exploratory Study in the Reception of News." *Cultural Studies* 8 (1): 162–182.

Montfort, Patrice. 2002. "Nigeria: Le raz-de-marée de la home video." *Africultures* 45 (February): 47–48.

Mookherjee, Nayanika. 2007. "The 'Dead and Their Double Duties': Mourning, Melancholia, and the Martyred Intellectual Memorials in Bangladesh." *Space and Culture* 10 (2): 271–291.

Morocco World News. 2015. "Morocco Bans Nabil Ayouch's Film on Prostitution." May 25. https://www.moroccoworldnews.com/2015/05/159322/morocco-bans-nabil -ayouchs-film-on-prostitution/.

Mottahedeh, Negar. 2008. *Displaced Allegories: Post-revolutionary Iranian Cinema*. Durham, NC: Duke University Press.

MPAA. 2016. *Theatrical Market Statistics 2016*. Los Angeles: Motion Picture Association of America.

Mudimbe, V. Y. 1988. *The Invention of Africa*. Bloomington: Indiana University Press.

Mugane, John. 2015. *The Story of Swahili*. Athens: Ohio University Press.

Mulvey, Laura. 1975. "Visual Pleasure and Narrative Cinema." *Screen* 16 (3): 6–18.

Muñoz, José Esteban. 2009. *Cruising Utopia: The Then and There of Queer Futurity*. New York: New York University Press.

Murch, Walter. 2001. *In the Blink of an Eye*. 2nd ed. Los Angeles: Silman-James.

Myers, Fred. 2001. "Introduction." In *The Empire of Things: Regimes of Value and Material Culture*, edited by Fred Myers, 3–61. Santa Fe, NM: School of American Research Press.

Nader, Laura. 1974. "Up the Anthropologist: Perspectives Gained from Studying Up." In *Reinventing Anthropology*, edited by Dell Hymes, 284–311. New York: Vintage.

Naficy, Hamid. 1993. *Making of Exile Culture: Iranian Television in Los Angeles*. Minneapolis: University of Minnesota Press.

Naficy, Hamid. 2012a. *A Social History of Iranian Cinema*, vol. 3: *The Islamicate Period, 1978–1984*. Durham, NC: Duke University Press.

Naficy, Hamid. 2012b. *A Social History of Iranian Cinema*, vol. 4: *The Globalizing Era, 1984–2010*. Durham, NC: Duke University Press.

Nagib, Lúcia, ed. 2003. *The New Brazilian Cinema*. London: I. B. Tauris.

Nagib, Lúcia, Chris Perriam, and Rajinder Dudrah. 2012. *Theorizing World Cinema*. London: I. B. Tauris.

Nakassis, Constantine, and Amanda Weidman. 2018. "Vision, Voice, and Cinematic Presence." *Differences* 29 (3): 107–136.

Nanni, Giordano. 2012. *The Colonisation of Time: Ritual, Routine and Resistance in the British Empire*. Manchester: Manchester University Press.

Ndhlovu, Finex. 2018. *Language, Vernacular Discourse and Nationalisms: Uncovering the Myths of Transnational Worlds*. Cham, Switzerland: Palgrave Macmillan.

Neale, Steve, and Murray Smith, eds. 1998. *Contemporary Hollywood Cinema*. New York: Routledge.

Nelson, Alondra. 2002. "Introduction: Future Texts." *Social Text* 20 (2): 1–15.

Ngũgĩ wa Thiong'o. 2009. *Something Torn and New: An African Renaissance*. New York: Basic Civitas Books.

Ninan, Sevanti. 2007. *Headlines from the Heartlands: Reinventing the Hindi Public Sphere*. New Delhi: Sage.

Nyawalo, Mich. 2016. "Afro-futurism and the Aesthetics of Hope in Bekolo's *Les Saignantes* and Kahiu's *Pumzi*." *Journal of the African Literature Association* 10 (2): 209–221.

Okorafor, Nnedi. 2019. "Africanfuturism Defined." *Nnedi's Wahala Zone Blog*. October 19. http://nnedi.blogspot.com/2019/10/africanfuturism-defined.html.

Oldham, Gabriella. 2012. *First Cut 2: More Conversations with Film Editors*. Berkeley: University of California Press.

Onuoha, Debbie. 2016. "Economies of Waste: Rethinking Waste along the Korle Lagoon." *Journal for Undergraduate Ethnography* 6 (1): 1–16.

Orpen, Valerie. 2003. *Film Editing: The Art of the Expressive*. London: Wallflower.

Ortner, Sherry. 2010. "Access: Reflections on Studying Up in Hollywood." *Ethnography* 11 (2): 211–233.

Ortner, Sherry B. 2013. *Not Hollywood: Independent Film at the Twilight of the American Dream*. Durham, NC: Duke University Press.

Ottaviani, Jacopo. 2015. "E-waste Republic." *Al Jazeera Interactives*. https://interactive .aljazeera.com/aje/2015/ewaste/index.html.

Ouamer-Ali, Tarik. 2018. "La théorie de l'art propre a encore de beaux jours devant elle!" Founoune Art Média, March 15. https://www.founoune.com/index.php/theorie-de -lart-propre-a-de-beaux-jours-devant-khadija-tnana-maroc/.

Page, David, and William Crawley. 2001. *Satellites over South Asia: Broadcasting Culture and the Public Interest*. New Delhi: Sage.

Pak-Shiraz, Nacim. 2011. *Shi'i Islam in Iranian Cinema: Religion and Spirituality in Film*. London: I. B. Tauris.

Pandian, Anand. 2012. "The Time of Anthropology: Notes from a Field of Contemporary Experience." *Cultural Anthropology* 27 (4): 547–571.

Pandian, Anand. 2015. *Reel World: An Anthropology of Creation*. Durham, NC: Duke University Press.

Parikka, Jussi. 2015. *A Geology of Media*. Minneapolis: University of Minnesota Press.

Park, Young-a. 2015. *Unexpected Alliances: Independent Filmmakers, the State, and the Film Industry in Post-authoritarian South Korea*. Stanford, CA: Stanford University Press.

Pauline. 2015. "Comment défendre le documentaire marocain?" *Telquel*, January 9. http://telquel.ma/2015/01/09/comment-defendre-documentaire-marocain_1429500.

Peterson, Mark. 2010. "Getting the News in New Delhi: Newspaper Literacies in an Indian Mediascape." In *The Anthropology of News and Journalism: Global Perspectives*, edited by S. Elizabeth Bird, 168–182. Bloomington: Indiana University Press.

Phillips, Rasheedah. 2015. *Black Quantum Futurism: Theory and Practice*, vol. 1. Philadelphia: Afrofuturist Affair/House of Future Sciences Book.

Picket, Mallory. 2017. "Action at a Distance: Why Hollywood's Most Thrilling Scenes Are Now Orchestrated Thousands of Miles Away." *New York Times Magazine*, May 7, 66.

Pinney, Christopher. 1992. "Future Travel: Anthropology and Cultural Distance in an Age of Virtual Reality; Or, A Past Seen from a Possible Future." *Visual Anthropology Review* 8 (1): 38–55.

Povinelli, Elizabeth. 2001. "Translation in a Global Market: Editor's Note." *Public Culture* 13 (1): ix–xi.

Powdermaker, Hortense. 1950. *Hollywood, the Dream Factory*. Boston: Little, Brown.

Powdermaker, Hortense. 1962. *Copper Town: Changing Africa*. New York: Harper and Row.

Powdermaker, Hortense. 1966. *Stranger and Friend: The Way of an Anthropologist*. New York: Norton.

Prakash, Gyan. 1999. *Another Reason: Science and the Imagination of Modern India*. Princeton, NJ: Princeton University Press.

Prasad, M. Madhava. 1998. *The Ideology of the Hindi Film: A Historical Construction*. Delhi: Oxford University Press.

Punathambekar, Aswin. 2013. *From Bombay to Bollywood: The Making of a Global Media Industry*. New York: New York University Press.

Punathambekar, Aswin, with Rohit Chopra and Manan Ahmed. 2012. "A Conversation." *Seminar: A Country of Our Own*, no. 632 (April).

Punathambekar, Aswin, with Shanti Kumar. 2012. "Television at Large." *South Asian History and Culture* 3 (4): 483–490.

Quayson, Ato. 1997. *Strategic Transformations in Nigerian Writing: Orality and History in the Work of Rev. Samuel Johnson, Amos Tutuola, Wole Soyinka and Ben Okri*. Bloomington: Indiana University Press.

Quid. 2018. "L'Impasse du cinéma national vue par le CNPF." November 21. https://www .quid.ma/culture/l%E2%80%99impasse-du-cinema-national-vue-par-le-cnpf.

Qureshi, Irna. 2010. "Destigmatising Star Texts—Honour and Shame among Muslim Women in Pakistani Cinema." In *South Asian Media Cultures: Representations, Audiences and Contexts*, edited by Shakuntala Banaji, 181–198. London: Anthem.

Rabinow, Paul. 2008. *Marking Time: On the Anthropology of the Contemporary*. Princeton, NJ: Princeton University Press.

Rahman, Harisur. 2017. "Bollywoodization or Ghettoization? The Bangladeshi Dream Factory Is in Disarray." *Studies in South Asian Film and Media* 8 (2): 109–123.

Rajadhyaksha, Ashish. 1990. "Beaming Messages to the Nation." *Journal of Arts and Ideas* 19: 33–52.

Rajadhyaksha, Ashish. 1999. "The Judgement: Re-forming the Public." *Journal of Arts and Ideas* 32–33: 131–150.

Rajadhyaksha, Ashish. 2009. *Indian Cinema in the Time of Celluloid: From Bollywood to the Emergency*. Bloomington: Indiana University Press.

Rajadhyaksha, Ashish. 2012. "A Theory of Cinema That Can Account for Indian Cinema?" In *Theorizing World Cinema*, edited by Lúcia Nagib, Chris Perriam, and Rajinder Dudrah, 45–59. London: I. B. Tauris.

Rajagopal, Arvind. 2001. *Politics after Television: Hindu Nationalism and the Reshaping of the Public in India*. Cambridge: Cambridge University Press.

Raju, Zakir Hossain. 2013. "Rickshaw Puller's Dreams: From a Cultural History to an Economic Geography of Bangladesh Popular Cinema." In *Bangladesh's Changing Media Landscape: From State Control to Market Forces*, edited by Brian Shoesmith and Jude William Genilo, 79–95. Bristol: Intellect.

Rancière, Jacques. 2007. *The Future of the Image*. London: Verso.

Rancière, Jacques. 2010. *Dissensus: On Politics and Aesthetics*. London: Bloomsbury Academic.

Rao, Ursula. 2010. *News as Culture: Journalistic Practices and the Remaking of Indian Leadership Traditions*. New York: Berghahn.

Rashiduzzaman, M. 1994. "The Liberals and the Religious Right in Bangladesh." *Asian Survey* 34 (11): 974–990.

Ray, Satyajit. (1976) 2005. *Our Films, Their Films*. New Delhi: Orient Longman.

Reisz, Karel, and Gavin Millar. 2010. *The Technique of Film Editing*. 2nd ed. Burlington, MA: Focal.

re:publica. 2017. "re:publica 2017—New Dimensions: Virtual Reality from Africa" [video]. YouTube. https://www.youtube.com/watch?v=mHZQNPyh-Sg.

Rerhaye, Narjis. 2013. "'Dialy,' une pièce de théâtre qui fait de la résistance." *Libération*, January 19. https://www.libe.ma/Dialy--une-piece-de-theatre-qui-fait-de-la-resistance_a34324.html.

Rheingold, Howard. 1991. *Virtual Reality*. London: Secker and Warburg.

Rhodes, John David, and Elena Gorfinkel, eds. 2011. *Taking Place: Location and the Moving Image*. Minneapolis: University of Minnesota Press.

Robertson, James C. 1993. *The Hidden Cinema: British Film Censorship in Action, 1913–1965*. London: Routledge.

Robiadek, Katherine M. 2016. "Worlding versus Worldview: Heidegger's Thinking on Art as a Critique of German Historicism." *Monatshefte* 108 (3): 383–394.

Rodrigues, Usha M., and Maya Ranganathan. 2015. *Indian News Media: From Observer to Participant*. Delhi: Sage.

Rofel, Lisa. 1994. "Yearnings: Televised Love and Melodramatic Politics in Contemporary China." *American Ethnologist* 21 (4): 700–722.

Rogez, Olivier. 2019. "L'industrie cinématographique marocaine, modèle pour l'Afrique sub-saharienne." RFI, April 8. http://www.rfi.fr/emission/20190409-industrie-cinematographique-marocaine-modele-afrique-sub-saharienne.

Roitman, Janet. 2013. *Anti-crisis*. Durham, NC: Duke University Press.

Rony, Fatimah Tobing. 1996. *The Third Eye: Race, Cinema, and Ethnographic Spectacle*. Durham, NC: Duke University Press.

Rossoukh, Ramyar. 2014. "An Anthropology of the Iranian Film Industry: The Making of *The Willow Tree*." PhD diss., Harvard University.

Rosten, Leo. 1941. *Hollywood: The Movie Colony, the Movie Makers*. New York: Harcourt, Brace.

Roth-Ey, Kristin. 2011. *Moscow Prime Time: How the Soviet Union Built the Media Empire That Lost the Cold War*. Ithaca, NY: Cornell University Press.

Roxborough, Scott. 2019. "Netflix's Global Reach Sparks Dubbing Revolution: 'The Public Demands It.'" *Hollywood Reporter*, August 13. https://www.hollywoodreporter.com/news/netflix-s-global-reach-sparks-dubbing-revolution-public-demands-it-1229761.

Roy, Srirupa. 2007. *Beyond Belief: India and the Politics of Postcolonial Nationalism*. Durham, NC: Duke University Press.

Rubin, Peter. 2014. "The Inside Story of Oculus Rift and How Virtual Reality Became Reality." *Wired*, May 20. https://www.wired.com/2014/05/oculus-rift-4/.

Ruby, Jay. 2005. "The Last 20 Years of Visual Anthropology: A Critical Review." *Visual Studies* 20 (2): 159–170.

Sabur, Seuty. 2013. "Post Card from Shahabag." ISA *E-symposium for Sociology*. http://www.isa-sociology.org/uploads/files/EBul-Sabur-March2012.pdf.

Sadana, Rashmi. 2012. *English Heart, Hindi Heartland: The Political Life of Literature in India*. Berkeley: University of California Press.

Sadr, Hamid. 2006. *Iranian Cinema: A Political History*. London: I. B. Tauris.

Safety for Sarah. n.d.a. "Safety Assistance." Accessed May 23, 2018. https://www.safetyforsarah.com/pledge-to-sarah.

Safety for Sarah. n.d.b. "Safety for Sarah End Credits Program." Accessed May 23, 2018. https://www.safetyforsarah.com/safety-for-sarah-explanation.

Salt, Barry. 2009. *Film Style and Technology: History and Analysis*. London: Starword.

Samaddar, Ranabir. 2002. *Paradoxes of the Nationalist Time: Political Essays on Bangladesh*. Dhaka: University Press Limited.

Savage, Thomas. 2016. "Qui veut la peau du Centre cinématographique marocain?" *Telquel*, November 7. https://telquel.ma/2016/11/07/veut-peau-du-centre-cinematographique-marocain_1522372.

Schaefer, Eric. 1999. *"Bold! Daring! Shocking! True!": A History of Exploitation Films, 1919–1959*. Durham, NC: Duke University Press.

Schatz, Thomas. 1981. *Hollywood Genres: Formulas, Filmmaking and the Studio System*. New York: Random House.

Schatz, Thomas. 2014. "Film Studies, Cultural Studies, and Media Industries Studies." *Media Industries Studies Journal* 1 (1): 39–43. doi:10.3998/mij.15031809.0001.108.

Schiller, Jakob. 2015. "Inside the Hellscape Where Our Computers Go to Die." *Wired*, April 23. https://www.wired.com/2015/04/kevin-mcelvaney-agbogbloshie.

Schwab, Klaus. 2016. *The Fourth Industrial Revolution*. Geneva: World Economic Forum.

Scott, Allen J. 2005. *On Hollywood: The Place, the Industry*. Princeton, NJ: Princeton University Press.

Sherouse, Perry. 2015. "Russian Presence in Georgian Film Dubbing: Scales of Inferiority." *Journal of Linguistic Anthropology* 25 (2): 215–229.

Shih, Willy, and Henry McGee. 2015. "Hollywood on the Yellow Sea." *Atlantic*, December, 45–51.

Simon, Jonathan. 2005. "Edgework and Insurance in Risk Societies: Some Notes on Victorian Lawyers and Mountaineers." In *Edgework: The Sociology of Risk-Taking*, edited by Stephen Lyng, 203–226. New York: Routledge.

Simonite, Tom. 2016. "Moore's Law Is Dead. Now What?" *MIT Technological Review*, May 13. https://www.technologyreview.com/s/601441/moores-law-is-dead-now-what.

Sinclair, Kamal. 2017. "Making a New Reality: Furthering Equality in Emerging Media." *Immerse*, October 31. https://immerse.news/making-a-new-reality-625b78aeb1c5.

Singhal, Arvind, and Everett Rogers. 2001. *India's Communication Revolution: From Bullock Carts to Cyber Marts*. New Delhi: Sage.

Smith, Stacy L., Marc Choueiti, and Katherine Pieper. 2018. "Inclusion in the Director's Chair? Gender, Race and Age of Directors across 1,100 Films from 2007 to 2017." Annenberg Inclusion Initiative. http://assets.uscannenberg.org/docs/inclusion-in-the-directors-chair-2007-2017.pdf.

Smolin, Jonathan. 2013. *Moroccan Noir: Police, Crime, and Politics in Popular Culture*. Bloomington: Indiana University Press.

Sobchack, Vivian. 1992. *The Address of the Eye: A Phenomenology of Film Experience*. Princeton, NJ: Princeton University Press.

Spitulnik, Debra. 1993. "Anthropology and Mass Media." *Annual Review of Anthropology* 22: 293–315.

Spitulnik, Debra. 1997. "The Social Circulation of Media Discourse and the Mediation of Communities." *Journal of Linguistic Anthropology* 6 (2): 161–187.

Srinivas, Lakshmi. 2016. *House Full: Indian Cinema and the Active Audience*. Chicago: University of Chicago Press.

Srinivas, S. V. 2000. "Is There a Public in the Cinema Hall?" *Framework: The Journal of Cinema and Media* 42 (summer). https://www.frameworknow.com/vol-42.

Srinivas, S. V. 2008. "Missing in the Original: Twin Dragons Remade in India." *Journal of Moving Image*, no. 7.

Standing, Guy. 2011. *The Precariat: The New Dangerous Class*. London: Bloomsbury Academic.

Stasik, Michael, Valerie Hänsch, and Daniel Mains. 2020. "Temporalities of Waiting in Africa." *Critical African Studies* 12 (1): 1–9.

Sunstrum, Pamela Phatsimo. 2013. "Afro-Mythology and African Futurism: The Politics of Imagining and Methodologies for Contemporary Creative Research Practices." *Paradoxa* 25.

Swartz, Lana. 2017. "Blockchain Dreams: Imagining Techno-economic Alternatives after Bitcoin." In *Another Economy Is Possible: Culture and Economy in a Time of Crisis*, edited by Manuel Castells, 82–105. Malden, MA: Polity.

Szeto, Mirana M., and Yun-chung Chen. 2013. "To Work or Not to Work: The Dilemma of Hong Kong Film Labor in the Age of Mainlandization." *Jumpcut* 55 (fall). http://ejumpcut.org/archive/jc55.2013/SzetoChenHongKong/.

Szklarski, Cassandra. 2015. "William Hurt Reflects on Crew Member's Death." *Canadian Press*, June 25. https://globalnews.ca/news/2074737/william-hurt-reflects-on-crew-members-death.

Tanvir, Kuhu. 2015. "Through the Digital Peephole: LSD and the Grammar of Transparency." *South Asian Popular Culture* 13 (1): 31–45.

Tapper, Richard, ed. 2002. *The New Iranian Cinema: Politics, Representation and Identity*. London: I. B. Tauris.

Thomas, Rosie. 2013. *Bombay before Bollywood: Film City Fantasies*. New Delhi: Orient Blackswan.

Thompson, E. P. 1967. "Time, Work, and Discipline in Industrial Capitalism." *Past and Present* 38: 56–97.

Thompson, Tade. 2018. "Please Stop Talking about the 'Rise' of African Science Fiction." *Literary Hub*, September 19. https://lithub.com/please-stop-talking-about-the-rise-of-african-science-fiction/.

Thussu, D. K. 2009. *News as Entertainment: The Rise of Global Infotainment*. New Delhi: Sage.

Tourabi, Abdellah. 2014. "Conservateurs contre modernistes: La guerre des valeurs." *Telquel*, July 13. https://telquel.ma/2014/07/13/conservateurs-contre-modernistes-guerre-valeurs_1409257.

Traube, Elizabeth. 1991. *Dreaming Identities*. Boulder, CO: Westview.

Tribeca Film Festival. 2017. "Virtual Arcade: The Other Dakar." https://tribecafilm.com/filmguide/other-dakar-2017.

Udupa, Sahana. 2015. *Making News in Global India: Media, Publics, Politics*. Cambridge: Cambridge University Press.

Urban, Greg. 2001. *Metaculture: How Culture Moves through the World*. Minneapolis: University of Minnesota Press.

Urry, John. 1990. *The Tourist Gaze: Leisure and Travel in Contemporary Societies*. London: Sage.

Van de Peer, Stefanie. 2012. "A Transnational Feminist Rereading of Post–Third Cinema Theory: The Case of Maghreb Documentary." *Journal of African Cinemas* 4 (2): 175–189.

Varzi, Roxanne. 2009. *Warring Souls: Youth, Media, and Martyrdom in Post-revolution Iran*. Durham, NC: Duke University Press.

Vasudev, Aruna. 1978. *Liberty and License in Indian Cinema*. New Delhi: Vikas.

Vasudevan, Ravi. 2010. *The Melodramatic Public: Film Form and Spectatorship in Indian Cinema*. Delhi: Permanent Black.

Vint, Sherryl, ed. 2016. *The Futures Industry*. 2nd ed. Vashon Island, WA: Paradoxa.

Vitali, Ali, Kasie Hunt, and Frank Thorp V. 2018. "Trump Referred to Haiti and African Nations as 'Shithole' Countries." NBC News, January 12. https://www.nbcnews.com /politics/white-house/trump-referred-haiti-african-countries-shithole-nations-n836946.

Vitali, Valentina, and Paul Willemen, eds. 2006. *Theorising National Cinema*. London: British Film Institute.

Vivarelli, Nick. 2015. "Sheikhdoms Spawn 'Star Wars': UAE Earns Reputation as International Hub for State-of-the-Art Productions." *Variety*, December 4, 109. http://variety .com/2015/film/spotlight/uae-earns-rep-as-international-hub-for-hi-tech-productions -1201652058/.

Waldrop, M. Mitchell. 2016. "The Chips Are Down for Moore's Law." *Nature* 530: 144–147. https://www.nature.com/news/the-chips-are-down-for-moore-s-law-1.19338.

Walzer, Graham. 2017. "Inside IMAX's Big Bet to Rule the Future of VR." *Wired*, January 18. https://www.wired.com/2017/01/imax-vr-theaters/.

Wasko, Janet. 2003. *How Hollywood Works*. London: Sage.

Weber, Max. (1922) 1958. "Science as a Vocation." In *From Max Weber: Essays in Sociology*, edited by H. H. Gerth and C. W. Mills, 129–156. New York: Oxford University Press.

Weber, Max. 1968. *Economy and Society: An Outline of Interpretive Sociology*, vol. 3, edited by Guenthr Roth and Claus Wittich, 956–1003. New York: Bedminster.

Welsch, Tricia. 2013. *Gloria Swanson: Ready for Her Closeup*. Jackson: University of Mississippi Press.

Wilder, Gary. 2009. "Untimely Vision: Aimé Césaire, Decolonization, Utopia." *Public Culture* 21 (1): 101–140.

Williams, Alan, ed. 2002. *Film and Nationalism*. New Brunswick, NJ: Rutgers University Press.

Williams, Raymond. (1974) 2003. *Television: Technology and Cultural Form*. London: Fontana.

Williams, Raymond. 1977. *Marxism and Literature*. Oxford: Oxford University Press.

Wilson, Craig. 2015. "The New Dimensions Virtual Reality Exhibition Will Blow Your Mind." *Stuff Magazine South Africa*, October 29. https://stuff.co.za/2015/10/29/the -new-dimensions-virtual-reality-exhibition-will-blow-your-mind.

Wilson-Goldie, Kaelen. 2007. "Training Morocco's Next Generation of Filmmakers." *Daily Star* (Lebanon), December 15. https://www.dailystar.com.lb/Culture/Art/2007 /Dec-15/115673-training-moroccos-next-generation-of-filmmakers.ashx.

Woolard, Kathryn, and Bambi G. Schieffelin. 1994. "Language Ideology." *Annual Review of Anthropology* 23: 55–82.

Yamato, Jen. 2014. "'Midnight Rider' Producer Made Controversial Remarks about Local Filming Days before Sarah Jones Death." *Deadline*, April 23. https://deadline.com/2014/04/midnight-rider-sarah-jones-death-producer-cbgb-717573.

Young, S. M., James J. Gong, and Wim A. Van der Stede. 2008. "The Business of Making Movies." *Strategic Finance* 89 (8): 26–32.

Zaloom, Caitlin. 2004. "The Productive Life of Risk." *Cultural Anthropology* 19 (3): 365–391.

Zeydabadi-Nejad, Saeed. 2010. *The Politics of Iranian Cinema: Film and Society in the Islamic Republic.* London: Routledge.

Zyad, Nouri. 2007. "La réglementation du secteur cinématographique s'impose à Ouarzazate." *Libération* (Casablanca), April 17. https://fr.allafrica.com/stories/200704170712.html.

Contributors

STEVEN C. CATON is the Khalid bin Abdullah bin Abdulrahman Al Saud Professor of Contemporary Arab Studies in the Anthropology Department at Harvard University. His fieldwork has focused on the Arabian Peninsula, where he has conducted research on Yemeni tribal poetry and the politics of water use and management in the Republic of Yemen and the Gulf (Abu Dhabi, Oman, and Saudi Arabia). His book *Lawrence of Arabia: A Film's Anthropology* (1999), as well as essays on media production, and on the imagery of T. E. Lawrence and its ideological ramifications, served as the foundation for his thinking about film industries as anthropological objects of study.

JESSICA DICKSON is a doctoral candidate in the Department of African and African American Studies at Harvard University. Her dissertation research focuses on the film-service sector of Cape Town's film industry and South Africa's changing position within global Hollywood. Her related areas of interest include media anthropology, postcolonial science fiction, South African cinema, new visual technologies, and visual effects industries.

KEVIN DWYER is an anthropologist and author of *Moroccan Dialogues: Anthropology in Question* (1982), *Arab Voices: The Human Rights Debate in the Middle East* (1991), and *Beyond Casablanca: M. A. Tazi and the Adventure of Moroccan Cinema* (2004), as well as articles on anthropological theory, human rights, and Moroccan society and culture. He has worked as head of Amnesty International's Middle East Research Department (London, 1978–1984), and as founder and director of the Institut de Recherches Appliquées (Tunisia, 1990–2001); his academic positions include professor of anthropology at the American University in Cairo (2001–2008), fellow at the Woodrow Wilson International Center for Scholars (Washington, DC, 2006–2007), and visiting professor of anthropology at Columbia University (spring 2010). He currently divides his time between New York and Tunis.

TEJASWINI GANTI is associate professor in the Department of Anthropology and core faculty in the Program in Culture and Media at New York University. She is the author of *Producing Bollywood: Inside the Contemporary Hindi Film Industry* (2012) and *Bollywood: A Guidebook to Popular Hindi Cinema* (2004; second edition, 2013). Her current research examines the politics of language and translation within the Bombay film industry and the formalization and professionalization of film training in India. In addition to her scholarship, she has written the English dubbing scripts for season one of the Netflix original series *Sacred Games* and season one of Amazon Prime's original series *Breathe*.

LOTTE HOEK is a media anthropologist at the University of Edinburgh. Her research focuses on South Asian film and media cultures. She is the author of *Cut-Pieces: Celluloid Obscenity and Popular Cinema in Bangladesh* (2014) and coeditor of the journal *BioScope: South Asian Screen Studies*. With Sanjukta Sunderason, she edited the volume *Forms of the Left in Postcolonial South Asia: Aesthetics, Networks and Connected Histories* (2021).

AMRITA IBRAHIM teaches in the Department of Anthropology at Georgetown University. Her research and teaching focus on media, politics, surveillance, gender, and sexuality. She is working on a book titled *Journalism, Surveillance, and Social Order in Post-Liberalization India* that explores how television journalists have shaped new discourses of crime and governance in India since the 1990s.

SYLVIA J. MARTIN is an assistant professor at the University of Hong Kong, where her research includes media, globalization, the state, and gender. She is the author of *Haunted: An Ethnography of the Hollywood and Hong Kong Media Industries* (2017), which is based on multisited fieldwork. Recent work examines how the U.S. state turns to Hollywood storytellers to help innovate military training and can be read in "Imagineering Empire: How Hollywood and the U.S. National Security State 'Operationalize Narrative'" in *Media, Culture & Society*.

RAMYAR D. ROSSOUKH spent time with the Bakhtiyari, a tribal group in southwestern Iran, before embarking upon a three-year fieldwork project on the Iranian film industry, which he got to know as an insider by working in a number of different jobs, including directorial assistant. His 2014 dissertation in anthropology and Middle East studies at Harvard University is the first in-depth ethnography of the Iranian film industry. He is currently completing a book manuscript based on his dissertation. He is a lecturer in the Princeton Writing Program and teaches a course on visual representations of Mars.

Index

Gore, Al, 2, 3
Govil, Nitin, 111
Gunning, Tom, 164
Griffith, D. W., 170
Grosz, Elizabeth, 201, 203
Guyer, Jane, 189

Habermas, Jürgen, 38n2, 39n6
Hansen, Miriam, 39n6
Harari, Yuval Noah, 197–199, 209n29
Hardt, Michael, 177
Hassan II, 218, 230
Heidegger, Martin, 201, 206
Hendricks, Riaan, 191, 200, 204, 206
Hoek, Lotte, 19, 21–22, 34, 133
Hollywood, 1, 4, 8; Bollywood and, 32, 41, 43–47, 56, 58–59; franchise or tentpole films, 41; Hong Kong film industry and, 170; personnel overlap with other national film industries, 5, 22, 67, 170; subsidiaries of studios in other countries, 43, 50, 170; subsidies and tax credits, 171; technology industry and, 193. *See also* film industries; virtual reality
Holt, Jennifer, 39n4
Horkheimer, Max, 14–15
Hunger Games, The (film), 49
Hurt, William, 171, 173

Ibrahim, Amrita, 15, 33
"image-object," 112–113. *See also* film censorship
Inconvenient Truth, An (film), 2, 3
independent cinema. *See* film industries
Indian television, 15, 33; advertisement and, 97–98, 100; cultural vectors in, 103–106; demographics of genres in, 96; history of, 94–96; interdependence of Indian film industry and, 98–99; journalists as bricoleurs in, 93, 99–103; mobile technologies as displacement of, 96; national programming and, 95; newspapers and, 96; ownership of entertainment channels and, 97; "sites of replication" in, 93; *tapori* in, 102–103; three Cs (crime, cricket, and cinema), 97; use of cinematic in crime stories of, 99–103
indigenous media, 6

Jaikumar, Priya, 9
Jones, Sarah, 170–174

Jungle Book, The (film), 54–59, 61n13
Jurassic Park (film), 41

Kaes, Anton, 30
Kamu, Kamruzzaman, 110, 115–120, 122–128
Kane, Selly Raby, 203, 204, 205
Kid "in" Africa (film), 163
Killer Elite, The (film), 147
Kipling, Rudyard, 198
Kopp, Ingrid, 187, 195, 206
Kracauer, Siegfried, 14
Kwan-ching, Moon, 170

Lamont, Charles, 163, 176, 179n1
language ideologies, 42
Larkin, Brian, 7
Lawrence of Arabia (film), 5, 21, 65, 161n4
Lean, David, 21, 223
Lee, Bruce, 170
Let This Be a Warning (film), 192, 202
Liang, Lawrence, 113
Lois, Jennifer, 178
Lukács, Gabriella, 107n2
Lyng, Stephen, 165, 177

magical realism, 190
Majid, Majidi, 63–64, 130
Markovitz, Steven, 181, 187
Martin, Sylvia J., 20, 35–36, 144
Mayer, Vicki, 10–11, 134
Mazzarella, William, 34, 112, 119, 124
Mbeki, Moeletsi, 196
Mbembe, Achille, 189, 204
media industry studies, 25, 39n4
#MeToo movement, 163, 173
Midnight Rider (film), 170–171, 177
Miller, Randall, 170–173
Mitter, Partha, 113
Miyao, Daisuke, 22
"mobile cinema," 4, 220
mobile devices and smartphones, 28, 96, 103, 186, 196
modularity, 3, 20–24, 30–31; hierarchy in, 22; linearity or sequencing in, 20, 22; location scouting, 5, 18; postproduction editing and outsourcing, 23, 67–70; spatial dispersion in, 22–24; transposability between media industries and, 23. *See also* dis-location shooting

Moore's law, 197, 209n30

Moroccan film industry, 7, 8–9, 37; Amazigh films and, 218–219; censorship of, 230–231; Centre Cinématographique Marocain (CCM, Moroccan Film Center) and, 214, 216; "clean art" and, 231–232; coproduction and regional cooperation in, 222–223; criticisms of CCM, 225–229; film clubs and, 221; film critics and, 221; film festivals and, 220–222; financing of, 216–220; Marrakesh International Film Festival and, 224; national and international aspects of, 214–222; television and, 217; theater exhibition, 214, 217, 236n3; training institutes for, 221

Motion Picture Association of America (MPAA), 1

Mudimbe, V. Y., 190

Muhammad VI, 219, 233

Mukii, Ng'endo, 200, 202, 204

Nairobi Berries (film), 200, 202, 204

Nakassis, Constantine, 26, 142

national film industries, 1–2; Bangladeshi, 8, 19–20, 21, 34, 110, 117; Cuban, 1, 19; Egyptian, 1, 18; Georgian, 60n12; Ghanaian video, 8; Hindi (Bollywood), 8, 32, 33, 43, 124; Hong Kong, 8, 36, 165, 167, 169–170, 174–176; Iranian, 19, 64, 65, 130; Moroccan (*see* Moroccan film industry); Nigerian (Nollywood), 7, 8; South Korean, 8; Soviet, 16, 19; Tamil (Kollywood), 8, 20–21, 23, 142; Yemeni, 35, 130

neoliberalism, television industries and, 107

New Day in Old Sana'a, A (film), 129, 143–145

Odyssey, The, 213, 235

on-location shooting, 5, 21, 130–134, 146–150, 155–160, 168; cityscapes and, 146–147; film set as sacred space in, 151–154; gendered norms of, 152–154, 167

optical unconscious, 74, 86

Ortner, Sherry, 8, 16, 39n3, 206, 209n24

Osman, Jean-Nesar, 109–110, 121–122, 128

Other Dakar, The (film), 203, 204, 205

Pandian, Anand, 20–21, 23

Pandora (film), 187–188, 203

Park, Young-a, 8

Peirce, C. S., 92, 142, 161n3

Perren, Alisa, 39n4

Pinney, Christopher, 201

Pinto, Jerry, 8

piracy, 43, 45

Povinelli, Elizabeth, 92

Powdermaker, Hortense, 4, 9, 10, 16

Prasad, Madhava, 124

production studies, 3, 7, 9–12, 24–25, 31, 133, 136; production culture, 166, 178

Quayson, Ato, 204

Rajadhyaksha, Ashish, 13

Raju, Zakir, 117

Rancière, Jacques, 203

Ray, Satyajit, 113, 118

realism, 142–143, 149, 191, 204, 206

"regimes of anticipation," 194

Roitman, Janet, 189

Roots (television series), 2

Rossoukh, Ramyar, 27, 32–33, 130

Rosten, Leo, 10

"runaway production," 165, 170–171

Safety for Sarah, 174, 179

Sana'a (Old City), 150–155

Sansom, Kevin, 168

Savin, Jody, 170, 172, 173

Seidu, Kabiru, 188

Selma (film), 2

semiotics: iconic-indexical, of editing and filmic text, 73, 92; indexicality and on-location shooting, 133, 142–144, 146–149, 160

shadow (lighting), 22

Shallows, The (film), 47

short films, 115, 118, 120, 125, 181, 219

Simon, Jonathan, 173

Slates for Sarah, 173

Sobchack, Vivian, 26

sound flashbacks, 82–83

sound-image, 26, 142

Spirit Robot (film), 188

"stolen shot," 20, 35–36, 144, 165, 170, 176, 177

studying up, 10, 39n3

stunt work: damsels in distress and, 172; fatalities in, 171; Hollywood and Hong Kong cinemas and, 167–168; vulnerability of children in, 174. *See also* edgework